Communication for Business

We work with leading authors to develop the
strongest educational materials in business,
bringing cutting-edge thinking and best
learning practice to a global market.

Under a range of well-known imprints, including
Longman, we craft high quality print and
electronic publications which help readers to understand
and apply their content, whether studying or at work.

To find out more about the complete range of our
publishing please visit us on the World Wide Web at:
www.pearsoned.co.uk

Communication for Business

A practical approach

Fourth edition

Shirley Taylor

PEARSON
Longman

Harlow, England • London • New York • Boston • San Francisco • Toronto • Sydney • Singapore • Hong Kong
Tokyo • Seoul • Taipei • New Delhi • Cape Town • Madrid • Mexico City • Amsterdam • Munich • Paris • Milan

Pearson Education Limited
Edinburgh Gate
Harlow
Essex CM20 2JE
England

and Associated Companies throughout the world

Visit us on the World Wide Web at:
http://www.pearsoned.co.uk

First published 1991
Second edition published 1993
Third edition published 1999
Fourth edition published 2005

ISBN: 978-0-273-68765-8

British Library Cataloguing-in-Publication Data
A catalogue record for this book is available from the British Library.

Library of Congress Cataloging-in-Publication Data
Taylor, Shirley.
   Communication for business : a practical approach / Shirley Taylor.-- 4th ed.
       p. cm.
   Includes index.
   ISBN 0–273–68765–4 (paperback)
 1. Business communication. I. Title.
HF5718.T38 2005
651.7--dc22

                                                        2005045908

10 9 8 7 6 5 4 3
10 09 08 07

Typeset in 10/12.5 pt Palatino by 30
Printed and bound in Malaysia (CTP-VVP)

Contents

Section One The nature of communication

Section Three Telecommunications

Section Four Internal communication

Section Five Persuasive communication

Section Six   Visual and oral communication

About the author

Shirley Taylor has established herself as a leading authority in business writing and communication skills.

Shirley is the author of several popular, best-selling books including the international best-seller *Model Business Letters, E-mails & Other Business Documents, 6th edition*; *Essential Communication Skills*; *Pocket Business Communicator*; *The Secretary in Training*, and *Guide to Effective E-mail*.

A trained teacher from the UK, Shirley took up her first teaching post in Singapore in 1983, where she spent several years as Training Consultant and Lecturer teaching on secretarial and business studies courses. She has also worked as Head of Department and Senior Lecturer in Bahrain, Arabian Gulf, as well as in Canada and the UK, where for many years she was Chief Examiner and Moderator for the LCCI Examinations Board.

Based in Singapore in recent years, Shirley enjoys travelling widely to conduct her popular public workshops and in-house training. She is also a regular speaker at international conferences.

You can find out more about Shirley, her books and her workshops by visiting www.shirleytaylor.com. Her website also contains a wealth of information and articles on writing and communication skills. Shirley sends out a monthly e-newsletter called **Shirley Says** containing tips, quizzes and articles on modern business writing and communication skills. To sign up for this popular e-newsletter, visit www.shirleytaylor.com and type your name in the sign-up box.

Preface to the fourth edition

Wow – a fourth edition! If anyone had told me way back in 1991 that my first book would become so successful that it would be used by many people all over the world, and that in 2005 I would be writing a Preface to the fourth edition, I would never have believed it. It's true though, and I'm very proud and happy about it.

So thanks to the teachers and students who have used this book in the past, and hello to everyone who will use the fourth edition. In compiling this new edition, I have taken into account feedback that I received from users of the third edition. I have tried to retain many of the popular features from previous editions as well as introduce many exciting new features.

Speaking and writing are the two main ways of communicating, of sharing ideas and conducting business. Writing in particular has become the main form of business communication throughout the world. Most employers would agree that two of the most crucial skills they look for in hiring new staff and in training current staff are the ability to think critically and to express themselves clearly both orally and in writing. Doesn't this confirm the importance of communication? Communication is and it always will be the lifeblood of any organisation, and just like any other endeavour, the more you put into it, the more you'll get back!

By using the tried and tested techniques, tips and guidelines presented in this book, I hope you will enjoy learning to communicate your ideas effectively and professionally, and so enhance your own career as well as the success of your organisation.

A COMPREHENSIVE TEXTBOOK, WORKBOOK AND REFERENCE BOOK ROLLED INTO ONE

The fourth edition of *Communication for Business* will be helpful to anyone who is working or training to work in a managerial, administrative or secretarial role that demands good communication and business English skills. A comprehensive textbook, workbook and reference book rolled into one, this book aims to:

- Stimulate interest in the use of business English so that it can be written more accurately, clearly and concisely.
- Provide specimen layouts of all business documents.

- Discuss essential theory on each topic to help develop understanding.
- Offer a wide range of authentic documents for interest and reference.
- Supply a variety of assignments to reinforce learning.
- Help readers to develop confidence and expertise in composing effective business communications.
- Highlight common errors in spelling and written expressions, to clarify correct use of language.
- Make learning fun!

CLEAR ORGANISATION

Each self-contained unit includes all the necessary theory, specimens, suggested layouts and explanations required to develop understanding and initiative. Units are flexibly organised so that you can choose an appropriate learning sequence. Each unit begins with objectives and the majority finish with key points to remember. Assignments help readers put theory into practice; they can be worked alone, with a partner or in a group discussion.

SIMPLE AND CLEAR WRITING STYLE

The first three editions of *Communication for Business* have been very popular with international audiences all over the world. This new edition will prove equally successful, with its use of straightforward, simple language and clear explanations.

SPECIMEN LAYOUTS

The fully-blocked method of display with open punctuation is stressed throughout this book. This is the most up-to-date, attractive method of presentation and it is widely used by many organisations. If you choose to adopt this style or use your company's house style, just remember the main rule: be consistent in presentation of all your communications.

NEW TO THIS EDITION

While retaining all the familiar and popular characteristics from the third edition, the current edition has been modified in the light of current practice and from personal experience. It has also been updated to reflect modern business language as well as communications expectations in today's workplace. Specific changes include:

- Expansion and development of Unit 1 – Business communication basics, in particular discussion on communication in a changing workplace, intercultural sensitivities, and steps to effective communication.
- Expansion and development of Unit 3 – Use of English, with extra examples of poor business language and how to put it right. Also, this unit includes an interesting list of 'The world's most irritating phrases' reproduced with permission from The Plain English Campaign.
- Unit 4 – Introducing the business letter, now lists categories of business letters and discusses their use.
- Unit 5 – Rules of good writing, now offers an expanded discussion of all the rules and examples, including an article discussing 'great-grandfather' language vs modern business writing.
- Unit 8 – Electronic mail, has been completely revised and updated, and now offers comprehensive coverage of the topic.
- Unit 10 – Reports, now contains information about proposals.
- Unit 18 – Oral presentation skills is brand new. This comprehensive unit is written by my good friend, communications and presentation skills expert, Ricky Lien.
- New features in the Appendix include: Frequently confused words, Commonly misspelled words, and The Plain English Campaign's A to Z of alternative words.

ROBUST PEDAGOGY

The book is filled with robust pedagogy, including new and updated illustrations, and the following features.

Remember

Tips, advice and suggestions are given throughout the text to reinforce learning.

Did you know?

This provides an interesting titbit of information to enhance knowledge.

Checkpoint

Suggestions for readers to do something either as a group or as additional research.

What's wrong?

This gives you an opportunity to criticise answers to some assignments. You can then rewrite the documents more appropriately.

Weblink

Weblinks provide useful links to website urls with further information on topics.

Shirley Taylor website articles

Want to dig deeper into a topic? Special articles from Shirley Taylor's own website are reproduced here.

STRONG END-OF-UNIT PEDAGOGY

Remind yourself of main points and prepare for your exam with confidence with the following superb end-of-unit materials.

Key points to remember

This feature lists of important guidelines to drive home the main points.

A–Z of bloopers, blunders, common errors and clichés

Avoid pitfalls and embarrassing business situations by studying these useful notes.

In the bin

Words and phrases to avoid at all costs.

Help yourself

This provides simple and quick tests to reinforce learning and build confidence.

Test yourself

Unbeatable examination preparation via sample examination questions.
This book should prove useful to students wishing to take the following exams:

- City & Guilds English for Business Communication
- LCCI Examinations Board English for Business
- RSA Examinations Board Communication in Business

The following abbreviations have been used throughout the text:

- City & Guilds EFBC1   City & Guilds English for Business Communication Level 1

- City & Guilds EFBC2   City & Guilds English for Business Communication Level 2

- LCCIEB EFB1 style   Assignments written in the style of the English for Business Level 1 examination from the LCCI Examinations Board*

- LCCIEB EFB2 style   Assignments written in the style of the English for Business Level 2 examination from the LCCI Examinations Board*

FINAL WORD

Everyone can improve their communication skills – I hope this book helps you to improve yours. Please also visit my website – www.shirleytaylor.com – where you will find a wealth of other articles and resources on communication, e-mail and business writing skills. I also send out a monthly e-newsletter packed with articles and tips. To receive your free copy just type your name in the sign-up box on my home page.

Shirley Taylor
Spring 2005

NB: The names, addresses, post codes, and other details of individuals and organisations used in examples and assignments in this book are fictitious. Any resemblance to existing individuals or organisations is coincidental.

* The author wishes to make it clear that LCCIEB-style exam examples are not copies of LCCIEB examination questions. They have been written in a style that the author considers to be similar to that of the examination and level stated, but they have not been approved by or used by the LCCIEB.

Acknowledgements

My thanks are due to a whole host of people for their help in bringing this fourth edition to print. First of all, thanks to Thomas Sigel, Senior Acquisitions Editor, at Pearson Education for your support and enthusiasm from the start. Thanks also to the many other people at Pearson whose contribution, innovation and creative flair is really evident in this new edition, in particular Peter Hooper, Editorial Assistant; Karen Mclaren, Senior Editor; Angela Hawksbee, Senior Production Controller; Andrea Bannuscher, Designer; Jo Barber, Marketing Manager, and Winek Kosior, International Sales Executive.

Thanks also to the great many friends I have made at Pearson Education throughout the world – you are far too numerous to mention, but you know who you are! I am very fortunate to be able to travel around and meet so many of the people who are responsible for making this book so popular in so many different countries – my grateful thanks for your friendship and support.

Many thanks go to Peter Leggott who very kindly produced some examination questions for me similar in style to LCCI Examinations Board English for Business Level 1 and 2. Thanks also to Jean Newland, former LCCIEB Examinations Manager, for her valuable advice and guidance on these questions. I am very grateful to you both for your help and expertise.

Special thanks go to my good friend and fellow-trainer Ricky Lien for contributing the unit on Oral Presentation Skills. And last but not least, three cheers to the very talented Edwin Ng, whose fabulous illustrations help to bring all the topics to life.

I am very grateful to the following organisations for providing permission to reproduce copyright material:

Acco UK Limited; Boots Group plc; Cadbury Trebor Bassett; The City and Guilds of London Institute; Civil Aviation Authority of Singapore; Corus Hotels; Department of Health; Lichtwer Pharma AG; Ministry of the Environment and Water Resources, Singapore; Mövenpick Gastronomie Uchwelz AG; National Pollen and Aerobiology Research Unit; Oyez Straker; Pat's Schoolhouse, Singapore; Pearson Education Limited; Plain English Campaign; Sheffield Wednesday Football Club; Singapore Airlines Limited; Singapore Exhibition Services Pte Ltd; Singapore MRT Ltd; SPH – *The Business Times*; Tim North; Unilever UK Foods; Ward Hi-Tech Ltd; Waterlow Business Supplies Limited; World Wildlife Fund UK.

Every effort has been made by the publisher to obtain permission from the appropriate source to reproduce material which appears in this book. In some instances we have been unable to trace the owners of copyright material, and we would appreciate any information that would enable us to do so.

Section 1

The nature of communication

Unit 1

Business communication basics

LEARNING OUTCOMES

After studying this unit you should be able to:

- Explain what effective communication is

- State the benefits of effective communication

- Discuss the developments taking place in today's workplace that increase the need for effective communication

- Describe the various methods of communication in today's workplace

- Discuss the factors to be considered in choosing the method of communication

- Explain the key stages in the communication cycle

- Discuss examples of barriers to communication

- Discuss the different ways communication flows in a business organisation

- Explain what culture is and discuss some ways in which you can improve cross-cultural communications

- Explain the seven step formula to achieve effective communication

EFFECTIVE COMMUNICATION – AN ORGANISATION'S LIFEBLOOD

All day, every day we are communicating – whether it is talking to people on the telephone or in person, taking dictation and transcribing business correspondence, liaising with colleagues and staff, writing letters, faxes, reports and e-mails. It is essential to learn from our communications, from our successes and our failures, and to develop and enhance our communication skills. The more we write and the more we speak, the more we improve our communication skills.

Communication may be defined as:

giving, receiving or exchanging information, opinions or ideas by writing, speech or visual means, so that the message communicated is completely understood by the recipient(s).

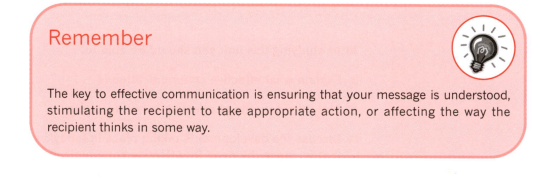

Remember

The key to effective communication is ensuring that your message is understood, stimulating the recipient to take appropriate action, or affecting the way the recipient thinks in some way.

BENEFITS OF EFFECTIVE COMMUNICATION

The most successful organisations understand that if they are to be successful in today's business world, good communication at all levels is essential. Here is a useful nmemonic to remember the benefits you and your organisation can achieve from effective communication:

Stronger decision-making and problem-solving
Upturn in productivity
Convincing and compelling corporate materials
Clearer, more streamlined workflow
Enhanced professional image
Sound business relationships
Successful response ensured

COMMUNICATION IN A CHANGING WORKPLACE

Today's workplace is constantly changing and developing, so effective communication is vital to enable you to meet numerous challenges, such as:

- *Advancing technology*

  Today we have a variety of technological tools to help us to communicate faster, more frequently and across an increased range. The Internet, e-mail, fax messages, voice mail, teleconferencing, videoconferencing and wireless devices have transformed the way people communicate. People can work together effortlessly whether they are in New York or New Zealand, Singapore or Seattle, Beijing or Bangkok; whether in a car, an office, a hotel or at home, even in an airport or on an aeroplane. With every phone call or e-mail your communication skills are revealed for everyone to see.

- *Global communications*

  More and more businesses are now working on a global scale across national boundaries. Many people now work for multinational companies, and today's workforce all over the world now includes increasing numbers of people from different ethnic backgrounds. If you are to communicate effectively in this environment, you must understand other people's backgrounds, beliefs and characters.

- *The information age*

  With an increase in the amount of information in today's business world, you must be able to make quick, effective decisions based on the information you receive. You must also know how to find, assess, process and communicate information efficiently and effectively. With so much information available today, it is a constant challenge to get your recipient's attention so that they will read and act appropriately on your message.

- *Team-based business environments*

  In today's fast-paced business world, the traditional management hierarchy has changed, and teamworking is now in vogue. In such a team-based environment, it is important to study and understand how groups work together. You must learn to listen and watch other people carefully so that you interpret all the non-verbal cues you receive.

Remember

Learning more about effective communication helps us all adapt to changing environments.

Did you know?

Teams are the norm in today's workplace. Effective communication is essential to both team membership and team leadership.

METHODS OF COMMUNICATION

The main methods of oral and written communication, both internal and external, are shown in the following diagrams.

Internal communication

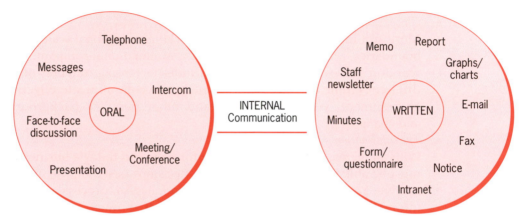

External communication

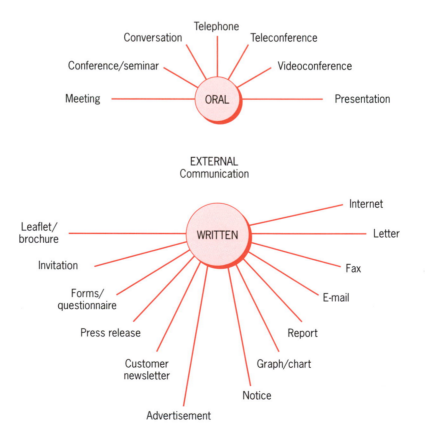

Checkpoint

How many of these forms of communication have you had experience with so far?

CHOOSING THE CHANNEL OF COMMUNICATION

The channel (or means) that is chosen to send a message is very important. The channel chosen can influence the message and how it is interpreted by the recipient. Each situation should be judged individually, and will depend on various factors such as:

Cost

- Consider how much the communication will cost in terms of the results expected.
- Can an internal message be handwritten or is a printed copy important?
- Is the postal service satisfactory, or is e-mail or fax justified?

Confidentiality

- E-mail or fax may not be appropriate.
- A telephone call could be overheard.
- An internal memo may need to be enclosed in an envelope.

Safety and security

- Should a special Post Office service be used, e.g. registered or recorded delivery?
- Would a courier service be justified?

Influence

- To convey a certain impression, would a congratulatory telegram or invitation be suitable?
- Multi-coloured letterheads on high quality paper convey a good image of a company.

Urgency

- Choose the method that will produce the desired results in the time available.
- Perhaps the higher cost of a fax will be justified by the results obtained through its speed.

Distance

- Is the communication within the building, in the same town, or the other side of the world?

Time of day

- This is particularly important when communicating with overseas countries.

Resources

- Consider the equipment and staff available (sender and recipient).

Written record

- Written communications carry more authority and are proof of a transaction.

Recipient

- Consider who is sending/receiving the message.
- Personal contact may be appropriate on certain occasions.
- Verbal communication may not be appropriate where complex information or bad news is concerned.
- Choose language appropriately, considering the situation and the relationship between sender/recipient.

Remember

A wrong decision about how a communication is expressed, and the method used to convey it, could have disastrous results. Think twice, and then think again!

SUMMARY OF COMMUNICATION CHOICES

Use oral channels when:
- your message is fairly simple
- you need an immediate response
- you don't need a permanent record
- you want to encourage interaction in problem-solving or decision-making
- you need to read the recipient's body language
- you need to hear the tone of your recipient's response
- your message has an emotional factor.

Use written channels when:
- your message is fairly detailed or requires careful planning
- you don't need an immediate response
- you need a permanent, written record
- you have a big, widespread audience
- you want to minimise the distortion that often occurs when messages are passed orally from person to person
- you don't need immediate interaction with your audience
- your message has no emotional factor.

Use electronic channels when:
- speed is important
- time zones differ
- you are physically separated from your audience.

KEY STAGES IN THE COMMUNICATION CYCLE

Sender

1 Conceive the message

'Don't open your mouth only to put your foot in it!' When you have something to say, consider the best means of putting your message across, and bear in mind that timing is important. Consider your recipient carefully and aim your message to suit their specific needs.

2 Encode the message

This stage involves putting the information into an appropriate form suitable to both the sender, the recipient and the aim. Think before reaching for your phone or putting fingers to keyboard. Decide first what specific outcomes you want from the communication. This will help you choose whether words will suffice, whether a printed record is necessary and whether graphics are appropriate. It will also help you choose appropriate language and tone.

3 Select the appropriate channel

This stage is where the message is actually sent and the information is transferred. The technological revolution has brought about a wide range of telecommunication methods. You must consider all aspects: speed, cost, quick receipt, printed record, confidentiality, etc., and make an intelligent decision before sending your message. Time and money can be wasted if the wrong medium is chosen.

Recipient

4 Decode the message

Because so many messages arrive in offices today, it is important to ensure that they are routed promptly and are given the attention they deserve. To achieve success at this stage it is also important to take the trouble to ensure that the recipient will understand the language and vocabulary used.

5 Interpret the message

Very often it is necessary to 'read between the lines'. It is always important to consider carefully the tone used in your communication so that the correct message is received. For example, you do not want to risk antagonising a good customer by using a harsh tone. Distortion of the message may occur if the sender has not carefully encoded the communication, in which case the recipient will interpret the message differently from how it was intended.

6 Feedback

The communication process cannot be successful without appropriate feedback. In oral communication this is often immediate, in meetings the audience may nod or smile to show understanding and agreement. But with written messages courtesy and discipline are important to acknowledge receipt of messages until a full and appropriate response can be given.

Did you know?

How well you communicate is determined not by how well you say things but by how well they are received.

BARRIERS TO COMMUNICATION

Many problems encountered in our business and personal lives result from miscommunication. What the recipient understands by a message may not always be the message which the sender intended. Several communication barriers exist between sender and recipient, and they may be responsible for a message not being understood correctly, or a message becoming distorted.

Communication may fail for a variety of reasons:

Non-verbal signals

Non-verbal signals, often referred to as 'body language', can provide valuable feedback where verbal communication is concerned. Such signals include facial expressions, gestures, movement, eye contact and nodding the head.

Language

Choice of words is vital to the effectiveness of any communication. Many words have different meanings. Our background knowledge and experience affect our understanding. Foreign languages, dialects, regional accents and the use of technical/specialist language should always be considered.

Listening

Anyone who has something valid to say deserves attention. Listening, however, is a skill. Careful concentration is demanded if a communication is to be understood. Success at gaining attention may depend on the words used, the way the communication is expressed, our interest in the speaker, our interest in the communication and various other factors.

Pre-judgement

What is understood is often conditioned by what we already know and by our background knowledge and experience. Often we hear what we want to hear, or what we think we have heard, instead of what has actually been said.

Relationships

The effectiveness of any communication may depend on our relationship with the person giving the message. If relationships between people are not good, communication may fail to be effective or may break down altogether.

Emotional responses

Communication cannot succeed if a person is highly emotional about the topic concerned. Problems may arise from insecurity, fear, anger, etc. If emotions are high on the part of the sender or recipient, then it would be better to wait for a while before trying to put the message across.

Systems

In any organisation there should be prescribed procedures for getting messages to the people who need them. Without such systems there can be no effective communication.

Apart from the barriers to communication already discussed, there are many other barriers that can be as simple as using words that are not easily understood by the recipient, or perhaps more complex issues such as not listening properly to a person because you don't really like them. Barriers to communication interfere with the process of sending or receiving a message. Barriers change a message. Here are some more common barriers that can alter a message.

accent	personal appearance
anger	personal space
background	physical barriers
biases	prejudices
culture	pronunciation
emotions	self-perception
expectations	self-talk
expressions	silence
facial expressions	slang
fear	smell
frowning	social background
gestures	smiling
group pressures	stress
individual differences	submissiveness
interruptions	taste
jargon	temperature
lighting	threatening motions
motivation	tone of voice
negotiation methods	visual distractions
noise	

Checkpoint

Spend a moment considering the items on this list and how they affect you as you send or receive messages. Can you think of any others?

THE FLOW OF COMMUNICATION

In small organisations of just a few people there may be few communication problems. In larger organisations the process is more complicated. Most larger companies produce an organisation chart which makes lines of communication quite clear.

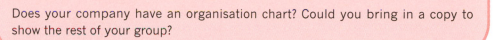

Checkpoint

Does your company have an organisation chart? Could you bring in a copy to show the rest of your group?

Organisation charts make it easier to see how communication can take place vertically (between levels), horizontally (between sections) and diagonally (between different levels and sections). It is important to keep all communication routes as open and as effective as possible.

Vertical communication

Vertical communication moves between individuals at different levels in an organisation. This is probably the most frequent form of communication. Sometimes messages are sent from the CEO to all employees, or from a department head to all employees in his or her department only. Generally, vertical communication follows the 'chain of command', i.e. the reporting lines that are reflected on a company's organisation chart. This means that a manager sends messages *downward* to those under his or her immediate supervision. Similarly, employees send messages *upward* to their immediate superior.

Horizontal communication

Horizontal communication occurs between people of the same status – sales staff, departmental heads, directors, supervisors. The senders and receivers can be in the same department or in different units. The common link is their need to cooperate and share. Messages that flow horizontally typically involve the exchange of information or data that is necessary to complete routine tasks. The information can be communicated during face-to-face discussions, via telephone, or through correspondence.

Diagonal communication

Diagonal communication takes place between people who work in different departments and at different levels within an organisation. Very often tasks frequently arise that involve more than one department, and there may be no

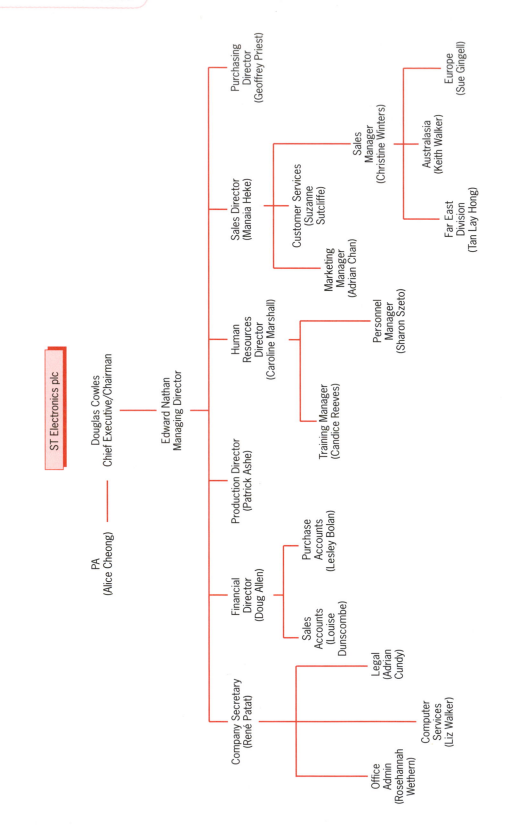

obvious line of authority. Very often diagonal communication involves committees, teams or task forces that are created to solve problems or complete special projects. Diagonal communication often relies largely on cooperation, goodwill and respect between the parties concerned.

The grapevine

When the correct lines of communication are not used, the grapevine often results. This term describes an unofficial communication system which is constantly changing. The grapevine is a vehicle for distortions of the truth, rumour and gossip. An active grapevine can cause much damage to an organisation by spreading incomplete, false or exaggerated information. It results in low morale, cynicism, fear and an unsettled workforce.

Although the grapevine may never be completely eradicated, management should take steps to reduce its influence by considering carefully ways in which information is communicated, particularly in times of uncertainty within the organisation. The confidence of an organisation's employees is vitally important, and adequate and accurate information should always be made available to the people concerned at the earliest possible opportunity, through the correct channels.

Checkpoint

Is there a grapevine in your organisation? Has any damage resulted from the spread of information through the grapvine? Discuss this with your colleagues.

INTERCULTURAL SENSITIVITIES

Many businesses today operate on a global scale. Therefore if communication is to be effective, it is important to be aware of cultural differences, and to be sensitive to them.

What is culture?

Culture is a shared system of beliefs, attitudes, values, expectations and norms of behaviour. Members of a culture have similar beliefs and theories on how people should behave, think and communicate, and they all tend to act on those beliefs in much the same way.

From group to group, cultures differ extensively. When you communicate with someone from a different culture, you do so using the theories and beliefs of your own culture. However, when your audience receives your message, they do so based on the assumptions of their own culture. As a result of basic cultural differences, misunderstandings could easily occur, and often do.

Remember

You can improve your cross-cultural communication skills by recognising cultural differences, by being willing to accept that other people have different beliefs and assumptions, by being open-minded enough to know that not everyone has the same standards and theories as you, and by constantly making an effort to improve your intercultural communication skills.

Acknowledging cultural differences

Many people assume that other people's attitudes and lives are like our own, but this is not so. Your aim should be to try to treat people not in the way you wish to be treated, but rather treat them the way they want to be treated.

If you are to communicate effectively across cultures, you must not judge other people by your own standards. It is essential to retain an open mind, and remember that our own cultural background is not necessarily superior to anyone else's.

Did you know?

The belief that one's own cultural background is superior to all others is known as **ethnocentrism**. This creates a barrier to effective communication because the mind remains closed to new information.

Ethnocentric people tend to form pre-conceived judgements of different cultures based on one experience, or based on limited evidence. Perhaps they tend to take stereotyping a little too far and don't keep an open mind so they cannot move beyond a certain stage. For example, when talking to Slavia Horsky, instead of looking at her as a special human being with unique qualities, ethnocentric people believe they are simply talking to 'an Israeli'. Perhaps they believe that all Israelis are Jews who are outspoken, crude, demanding and aggressive, simply because of pre-conceptions and maybe limited previous experience. Therefore, despite Slavia's many unique personal qualities, the ethnocentric person cannot see beyond their fixed ideas, even when those ideas are wrong, so their mind remains closed.

If you want to avoid ethnocentrism, you should:

- Recognise differences. Accept and acknowledge that there are distinctions between your own cultures and those of other people.
- Avoid assumptions. Bear in mind that others may not act in the same way as you, nor will they have the same fundamental theories or beliefs.
- Do not pre-judge. If people act differently to you, do not automatically assume that they are wrong, that their way is unacceptable, or that your cultures and customs are more superior to theirs.

Checkpoint

What is your experience of communicating across cultures? Have there been any misunderstandings, prejudices, assumptions or ethnocentrism?

CHECKLIST FOR COMMUNICATING EFFECTIVELY ACROSS CULTURES

Today's culturally diverse workforce is made up of people from different countries, ethnic backgrounds, races, religion and family structure. If you are to communicate effectively with all these different people, it is important to keep an open mind and try to learn as much as possible about their various cultures.

If you are to communicate effectively in a culturally diverse workforce, here is a checklist of points to remember. If you follow these tips you will be able to communicate with anyone from any culture.

1 Show respect. Learn how respect is communicated in different cultures (gestures, eye contact, symbols, signs, etc.).
2 Show empathy. Put yourself in the shoes of the recipient and imagine their feelings and their point of view.
3 Do not pre-judge. Accept differences without judging, and learn to listen.
4 Be open-minded. Accept that you may have to change your habits or mindset when communicating across cultures.
5 Avoid distractions. Do not be distracted by things like appearance or dress.
6 Be patient. Sometimes persistence will be necessary when communicating with someone from a different culture.
7 Look for similarities. Try to find common ground, parallels, connections.
8 Send clear messages. Make sure all your written as well as your verbal and non-verbal communications are quite clear, reliable and consistent.
9 Recognise your prejudices. Learn to appreciate and accept when your theories and beliefs are different from other people's.
10 Treat people as individuals. Do not treat one person as being a stereotype of a particular group, but rather as a unique human being with individual qualities and attributes.

SEVEN STEPS TO EFFECTIVE COMMUNICATION

Communication, whether oral or written, is all about understanding. Your aim should be to communicate your message successfully so that it is received as you intended, without any misunderstanding. You can achieve effective communication by having a through knowledge of the communication cycle, by being aware of the barriers that exist, and by following this seven-step process:

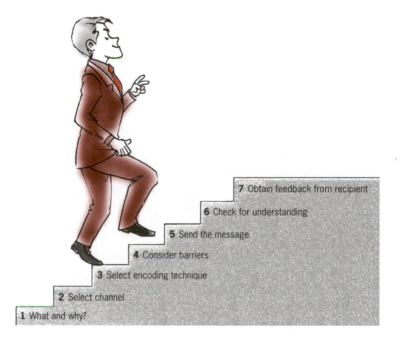

Step 1: What and why?

Your first step is to consider what is the objective of your communication and why you have to communicate the message. Are you aiming to give information, to persuade, to request, to inform?

Step 2: Select channel

The next step is to consider what channel (or means) of communication would be appropriate. Consider the relationship between the sender and the recipient, as well as the recipient's background knowledge, culture and experience.

Step 3: Select encoding technique

Encoding is choosing the manner in which we send our message. For example, the language you choose, an angry or soft voice, harsh tone or courteous tone. Consider why the communication is happening. Is it urgent, serious, dangerous, emotive, informative?

Step 4: Consider barriers

You must consider all possible barriers that may influence the recipient's understanding of the message. Is the communication likely to achieve the desired aims in the given circumstances? If the barriers are likely to interfere with the recipient's understanding, you may need to return to step 1 or 2 and think again.

Step 5: Send message

Having considered all these aspects, you may now send your message.

Step 6: Check for understanding

After sending the message, it is important to check whether the recipient has understood the message as you intended.

Step 7: Obtain feedback from recipient

The final stage is essential – you must obtain feedback from the recipient so that you know if your communication has been effective. If the message is not understood, rather than blame the recipient, ask yourself why the communication failed and how it could have been improved in order to be effective. Some questions you might ask are:

- Did your expressions or language create confusion or misunderstanding?
- Was your timing poor?
- Was your message too long so that the main points were lost?
- Were your tone and manner appropriate?
- Did you not structure the message logically?

THE IMPACT OF INFORMATION TECHNOLOGY

In recent years there has been an information technology revolution. While paper-based manual systems for processing information and communicating are still very much evident, more and more office functions and procedures are now being undertaken by computer-based technology. The implications of such information technology on communication methods cannot be ignored. However, the technology will always require people, and in communication it is the input of the operator that will ensure effective communication (or otherwise).

In the area of text creation, computer experts are trying to make the task of creating documents much easier. Programs are available that will produce standard layouts for most business documents when the inputs or variables are keyed in. In other words, the originator does not decide on the layout, the computer program does. Sadly, many computer programs are written by computer experts who may not be so expert in the modern display of business documents. Some of these standard layouts leave much to be desired.

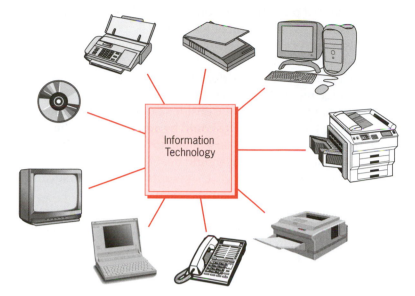

The fundamental skills of structure, tone and composition will always be of vital importance in ensuring effective communication. As an originator of printed communications, you have control over these factors. However, while technological developments are making your role more interesting and challenging, the basic presentational conventions should not be allowed to suffer. No matter how technology develops in the future, high standards must be set and maintained in order to ensure that all your communications are not only appropriately worded and logically structured, but are also consistently and attractively presented.

Checkpoint

How do you think information technology will develop in the future? Are there any dangers in our reliance on such technology? How will developments affect the process of communication?

SUCCESSFUL COMMUNICATION – KEY POINTS TO REMEMBER

1 *Read*. Extend your knowledge of language by reading.
2 *Listen intelligently*. Remember that communication is a two-way process. Listening is just as important as speaking. Similarly, try reading your written message as if you were the recipient, and consider if it will be effective.

3 *Think and plan.* Think before you speak or write. Plan all your communications carefully, whether oral or written.

4 *Use appropriate language.* Use clear, simple language, and appreciate the same used by others.

5 *Be open-minded.* Consider other people's viewpoints, be willing to adapt and change methods or procedures if necessary.

6 *Select appropriate media.* Consider carefully the method to be used for communicating your message. It should be appropriate to the desired objective.

7 *Time your communication appropriately.* Consider the best time for the communication and how long it should be.

8 *Use appropriate language.* Use words which are relevant to the topic and which will be understood by the recipient.

9 *Obtain feedback.* Obtain feedback to ensure that the communication was effective.

10 *Aim high.* Set and maintain high standards in all your methods of communication, both in terms of language and presentation.

A–Z OF BLOOPERS AND BLUNDERS, COMMON ERRORS AND CLICHÉS: A

A lot

So many people write *a lot* as one word instead of two. If you do this, ask yourself if you would write *a little*. Of course not. So, please don't write *alot*! The same goes for *in spite of* and *in fact*.

Above-mentioned

This is one of those old-fashioned phrases made up by our great-grandfathers to refer to whatever was in the subject heading or the paragraph(s) above. This phrase should not be used in our twenty-first century business writing.

Instead of

Thank you for registering for the above-mentioned workshop.

say

Thank you for registering for this workshop.

If whatever is above is plural, then use *these* instead of *this*. But never 'above', 'above-mentioned' or 'above-captioned' or even 'said'.

Accede to

This is a stuffy, great-grandfather phrase that should not be used in twenty-first century writing. Say 'We cannot agree to' instead.

Affect/effect

Affect is a verb meaning 'to influence', for example:

>*The fall in productivity will affect our profits this quarter.*

>*How did the business writing workshop affect your work performance?*

Effect is a noun meaning 'result', for example:

>*The fall in productivity will have an effect on our profits this quarter.*

>*What effect will these changes have on your department?*

IN THE BIN: A

a total of
abundantly
above
above-mentioned
absolutely
aforementioned
all things being equal
as a matter of fact

HELP YOURSELF

Choose the correct word from those shown in brackets.

1 Ten years have .... since the two companies merged.
   (past/passed)

2 When you take a problem to your manager, be sure to offer an ....
   solution.
   (alternate/alternative)

3 Good teachers should try to .... answers from their students,
   rather than telling them everything.
   (illicit/elicit)

4 Perhaps you can ask the chairman to .... the decision until the
   next meeting.
   (defer/deter)

5 When the company received a lot of adverse publicity, the staff ....
   was very low.
   (moral/morale)

6 Always .... that you proofread your documents carefully before
   sending them out.
   (insure/ensure)

7 I have asked Martha to write .... to John Lim giving him a disciplinary warning.
(formally/formerly).

8 Mark has always .... to being manager of his own company.
(aspired/inspired)

9 The CEO's speech had a great .... on staff motivation.
(affect/effect)

10 Please let me have your expert .... on this issue.
(advice/advise)

TEST YOURSELF

1 Why is communication the lifeblood of a business organisation?

2 What are the benefits to you and your organisation of effective communication?

3 Explain three of the factors that you must consider when choosing the method of communication.

4 Discuss three reasons why you would use oral channels of communication, and three reasons why you would use written channels.

5 What are barriers to communication? Discuss briefly, stating a variety of different barriers that exist.

6 How is the growth of teamworking affecting communication?

7 Discuss some ways in which you can improve intercultural communications.

8 State the communication methods you would use to:
(a) Congratulate an employee on passing an important examination.
(b) Inform employees about your annual dinner and dance.
(c) Put a nervous applicant at ease while waiting for an interview.
(d) Display the past five years' sales figures.
(e) Confirm a lunch appointment with a client next week.
(f) Describe the location of a hotel where your company is hosting a seminar next month.
(g) Remind staff of the security procedures at your company.
(h) Obtain reactions from staff to a new telephone system recently installed.
(i) Put forward a proposal for a change in company policy.
(j) Send an urgent message to an overseas client.

Unit 2

Speaking, listening and non-verbal communication

LEARNING OUTCOMES

After studying this unit you should be able to:

- **Explain why communication skills are important**

- **Discuss various types of oral communication in the workplace**

- **Describe the six stages of the listening process**

- **Discuss the barriers to effective listening**

- **Identify the differences between good listeners and bad ones**

- **Explain some techniques for effective listening**

- **Discuss various types of non-verbal communication**

- **State some ways in which non-verbal communication can be improved**

- **Discuss techniques to make you more effective on the telephone**

- **Appreciate the importance of voice mail, including how to record a greeting and how to leave an effective message**

WHY ARE COMMUNICATION SKILLS IMPORTANT?

Communication is the heart of every organisation. Everything you do in the workplace results from communication. Therefore good reading, writing, speaking and listening skills are essential if tasks are going to be completed and goals achieved. As you develop your career you will find various reasons why successful communication skills are important to you, for example:

- To secure an interview. You will need good communication skills to make sure your application letter is read and acted upon.
- To get the job. You will need to communicate well during your interview if you are to sell yourself and get the job you want.
- To do your job well. You will need to request information, discuss problems, give instructions, work in teams, interact with colleagues and clients. If you are to achieve cooperation and effective teamwork, good human relations skills are essential. Also, as the workplace is also becoming more global, there are many factors to consider if you are to communicate well in such a diverse environment.
- To advance in your career. Employers want staff who can think for themselves, use initiative and solve problems, staff who are interested in the long-term success of the company. If you are to be seen as a valued member of the organisation, it is important not just to be able to do your job well, but also to communicate your thoughts on how the processes and products or services can be improved.

Remember

Effective communication will help you to:

- get a job
- do your job
- keep your job
- earn promotions

ORAL COMMUNICATION IN THE WORKPLACE

In your business life you will probably spend much more of your time talking and listening to colleagues and clients than you will writing and reading. Oral communication can take a variety of forms. It can be over the telephone or face to face. It can be:

- a private discussion
- a conversation over lunch
- a gossip in the lift
- a telephone conversation
- a chance meeting in the corridor
- an informal gathering of staff
- instructing subordinates
- dealing with clients
- formal meetings
- interviews
- training sessions
- giving a presentation
- conferences/seminars

SPEAKING SKILLS

Most people find talking easier than writing because phrases can sometimes be used in speech that would not be appropriate in written communication. However, if understanding is to be complete and effective, your spoken language needs to be chosen carefully.

In today's workplace, everyone will, at some time or another, be required to give a presentation of some kind – it may be a formal presentation at a conference or perhaps an impromptu or prepared speech. Maybe it will be something as simple as being asked for your ideas or opinions on a specific topic.

In view of the importance of speaking and presentation skills, I have devoted Unit 18 to this topic, see page 368. I hope this will help you in compiling and presenting a speech, and in improving your confidence in doing so.

LISTENING SKILLS

There is hardly any point in someone talking if no-one listens to what is being said. Listening is half of oral communication, and it is a skill that needs to be practised and taken equally as seriously as speaking and writing. All effective leaders and managers realise the importance of acquiring good listening skills, so if you aim to climb the ladder of success this is something you need to take seriously. The consequences of not listening carefully could be disastrous.

Remember

Don't ignore the two-way nature of communication – it's important that both sides understand each other. Listening is essential, because how you listen conveys meaning to the other person and it helps to make the exchange successful.

The listening process

If you are to understand why oral messages are so often unsuccessful, you must understand the listening process. Here are the six stages of the listening process:

1   Receiving
2   Interpreting
3   Remembering
4   Evaluating
5   Responding
6   Acting

1   *Receiving.* Here, you physically hear the message and take note of it. The efficiency of this stage will be affected by various external factors, such as noise, poor hearing, lack of attention.

2   *Interpreting.* This is where you infer the speaker's meaning, based on your own experiences and expectations as well as your own values, beliefs, ideas and needs. You may need to consider whether the speaker's frame of reference is similar or different to yours and how this will affect your understanding of his/her meaning.

3   *Remembering.* Now you store the message for future reference. Perhaps you will take notes as you are listening, or make a mental note of the key points as they are mentioned.

4   *Evaluating.* Now it is important to consider the points mentioned and assess their and importance. You will need to separate fact from opinion and assess the quality of the facts provided by the speaker.

5   *Responding.* When you have had chance to evaluate the speaker's message, it is usual to react in some way. In a one-to-one or group situation, perhaps you will give verbal feedback, or nods or sounds of agreement. In a larger audience, your initial reaction to a message may be to laugh or applaud, or perhaps to make some notes, and you may not act on what you have heard until much later.

6   *Acting.* On some occasions, communication is an end in itself – perhaps an update or progress report. However, very often action is vital. It is important to put all promised action in writing so as to avoid any misunderstandings, and make sure you always deliver your promises.

Did you know?

The ability to communicate effectively is often listed as a required attribute in many job advertisements. This shows the positive relationship between communication and a company's success.

Checkpoint

In pairs, present to your partner something that you did recently – a movie you saw, an interesting story or joke. Your talk should last 2–3 minutes. Your partner should then tell you the content of your talk. How good were your partner's listening skills? Next, change over and you do the listening. How good are your listening skills?

Barriers to effective listening

If you are to become a good listener, it is important to be familiar with and conquer a number of physical and mental obstacles. These include:

- *Pre-judgement.* Most people function in life through some basic principles and assumptions, so some listeners jump to conclusions or close their mind to new information on anything that does not agree with their beliefs. It is important to remember that in new situations and with new facts, our fundamental assumptions may be challenged, and listeners should try to keep an open mind.
- *Selfishness.* Some people prefer not to listen but to take control of conversations. It doesn't matter what the subject is, the selfish listener believes he/she knows more than the speaker, and they set about to prove it by relating their own experiences and their own problems, and belittling the speaker's comments.

Did you know?

Your mind can process information more than four times faster than the rate of speech. This huge difference between the rate of speech and the rate of thought means that many listeners get easily distracted and simply tune out.

- *Selective listening.* Selective listeners let their minds drift around all over the place – perhaps wondering where they will go for lunch, or what they will do after work. They tune out until they hear something that attracts their attention, and then they tune back in again temporarily.

What's the difference between a good listener and a bad one?

A bad listener	A good listener
• is easily distracted	• makes the most of the opportunity • fights distractions
• daydreams	• makes an effort to concentrate
• fakes attention	• uses body language to show attention
• tunes out dryer subjects	• asks 'What's in this for me?' • considers the facts and data
• tunes out if delivery is poor	• forgives delivery errors • judges content over delivery
• tends to argue	• interrupts only to clarify • gives speaker a chance before judging
• reacts to emotions	• is not obsessed with emotional words • considers evidence

Techniques for effective listening

Good listening skills will give you an edge in life and at work. However, if you are to become an effective listener, it's going to take more than just desire and enthusiasm – it's going to take a huge conscious effort. Here are my suggestions for how you can improve your listening skills:

1 Prepare to listen. Clear your mind so that your attention is assured.
2 Avoid pre-judgement. Do not pre-judge the speaker because of appearance or occupation, and do not jump to any conclusions before hearing what is said.
3 Be open-minded. Appreciate the speaker's point of view and accept that it may not necessarily agree with your own.
4 Establish eye contact. This shows that you are listening, as does your posture and your facial expressions.
5 Don't interrupt. Try to keep emotions out of it and hold any counter-arguments until the speaker has finished.
6 Watch for signals. Pick up aspects that the speaker considers important by watching posture and gestures, as well as listening to intonation in the speaker's voice. This is like listening to the 'music' as well as to the words.
7 Judge content, not delivery. Appraise the content instead of the speaker. Consider the main points and ask if they make sense.

8   Extract key points. Pick out and repeat to yourself some key words or phrases. This will help to fix in your mind what is being said.

9   Give feedback. Learn to give positive feedback non-verbally, perhaps by nodding or smiling, to let the speaker know you are following what is being said. Be alert and make an appropriate comment or ask a question if it will help your understanding.

10   Block out distractions. Fight distractions and competing thoughts, by working hard at listening. You may need to close doors, turn off a television or radio, or move closer to the speaker.

Remember

Listening to what other people are saying is essential to your success in business – whether it is talking to someone on the phone, having an informal discussion in the corridor, or listening to a speaker at a meeting.

NON-VERBAL COMMUNICATION

In face-to-face encounters non-verbal communication is often just as important as verbal communication. As you are speaking information can be conveyed non-verbally as well as verbally. The non-verbal signals of listeners will provide instant feedback. Non-verbal communication is often referred to as body language.

Non-verbal communication techniques are often used unconsciously, for instance while speaking we may throw our arms around; while listening a sudden shock may result in a sharp intake of breath. Such non-verbal signals add impact to a meaning, and they combine to provide an instant impression in a way that written communication or telephone calls cannot. Actions of this sort are an important part of the communication process.

Posture

The way people stand or sit can say an awful lot about how they feel. Someone who is nervous or anxious will fidget with their hands, tap their feet, drum the table with their fingers. Someone who is sitting well back in their chair, legs crossed at the ankle, may be seen as being relaxed and confident. Someone with a gloomy expression, head down and

lifeless is probably feeling depressed or dejected. Someone sitting forward in their chair looking intently at the speaker, is showing a great deal of interest. The ability to interpret such signals and act as necessary is important in developing good human relations.

Facial expressions

Human faces are capable of communicating a wide range of expression and emotion. A smile conveys good humour, raised eyebrows denote questioning and disbelief, a frown denotes upset or worry.

Gestures

Many gestures are used as we speak, for example, shaking a fist to denote anger, sweeping arms in excitement, using hands for emphasis. In listening, too, gestures are used, like nodding in agreement, shaking your head in disapproval, putting your hand to your chin in consideration, folding your arms in boredom. These are all valuable signs in communicating and you should learn to read such gestures carefully.

Eye contact

The importance of eye contact is paramount. Looking someone directly in the eye suggests openness, honesty, confidence and comfort. Looking away gives an impression of being conniving or sly, or perhaps just unsure and uncomfortable. When speaking to one person try to look them in the eye. When speaking to a group avoid fixing your gaze on one or two people – let your eyes roam regularly to all corners of the room so that everyone feels involved.

Touching

Touch is an important tool to convey warmth, reassurance, support, encouragement and comfort. In some cultures, because touching implies intimacy and familiarity, there are very strict rules that govern who may touch whom and how. These norms of behaviour may change according to age, status, cultural background, etc. In today's workplace, touching has become rather a contentious issue, as it could sometimes be construed as sexual harassment.

Checkpoint

Discuss the body language and facial expressions that may be used to express:

anger	*jealousy*	*impatience*
love	*surprise*	*alertness*

Did you know?

Studies show that it takes just 15 seconds for a person to judge you when you first meet and greet someone new. It is in these 15 seconds that the other person will decide if they will listen to you, believe you and trust you. Your body language, tone of voice and the words you say to people all contribute to your first impression. Take a look at the following pie chart and you may be surprised to know exactly what impact these three areas have in those first 15 seconds.

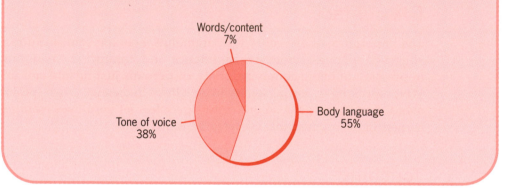

How to improve your non-verbal communication skills

Here are some ways in which you can improve your non-verbal communication skills:

1 Be honest, especially when communicating emotions.
2 Use a firm, friendly handshake when meeting new people.
3 Maintain eye contact with your entire audience.
4 Reinforce your words with tones and gestures.
5 Be aware of your posture.
6 Use appropriate gestures to support your points.

7 Imitate the posture and appearance of people you want to impress.

8 Show respect for speakers and listeners.

9 Touch people only when appropriate and acceptable.

10 Smile genuinely, as a fake one will be obvious

THE TELEPHONE

Most people use the telephone several times a day to talk with friends or to make social arrangements. These calls are usually quite straightforward and require little planning. Using the telephone for business purposes is very different. In any organisation, the person on the telephone represents the company and gives an impression of the company to the outside world. If you are to ensure good public relations, you must master effective telephone techniques.

When using the telephone and voice mail, your communication loses a lot of the impact that would be present with face-to-face communication. On the telephone, therefore, it's important to use tone of voice, inflections and attitude carefully, to show your professionalism, your readiness to listen carefully, and your ability to communicate clearly.

Remember

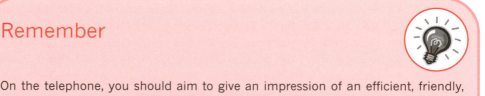

On the telephone, you should aim to give an impression of an efficient, friendly, progressive company, eager to give good service.

Making effective telephone calls

The key to making effective telephone calls is, as in most things, planning. Here are some tips that will ensure you are as effective as possible on the telephone:

Before calling

- *Choose the right time to call*. Consider both cost, urgency and convenience. When calling overseas you must also consider the time difference.
- *Check the number*. A great deal of money is wasted each year on dialling wrong numbers.
- *Plan your call*. Make a list of points and questions to be raised during your call.
- *Be prepared*. Gather together any files, papers or other information which may be needed during the call. It is unprofessional to have to say 'Hold on while I look for that.'
- *Avoid interruptions*. Call at a time when you are unlikely to be distracted.

During the call

- *Be courteous and establish a rapport*. Make time for suitable pleasantries like 'How are you today Jim?', 'Did you enjoy your holiday?'
- *Put a smile in your voice*. Remember your caller cannot see you so use intonation to good effect and try to sound confident, decisive, helpful, interested.
- *Check your notes*. Look back at your notes to ensure you have covered everything and quote figures and other data correctly.

- *Obtain feedback*. Make sure the caller understands the message correctly, especially where deadlines and actions are involved.
- *Close in a positive. courteous manner*. Double check any essential details, then finish by thanking the caller for his or her time and trouble.

Remember

If you have to ask the caller to hold on, keep going back and assuring him/her that you will be as quick as possible.

After the call

- *Make notes*. Let it become a habit to make notes of the call and place them in the appropriate file.
- *Take action*. If you need to send a letter of confirmation or inform someone in your organisation about any details of the call, do so immediately so that you do not forget important points.

Taking messages

Taking telephone messages requires both oral and written communication skills. A pencil and telephone message pad should always be kept by the telephone. A message pad like the one shown overleaf provides headings which act as a reminder to obtain the necessary information from the caller.

When taking messages, remember that the caller cannot see you. You will need to give verbal signals to know that the message is being understood. Repeat the

Reproduced courtesy of Oyez Straker

information given, confirm telephone numbers and spellings, to check all the details are received correctly.

A telephone message should be passed to its recipient immediately, or placed on his or her desk if the recipient is out.

VOICE PROCESSING

Answering machines are now a thing of the past, and voice mail is now part of what is known as 'voice processing'. This includes an automatic attendant, automatic call distribution, call forwarding, call screening, and many other features.

Voice mail is more than just an answering machine – it allows you to send, store and retrieve verbal messages. It is often used in business to replace brief inter-office notes or e-mails and messages that need no response.

Recording your voice mail greeting

Very often you will be required to record your own outgoing greeting on your voice mail system, so here are my tips to help you to record an effective voice mail greeting:

- Keep it brief. Your message should not be longer than 20–30 seconds.
- State action clearly. Be precise about what you want callers to do.
- Be professional. Keep your voice businesslike but bright and friendly. Speak slowly and precisely, pronouncing all your words carefully, especially any names or numbers.
- Give helpful options. Don't give too many options, no more than two or three. One option should be for callers to be transferred to a live operator – there is nothing more frustrating than being bounced around from one menu to another.
- State logical actions. When explaining the options, keep them logical – state the action first and then the key to press.
- Respond promptly. Check your voice mail messages regularly, and be sure to return appropriate calls quickly, at least within 24 hours.
- Update your personal greeting. As your schedule changes, make sure your greeting reflects such changes, and give any special announcements. When you are on vacation or know you will be away from your desk for a while, be sure to reflect this in your greeting.

Remember

Organise your thoughts before you start recording, so you can try to get it right first time.

Leaving a voice mail message

There is nothing more annoying than when a caller hangs up when reaching a voice mail service. It shouldn't be too difficult if you plan your message carefully in advance. Here are my tips to help you to leave an effective voice mail message:

- Keep it simple. Give just enough detail so that the recipient gets the main gist, and don't forget your name and number. Mention a time when it would be best to call you back, or when you will call the person back.
- Be professional. Speak slowly, precisely and clearly, especially when giving a number. Repeat the number at the end of the message too.
- Replay your message. Sometimes there is an option to listen to your recorded message, so you can listen to it and make sure it is clear and contains all the essential details.

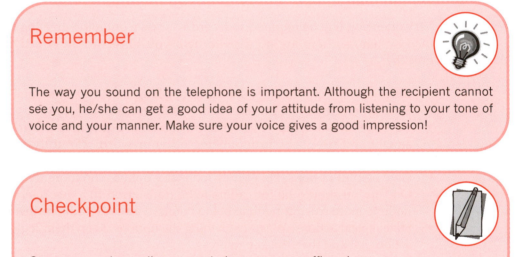

Remember

The way you sound on the telephone is important. Although the recipient cannot see you, he/she can get a good idea of your attitude from listening to your tone of voice and your manner. Make sure your voice gives a good impression!

Checkpoint

Compose a voice mail message to leave on your office phone.

A–Z OF BLOOPERS AND BLUNDERS, COMMON ERRORS AND CLICHÉS: A

Alphabet

So many people use the word alphabet wrongly. It is not correct to say '*There are seven alphabets in my name.*' This is wrong. There are *seven letters* in my name – Shirley.

There is only one *alphabet* in the English language – *abcdefghijklmnopqrstuvwxyz* – and there are 26 *letters* in the alphabet.

Mind you, I thought one of my workshop participants had a very funny answer, when he said *'No Shirley, there are only 24 letters in the alphabet – ET went home!'* Nice one!

Although

When you start a sentence with *Although*, you do not need the word *but*. For example: *'Although it is very late, I will still come over to see you.'*

Attached/enclosed herewith please find

Why do you need *herewith*? – If it's not herewith, where the heck is it? Get rid of it! Also get rid of *Please find* – it's passive and impersonal. Use the remaining words in any of these ways:

I enclose/I attach

I am enclosing/I am attaching

I have enclosed/I have attached

Enclosed is/Attached is

NB: Use *attach* for e-mails. Use *enclose* for letters.

Anytime/any time/anymore

Anytime is an adverb. *Anymore* is an adverb. *Any time* as two words are adjective and noun. For example:

You can discuss this with me anytime.

Do you have any time to discuss this with me?

I can't do this anymore.

As per

This is a simple cliche that is old-fashioned and overworked. We should not use 'per' in our writing.

Instead of

As per your request ... say 'As you requested'

As per our agreement ... say 'As we agreed'

As per your instructions ... say 'As you instructed'

As per our telecon ... say 'As discussed'

IN THE BIN: A

as far as I am concerned
as the case may be
as to whether
at hand
at the end of the day
at this moment in time

HELP YOURSELF

Identify *one* error of grammar or syntax in these sentences.

1 I'm not sure who's fault it is that this problem happened.
2 Do you ever wished you could type faster?
3 I prefer the cinema than the theatre.
4 John must of been to Rawa, as he knew it so well.
5 I use to do the filing every week, but now I do it daily.
6 The girl couldn't have spoken more quick if she had tried.
7 The assignments in the book was too demanding for the students.
8 Whose to blame for this accident?
9 Although the cleaner had finished her work, but the desk was still dusty.
10 Do you have anytime to discuss this with me?

TEST YOURSELF

1   Explain the importance of listening in oral communication.
2   Discuss the points to be remembered when communicating with someone orally.
3   What does the expression 'non-verbal communication' mean? Give examples of some non-verbal communication signals which you might associate with:

   disagreement

   discomfort

   attentive listening

   sympathy

   boredom

4   You work at a local health centre. Compile the text of a message that you will record on the voice mail when the surgery is closed. Mention normal surgery hours and give a number for emergencies.

5   Miss Louise Farney had arranged to meet your employer, Mr Simon McLoughlin at his office at 10.30 am today. At 9.45 am she telephoned (before your employer had arrived at the office) to say that trains into the city had been delayed due to a fallen tree. She has no other form of transportation so she would not be able to attend the meeting. She suggested an alternative date and time next week, and asked if your employer would confirm this. Miss Farney asked you to pass on her apologies. Write out an appropriate message for Mr McLoughlin.

6   Discuss the errors made in the following telephone conversation and decide what should have been said instead. Then write out the telephone message as it should have been written if the call had been dealt with efficiently.

Operator	Aurora, hello.
Customer	I'd like to speak to Alan Hill, the MD please.
Operator	Who's calling?
Customer	Kim Birch
Operator	Sorry he's not in.
Customer	Really? And when will he be back?
Operator	Actually he went out for lunch 2 hours ago and I was expecting him back ages ago.
Customer	Would you please pass on a message that I called?
Operator	Hang on, I'll find a pen. OK, fire away.
Customer	My number is 4537876 and I want to talk to him about my order number EM1423 dated 12 June.
Operator	Okey dokey. I'll pass it on. Cheers.
Customer	Goodbye!

Use of English

LEARNING OUTCOMES

After studying this unit you should be able to:

- Understand why it is important to ensure the accuracy of language

- Identify different parts of speech

- Explain the composition of a grammatically correct sentence

- Identify subjects and verbs in a variety of sentences

- State the purpose of the various punctuation marks

- Punctuate sentences and passages correctly

- Explain the uses of the apostrophe and use it correctly

- Understand some basic rules of English grammar

- Appreciate some commonly made errors in English language and identify where such errors are made

MODERN BUSINESS LANGUAGE

In any business dealing positive results can only be achieved through effective use of language. It has become universally accepted that English today should be simple, courteous, relaxed and straightforward. Good communicators go to considerable trouble to become competent in the English language. This is often achieved only gradually through a life-long learning process. However, the time, patience and hard work which go into mastering such skills do bring enormous rewards and satisfaction.

It is important to ensure that your language in all business communications is accurate for several reasons:

1   *To establish a relationship.* It is important to aim for a good relationship with people you communicate with regularly. Unsuitable and inaccurate language could be quite damaging to these relationships.
2   *To communicate your ideas precisely.* Unsuitable or incorrect expressions may mean that your meaning is not clear to the reader.
3   *To convey a good image of your organisation.* Clear, concise and accurate language will give an impression of efficiency and will fill the reader with confidence. Careless expressions which contain errors will do exactly the opposite; the reader may wonder if such carelessness will extend to other business dealings.

In this unit we will look at the fundamentals of English language and at some common errors.

GRAMMATICAL TERMS

Many people are able to speak and write perfectly well without knowing a lot about traditional rules of English language. It has become automatic for them to apply the rules without consciously thinking about them. However, many people make grammatical errors because they do not understand the rules properly or simply through carelessness. Such errors can lead to misunderstanding and failure in communication. It may help you to understand why errors are made if you make sure you know the names of the various parts of speech and grammatical terms and how they all work together.

Here is an alphabetical list of all the parts of speech together with other terms you may find useful to know:

- *adjective:* a word that says more about a noun, qualifying or describing it.

    an *efficient* secretary, a *fast* typist, a *fair* manager

- *adverb*: a word that is to a verb what an adjective is to a noun. It modifies or describes a verb, describing how/when/where/why the action (in the verb) is happening.

  she thinks *logically*, I walk slowly, he screamed *loudly*

- *clause*: a group of words with a subject and a predicate. A main clause stands alone as a sentence. A subordinate clause is incomplete and is used with a main clause to express an idea.

  Main clause: I like watching television

  Subordinate clause: when I have time

- *collective noun*: a word used in the singular to express many individuals.

  furniture, committee, crowd, equipment, baggage, luggage

- *conjunction*: a word that links other words (or groups of words) together.

  and, but, so, then, or

- *infinitive*: the verb form introduced by the word 'to'.

  to walk, to go, to finish, to play

  Mrs Lim wants *to speak* to her daughter

- *interjection*: a word which expresses exclamation.

  Ouch! Wow! Gosh!

- *noun*: a word used as a name of a person, thing, idea or quality.

  computer, money, desk, secretary, manager, frustration, street

- *participle*: a verb form that can also be used as an adjective to qualify a noun.

  the *laughing* policeman, the *speaking* clock, the *hard-working* student

- *pronoun*: a word used in place of a noun, to avoid repeating the noun.

  we hurried, *they* are pleased, I need *it* now, this is *my* computer

- *preposition*: a word used in front of a noun or pronoun to show its connection to another word.

  my mother hid *behind* the door

  I left the book *at* work.

  I wish to speak to you *about* your report.

- *sentence*: a group of words that expresses a complete thought.

  She cried.

  Mary went to the market.

- *subject*: one of two main components of a sentence; this is the person, place or thing that you are speaking about. It may be a noun, pronoun or a phrase used as a noun.

    The *consultant* charged a fair price.

    Sex and the City is a popular TV show.

    Choosing the right *computer* can be a difficult process.

- *verb*: a word that expresses action or condition.

    I *wish* I could go to California for my holiday.

    The computer *developed* a fault.

    You will *enjoy* learning about modern business writing.

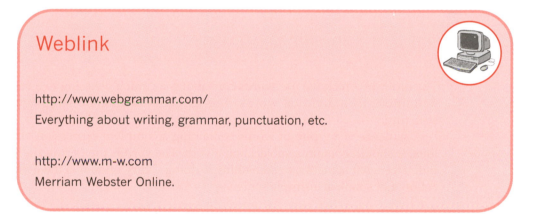

Weblink

http://www.webgrammar.com/
Everything about writing, grammar, punctuation, etc.

http://www.m-w.com
Merriam Webster Online.

Checkpoint

State which parts of speech are represented by each of the following words:

1 book _____   6 equipment _____

2 to _____   7 quickly _____

3 generate _____   8 concerning _____

4 genuine _____   9 innocent _____

5 machine _____   10 study _____

SUBJECT AND VERB AGREEMENT

The order in which we use words contributes as much meaning to a sentence as the definitions of individual words. The first rule of English language is sentence structure.

A sentence is a group of words containing a complete expression of a thought or idea. It should contain a subject and a verb. The verb is the part of the sentence that indicates what someone or something is doing – very often it is the word that shows action. Let's look at a simple sentence:

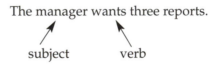

In this longer sentence you will note that the subject and verb are quite far apart:

Very often in long sentences errors are made with subject/verb agreement. This happens when the verb ends up quite far from the subject. Look at these examples:

✘ The Chairman of the board of directors plan to announce a large profit at the meeting.
✓ The Chairman of the board of directors plans to announce a large profit at the meeting.

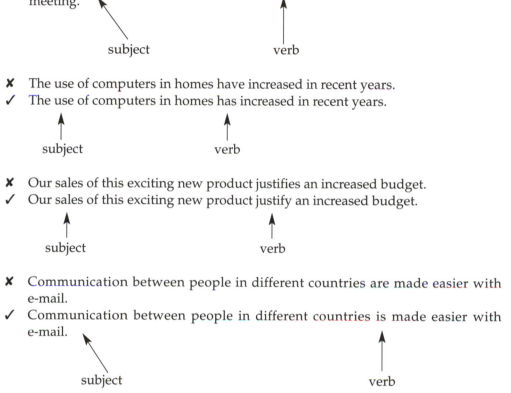

✘ The use of computers in homes have increased in recent years.
✓ The use of computers in homes has increased in recent years.

✘ Our sales of this exciting new product justifies an increased budget.
✓ Our sales of this exciting new product justify an increased budget.

✘ Communication between people in different countries are made easier with e-mail.
✓ Communication between people in different countries is made easier with e-mail.

Remember

Keep your sentences short and simple. In this way you will avoid subject/verb agreement errors and failure in communication.

Checkpoint

Identify the subject and choose an appropriate verb in each of these sentences.

1 This problem _____ easy to resolve.

2 The fault with our computers _____ rectified yesterday.

3 The notice in all yesterday's newspapers _____ the news.

4 A representative from all departments _____ presented at the meeting.

5 A questionnaire comprising three pages _____ completed by all participants.

6 A list of items for discussion at the meeting _____ to be circulated today.

7 The minutes of the meeting _____ an important record.

8 Your report to the directors _____ discussed at yesterday's meeting.

9 The announcement to staff _____ going to be made later this afternoon.

10 Make sure that the car belonging to the new Chairman _____ cleaned carefully.

PUNCTUATION

The sole purpose of punctuation is to help the reader to understand clearly the meaning of what is written. Errors in punctuation can create confusion and lead to failure in communication. If you are using rather a lot of punctuation marks in your writing, you can be sure that errors are being made and you should begin again.

Full stop/question mark/exclamation mark

All these symbols indicate the end of a sentence.

.   A full stop marks the end of a sentence.

?   The question mark is obviously used at the end of a sentence which asks a question.

!   The exclamation mark is used at the end of a word, phrase or sentence which indicates strong emotion.

Commas

Today's business writing is simple, concise and uncluttered. That means as few commas as possible. However, commas are used:

* to separate two or more nouns

    Please order some paper, envelopes and ribbons.

* to mark off two separate clauses

    I did not realise it was poor quality, otherwise I would not have bought it.

* to separate a descriptive group of words

    Teresa Long the new teacher, started work today.
    The Sales Manager, Ms Sherran Finney, is in a meeting.

* to separate a word or group of words from the main part of the sentence

    A word processor is, in my opinion, all I need for my work.
    A computer, on the other hand, has many more uses.

* to mark off words like 'therefore', 'however', 'consequently', 'unfortunately' at the beginning or in the middle of sentences

    Unfortunately, I have an appointment on Friday. I can, however, see you on Thursday.

Semi-colons

It is possible to write perfect English without any semi-colons but they can sometimes be useful.

- Semi-colons represent a pause longer than a comma and shorter than a full stop. They are used to separate two parts of a sentence where a comma would be insufficient.

    We must buy the new book; it will be very valuable for reference purposes.

- A semi-colon is also used to separate items in a list which already contains commas:

    Three new employees will be needed in personnel, purchasing and sales; one in marketing; two in administration and one in computing.

Colons

A colon is most commonly used to indicate that something will follow, for example a list or a quotation:

Many qualities are required: tact, diplomacy and patience.

Confucius said: 'Success can only be achieved through thorough preparation. Without such preparation there is sure to be failure.'

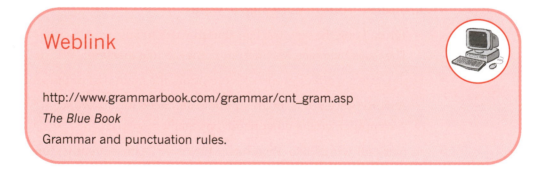

Weblink

http://www.grammarbook.com/grammar/cnt_gram.asp

The Blue Book

Grammar and punctuation rules.

Hyphens and dashes

Hyphens are mainly used in compound words, where two or more words are treated as one. For example:

self-centred
user-friendly
large-scale
up-to-date
self-taught
one-to-one
career-minded

A *dash* is used to show a change in thought in a sentence, or as an alternative to brackets. Sometimes a dash is useful because *it adds more emphasis* than a comma would add. For example:

- Communication is a two-way process – listening is just as important as speaking.
- Staff attended the anniversary celebration from all over the world – it was great to meet them all.
- She's a real self-starter – she's aiming for the top of the ladder.
- I was in Shanghai recently – what an exciting and cosmopolitan city it is.
- Today's employers are looking for real people with real abilities – not robots!

Remember

Leave one space before and one space after a dash, but no spaces are used in hyphenated words.

Checkpoint

1 Insert capital letters, full stops, commas and colons in the following passage:

The unit of the book on meetings that is Unit 13 includes the following Notice Agenda Chairman's Agenda Minutes and a series of practical assignments more practical assignments on meetings as well as many other topics are included in a separate section minutes should of course by written in third person and past tense they are an important record of what happened at a meeting.

2 Insert dashes and hyphens in the following passage:

The audio transcription programme the new one by Shirley Taylor has proved an enormous success. It was introduced in this college earlier this year January to be precise. Teachers have found that it enhances the student centred learning system at the college. All students both part time and full time have found the programme very user friendly.

3 Insert necessary punctuation marks in this passage:

A the meeting today the Chairman Mr Steven Coles suggested that a training course should be held for all sales staff members agreed that a two day seminar would be most appropriate it will be held in October. It is therefore important that you and I should meet to decide on topics suggestions for speakers will also be needed of course your expertise and help in making the necessary arrangements will be very valuable please let me know when it will be convenient for us to meet any afternoon next week would be suitable for me.

Apostrophes

Apostrophes are used to indicate:

- omission of a letter or letters

  It's important that you don't forget your textbook for all lessons.
  (It is)   (do not)

- singular possession or ownership

the toy belonging to the child	the child's toy
the purse belonging to the woman	the woman's purse
the car belonging to the director	the director's car
the desk belonging to the manager	the manager's desk

- plural possession or ownership

the toys belonging to the children	the children's toys
the purses belonging to the women	the women's purses
the cars belonging to the directors	the directors' cars
the desks belonging to the managers	the managers' desks

Note that sometimes the apostrophe is placed before the 's', sometimes after the 's'. A good rule of thumb is to separate the root word, as in these examples:

| the child's toy | the children's toys |
| child = singular | children = plural |

| the director's car | the directors' cars |
| director = singular | directors = plural |

Checkpoint

Rewrite these sentences inserting the apostrophe correctly.

1 Im going to town because I havent bought my mothers birthday present yet.

2 The course is hard work but its going to be worth it in the end.

3 I wouldn't do that if I were you. Youre bound to get caught by the boss.

4 Im delighted to hear that theres a party tonight. Its going to be fun.

5 The Boards decided to introduce flexitime. The decision was theirs.

6 I hear youre moving to a new office today. Which one is yours?

7 Whose coat is this? Does it belong to the girl whos going out with Mark?

8 Its hard to persuade the Board to change the policy but Im sure well succeed.

9 The dogs coat shines. Its collar says its names Ziggy.

10 Is this coat yours or is it Marks? I'm sure its not Iriss.

Checkpoint

Rewrite the following sentences inserting the apostrophe correctly.

1 Im going to Carols house for dinner tonight; Sues coming too.

2 There are 2 cs and 2 ms in accommodation.

3 The mans shoes are very old but the womans sandles are brand new.

4 Mens shirts are on the second floor; womens dresses on the third.

5 The two girls dresses are identical but thats because they are twins.

6 The boys attitude will have to change. Hes very rude to his teachers.

7 The teachers desk is at the front and there are 25 students desks.

8 Rosie loves Westlife but her brothers favourite pop group is Blue.

9 Eminems new single went straight to number one in this weeks charts.

10 The sales directors memo said that a regional managers meeting will be held next month.

SOME BASIC GRAMMATICAL RULES

Split infinitives

Avoid placing an adverb between *to* and the verb which follows:

    ✗ to *quickly* go   ✗ to *cautiously* enter   ✗ to *carefully* contemplate

    ✓ to go *quickly*   ✓ to enter *cautiously*   ✓ to contemplate *carefully*

Remember

If the construction becomes awkward, then ignore this rule,
e.g. ✓ ... to *seriously* expect ...

Participles

Phrases using participles can act as adjectives and must be attached to the correct noun or pronoun:

    ✗ Walking into the room, the light was bright.
    ✓ Walking into the room, she found the light was bright.
    ✗ Having gone to bed, the door bell rang.
    ✓ Having gone to bed, the boy heard the door bell ring.

Phrases like *Hoping to bear from you soon* and *Looking forward to bearing from you* are old-fashioned as well as incomplete sentences. They should not be used. Instead say:

    ✓ I hope to hear from you soon.
    ✓ I look forward to hearing from you.

Singular collective nouns

When thinking of the group as a whole, use a singular verb:

    ✗ A committee of eight members are to be formed.
    ✓ A committee of eight members *is* to be formed.

When thinking of individuals forming the group, use a plural verb:

    ✗ The committee was talking quietly among themselves.
    ✓ The committee *were* talking quietly among themselves.

Prepositions

Avoid ending a sentence with a preposition:

✗ Is there a book which I can find this information in?

✓ Is there a book *in which* I can find this information?

Did you know?

This rule occasionally leads to awkwardness so you can ignore this rule, e.g.:

✗ This is behaviour up with which I will not put.

✓ This is behaviour which I will not put up with.

Better still: This is behaviour which I will not *tolerate*.

Either/neither/every

All these words take singular verbs:

✗ Neither of the applicants are suitable.

✓ Neither of the applicants *is* suitable.

✗ Either one of the girls are willing to help you.

✓ Either one of the girls *is* willing to help you.

✗ Every student in the class have a computer.

✓ Every student in the class *has* a computer.

Each

When each precedes the word to which it refers it should be followed by a singular verb.

When each follows the word to which it refers it should be followed by a plural verb.

✗ Each of the students have six books.   ✗ The students each has six books.

✓ Each of the students *has* six books.   ✓ The students each *have* six books.

Shall/will

Shall/will are used in statements expressing the simple future tense:

Use shall with *I* or *we*:   ✓ I shall be pleased to visit him tomorrow
                                ✓ We shall need to go to the drug store.

Use will with *you, be, she, they, it*   ✓ They will make a decision soon.
                                          ✓ She will take her exams next month.

Will is used to express determination or intention:

✓ I will pass my exams this time.
✓ We will go straight to the disco after class.

Shall is often used with I and we to express a speaker's firm intentions or instructions:

✓ We shall fight them on the beaches.
✓ Shall I tell him or not?
✓ We shall overcome this problem.

Should/would

Should and would are used as past tense equivalents of shall and will.

I/We = shall/should   You/he/she/they/it = will/would

✓ I shall see him tomorrow.   ✓ He will see me tomorrow.
✓ I said I should see him tomorrow. ✓ He said he would see him tomorrow.
✓ Shall I help her?   ✓ What will happen on national day?
✓ He asked if he should help her.   ✓ He asked what would happen on
                                      national day.

The same distribution of should and would is used in main clauses linked to conditional clauses (e.g. clauses beginning with *if*).

✓ If we had not taken the train, we should not have arrived on time.
✓ If he had missed the train, he would have been late.
✓ If they had caught a train instead of the bus, they would have been early.

Use should when you mean 'ought to'.

✓ You should be able to do this.
✓ Why did they do that? They should know better.

Use would with *rather* and *sooner*.

✓ I would sooner go to the movies tonight.

✓ He would prefer a CD rather than a cassette.

✓ They would rather go to Australia for their vacation.

Do not confuse *would* and *could*. *Would* means 'if you are willing to' but *could* means 'if you are able to'.

✓ I should be grateful if you would deal with this matter urgently.

✓ I wonder if you would accompany me to the party?
  (would = if you are willing to)

✓ Do you think you could clean my windows?

✓ Could you help me with my homework?
  (could = if you are able to)

Weblink

http://www.grammardoctor.com/
Tips on grammar and style.

www.shirleytaylor.com

The world's most irritating phrases

At the end of the day ... we're fed up with clichés! So says The Plain English Campaign.

Plain English supporters around the world have voted 'At the end of the day' as the most irritating phrase in the language. Second place in the vote was shared by 'At this moment in time' and the constant use of 'like' as if it were a form of punctuation. 'With all due respect' came fourth. The Plain English Campaign (an independent pressure group launched on 26 July 1979) surveyed its 5000 supporters in more than 70 countries as part of the build-up to its 25th anniversary.

Spokesman John Lister said over-used phrases were a barrier to communication. 'When readers or listeners come across these tired expressions, they start tuning out and completely miss the message – assuming there is one! Using these terms

Checkpoint *continued*

in daily business is about as professional as wearing a novelty tie or having a wacky ringtone on your phone.'

The following terms also received multiple nominations in the survey to find the most irritating phrases:

24/7	going forward
absolutely	I hear what you're saying.
address the issue	in terms of …
around (in place of 'about')	it's not rocket science
awesome	literally
ballpark figure	move the goal-posts
basically	ongoing
basis ('on a weekly basis' in place of 'weekly' and so on)	prioritise
	pushing the envelope
bear with me	singing from the same hymn sheet
between a rock and a hard place	the fact of the matter is
blue sky (thinking)	thinking outside the box
boggles the mind	to be honest/to be honest with you/to
bottom line	be perfectly honest
crack troops	touch base
diamond geezer	up to (in place of 'about')
epicentre (used incorrectly)	value-added (in general use)
glass half full (or half empty)	

In the weekly e-newsletter from The Plain English Campaign, they reported:

> The widespread coverage of the survey (including an appearance on the front page of *The Times* and national television pieces on BBC1, BBC News 24 and Sky News) suggests we have struck a nerve, opened a can of worms, heard what people are saying, scored a home run, and any other cliché you wish to use!

John Lister took part in interviews for radio stations in Ireland, Canada, the United States, South Africa, Australia and New Zealand. Given the subject, it's probably not surprising that only one presenter ended an interview with the phrase we hear so often in these situations: 'more power to your elbow'. We received so many suggestions since publishing the list that we are thinking of holding a similar survey each year to see which of today's fresh buzzwords have become tomorrow's tired clichés.

We also received several e-mails that simply read 'Get a life.' We're not sure if these were intended to be general comments about us or nominations for clichés!

(This article was reproduced with permission from The Plain English Campaign, www.plainenglish.co.uk.)

A–Z OF BLOOPERS AND BLUNDERS, COMMON ERRORS AND CLICHÉS: B

Back

Do you use expressions like *return back* or *exchange back*? If so, you don't need the word *'back'* – it's completely redundant!

Bathe/bath

In England I often *have a bath* (in the bathtub) but in Singapore I mostly *take a shower* (standing up underneath a shower). I often hear people saying they are going to have a *bath* or they are going to *bathe*, when really they don't even have a bathtub. So how? In this case we should use the word *'shower'*.

Because, although, since, unless, if, when

When you start a sentence with any of these words, remember to attach an independent clause to it so that it becomes a complete sentence. We cannot have a sentence like 'Because it is raining.' This is a simple clause, but it is not complete until you attach an independent clause to it. For example, 'Because it is raining, I must take my umbrella.' The same goes for the other words mentioned in the heading. For example, 'Although I found the course hard, I still passed.' (Note that we don't need the word *but* when we use *although* – use a comma instead!)

Between or to

'Between' must be followed by 'and'. 'From' must be followed by 'to'. For example:

There were between 200 and 300 people at the concert.

The seminar will be conducted from 0930 to 1730.

Bored/boring

I often hear people use *boring* instead of *bored*. One workshop participant was blatantly honest with me when she said 'My boss made me come here but I didn't want to attend because I think I'm going to be very *boring*.' Hmmm . . .. I think she meant she thought she was going to be very *bored*. She could only be bored if *I* was boring! For example:

The lecture is *boring* so I am *bored*.

Bring and fetch

Use *bring* when the other person is at a different point to you and you want them to get you something. For example:

Please *bring* me the book when you come over to my place later.

Use *fetch* when the other person is at the same point as you are. For example:

Please *fetch* me a cup of coffee from the canteen.

Now the other person will have to physically go to the canteen, get the coffee and bring it back to where you are.

NB: *Fetch* is commonly used with dogs when we throw a stick . . .

IN THE BIN: B

basically
be that as it may
bear with me
beg to (differ/state)
bottom line

HELP YOURSELF

Choose the correct word from those shown in brackets.

1 It is always essential to ……….. your work carefully before finalising it.
   (check/cheque)
2 I ……………. wrong, but I thought Alison said she was on leave today.
   (maybe/may be)
3 The staff were very pleased with …………….. performance.
   (their/there)
4 I do not have ………………… to consider this matter today.
   (any time/anytime)
5 What sort of …………………… will this new book have on your work performance?
   (affect/effect)
6 It is important to ………………… all staff in your department of these new procedures.
   (advice/advise)
7 How will the new procedures ………………… safety in the company?
   (affect/effect)
8 You can discuss this with me ………………… you like.
   (any time/anytime)
9 I told John to ………………… the book here.
   (bring/take)

10 When you go to the meeting in Jurong, please .... this
report for Mr Koh.
(bring/take)

TEST YOURSELF

1   Infinitives, participles, collective nouns and prepositions

Rewrite the following sentences correctly.

(a) The team are playing very well this season.
(b) Which unit can I find information about grammar in?
(c) The cook asked him to slowly pour the cream into the mixing bowl.
(d) The new equipment are being delivered today.
(e) Walking down the street, the Christmas lights looked beautiful.
(f) The furniture for the new offices are being delivered today.
(g) Having declared the meeting closed, no other business could be discussed.
(h) Looking forward to seeing you at the meeting.
(i) My luggage are in the luggage rack above you.
(j) The new cutlery for the canteen have just arrived.

2   Neither/either/every/each

Choose the correct verb to complete these sentences.

(a) Neither of the students _____ ready for the examination.
(b) Some of the books that the students need to buy _____ expensive.
(c) Every student in the class _____ learning accurate keyboarding skills.
(d) All the male students in the class _____ hoping to find jobs in big companies.
(e) This student accommodation is popular because each student _____ a single room.
(f) All the students each _____ their own rooms.
(g) Either of the applicants _____ suitable for the position.
(h) Each of the orders _____ in excess of $1000.
(i) You will find that either of these dictionaries _____ very good.
(j) Neither of these machines _____ in good condition.

3   Shall/will and should/would

Choose the correct word to fill in these blanks.

(a) I _____ be going to the student disco next week.
(b) I said I _____ be going to the student disco next week.
(c) Mark said he _____ not be going to the student disco next week.
(d) _____ I give you some help with your homework?
(e) She asked if she _____ help her.
(f) When _____ you be teaching us how to write reports?
(g) The student asked when I _____ be teaching her how to write reports.
(h) He _____ see his father tomorrow.

(i) If you had done your homework you _____ have known the answer.

(j) If I hadn't done my homework I _____ not have known the answer.

4   Correct the errors

Each of the following sentences contains at least one error of grammar or sentence construction. Rewrite the sentences correctly.

(a) Neither of the girls are willing to help me.

(b) Lady's clothes are on the second floor.

(c) Although I didn't think it was possible, but I still passed my examination.

(d) Running to catch the bus, the car hit me.

(e) Each of these sentences contain one error.

(f) I shall appreciate if you would look into this matter urgently.

(g) If you could help me to carry my bags, I shall be very grateful.

(h) Having signed the minutes, no corrections could be made.

(i) A lot of new equipment are being bought this month.

(j) It is easy to sometimes disregard the importance of friendship.

5   Correct the errors

The following letter contains a number of errors. Rewrite it correctly.

Thank you for your letter of complaint dated on 21 July.

I feel very disturbing that you have a problem with the television recently purchased from us. One of our representatives, Mrs Joanne Gregory will call on you next Monday between 2 to 4 pm, he will endeavour to immediately rectify the fault. If he is unable to do so however, he will arrange to replace you with another television.

If this appointment is inconvenient for you please call my secretary, Alison Lester to make alternative arrangements.

Please let me know if I could be of further assistant.

6   The following letter contains a number of grammatical, punctuation and sentence construction errors. Rewrite it correctly.

You will be please to know that we are planning another seminar. This time for Executive Secretaries, it will be held at Mandarin Hotel, Orchard Road between 9.30 am to 5.30 pm. The date would be 8 October 2005.

This conference would be a practical conference, it aims to improve secretary's managerial skills and increase her productivity. A panel of professional speakers are been invited to give lectures on their specialisms, however, delegates will be able to take part in smaller practical sessions also. Latest equipment will be demonstrated too, during breaks delegates will be able to easily operate them.

Copies of the detailed programme is enclosed. A registration form is also enclosed which you should fill up and return it to me. Don't delay – act immediately so that your registration can be attended to. Reserving a place at this seminar, your money will be spent.

Remember, first come, first serve!

Business letters

Unit 4

Introducing the business letter

LEARNING OUTCOMES

After studying this unit you should be able to:

- State the main details found on letterheaded paper

- Design letterheaded paper

- Discuss the various parts of a business letter and continuation sheet

- Describe the basic presentation requirements in fully blocked layout with open punctuation

- Understand the importance of consistent presentation

- Explain how business documents should be structured

- Describe the four-point plan for structuring business communications

- Compose a variety of simple business letters

- State the main points to remember about business letters

Communication with people outside your organisation is vitally important. This is your means of establishing contact with the outside world. For this reason a high standard should be set and maintained in all your communications. High standards in an organisation's correspondence suggest high standards in business generally.

Despite the many modern communication methods available today, business letters are still very often the main means of establishing business relations with other organisations. Business letters are an ambassador for your company, so a good first impression is essential.

Business letters convey an impression of the company in many different ways:

When writing a business letter (or any other business communication) your aim should be to ensure a high standard in each of these four key areas. A well-presented business letter may lead to an important business contact.

These four key areas – printed stationery, presentation, structure, language and tone – will be considered in this unit.

PRINTED STATIONERY

Letterheaded paper

Good quality letterheaded paper is generally used for business letters. An attractive, well-balanced letterhead enhances the prestige of an organisation. Various details are included on letterheaded paper, as shown in this example:

Shirley Taylor Training and Consultancy
391B Orchard Road
#13-09 Ngee Ann City Tower B
Singapore 238874

Tel	**(+65) 64726076**		
Fax	**(+65) 63992710**	**E-mail**	**shirley@shirleytaylor.com**
Mobile	**(+65) 96355907**	**Website**	**www.shirleytaylor.com**

Logos

A logo is a graphic symbol on the letterhead, very often the same as a trade mark used on packaging, delivery vehicles, etc. These logos are often unusual or amusing so that customers remember them easily and become familiar with them. With effective design, a company's logo can become a widely circulated medium through which a company can confirm and sustain its corporate identity.

Reproduced courtesy of (a) WWF, (b) Boots Group plc, (c) Cadbury Trebor Bassett

PRESENTATION: FULLY-BLOCKED LAYOUT

The fully-blocked layout is now the most widely used method of display for all business documents. Open punctuation is usually used with fully blocked layout. This combination is thought to have a very businesslike appearance. In this example note that it is only necessary to leave one clear line space between each section of the letter.

Logo. A special logo can help to identify a company

Letterhead. Company's name, address and telephone/fax numbers, and email address

Reference. Initials of writer/typist (maybe also a filing reference)

Date. UK style is day month year. Alternative styles may be preferred in other countries

Inside address. Name, full postal address, town and post code

Salutation

Heading. Give the gist of what the letter is about

Body of letter. Separate into paragraphs with a new idea in each. Leave one clear line space between each paragraph

Complimentary close. Make sure it matches the salutation

The writer will sign the letter here

Sender's name (indicate females with a courtesy title in brackets)

Designation or department

Enclosure indication if necessary (if more than one use 'Encs')

Indicate anyone receiving copies here (if more than one use alphabetical order)

Shirley Taylor Training and Consultancy

394B Orchard Road
#13-09 Ngee Ann City Tower B
Singapore 238874

Tel	(+65) 64726076		
Fax	(+65) 63992710	E-mail	shirley@shirleytaylor.com
Mobile	(+65) 96355907	Website	www.shirleytaylor.com

ST/CFB

2 May 200-

Mr Dennis Harhalakis
38 Chancery Avenue
Singapore 309656

Dear Dennis

FULLY BLOCKED LAYOUT

The fully blocked layout for displaying business documents is now widely used, but do you use it correctly? The main feature of this modern display is that all lines start at the left margin – with no exceptions.

Most people combine fully blocked layout with open punctuation – this means that no punctuation marks are used outside the body of the message itself. Of course we need commas and full stops in the main text, but no punctuation is used in the date, inside address, salutation, complimentary close, etc.

If you use fully blocked layout for the first page of a letter, you should also block the second or subsequent pages. Continuation sheets should show the page number, date and reader's name – all blocked at the left margin. An example of a fully blocked continuation sheet is enclosed.

Remember to use fully blocked layout with open punctuation in all your business documents.

Yours sincerely

Shirley Taylor

Shirley Taylor (Miss)
Manager

Enc

Copy Suzanne Walker, Human Resource Manager

Did you know?

I'm often asked 'When should we use Dear (first name) and when should we use Dear Mr/Mrs/Ms xxxxx?' Well the answer is easy.

When you are writing to someone, consider how you would address them if you were to meet. For example, if you are writing to Marion Goldacre, imagine you are walking along the street and you meet Marion. Would say to her 'Hello Marion' or 'Hello Mrs Goldacre'? It's that simple. Remember, write as you speak!

OTHER PARTS OF A BUSINESS LETTER

Confidential/airmail/urgent

If a letter is confidential this should be indicated between the date and inside address, just as it would be shown on the envelope:

CONFIDENTIAL   AIRMAIL
Mr Tom Ong   Mrs Lily Ng
Managing Director   54 Taman Warna
Carona Press plc   10890 Johor Bahru
56 Walker Avenue   West Malaysia
Leeds
LS3 5GJ

Attention line

Traditionally an attention line was used when the writer wanted to ensure that the letter is directed toward the desk of a specific person. The letter was addressed to the company in general and always began 'Dear Sirs'.

FOR THE ATTENTION OF MRS MARISA BERTOCCHI, CULINARY DIRECTOR
Original Sin
Blk 43
#01–62 Jalan Merah Saga
Singapore 278115

Dear Sirs

In today's business communications when we usually know the name of the person to whom we are writing, it is rarely necessary to use an attention line. Simply include the recipient's name and designation in the inside address and use a personalised salutation.

Mrs Marisa Bertocchi
Culinary Director
Original Sin
Blk 43
#01–62 Jalan Merah Saga
Singapore 278115

Dear Marisa

Copies

When a copy of a letter is to be sent to another person (usually someone in the sender's organisation) this may be indicated by either of the following methods:

cc	Hanindah Zainomum, Training Manager	cc stands for courtesy copy
Copy	Rosehannah Farrelly, Personnel Manager Patricia McInally, Training Manager Karen Murphy, Welfare Officer	Use alphabetical order when more than one person is on the circulation list

Blind copies

If the sender of the letter does not wish the recipient to know that other people are receiving copies, a blind copy may be sent. In this case the indication bcc is used on the copies only – not on the original.

bcc   Patrick Ashe, Personnel Director   bcc stands for blind courtesy copy

Signing on someone else's behalf

You may have to sign a letter on behalf of someone else. This can be done in either of the following ways:

Yours sincerely

Sally Turner

pp STEVEN WONG
Managing Director   ◀——————   pp means *per procurationem* or *on behalf of*

Yours sincerely

Sally Turner

for STEVEN WONG
Managing Director

OPEN PUNCTUATION

Open punctuation is commonly used with the fully-blocked layout. Only punctuation marks which are essential to ensure grammatical sense are included within the text of correspondence. All other commas and full stops are omitted. When using open punctuation it is important to be consistent:

Dates

12 July 200–   No st, th or rd
                                          No comma

Names

Mr & Mrs Richard Reeves   No full stops

Addresses

Mrs Michelle Dietrich   No full stops after abbreviations
Production Manager   No commas at the end of lines
JCL Engineering Ltd
245 Upper Jurong Road West
Singapore 226767

Salutation and complimentary close

Dear Mrs Dietrich   No commas
Yours sincerely

Abbreviations

	Mr	BA	MRT		Mr.	B.A.	M.R.T.
✓	Dr	BEd	IBM	✗	Dr.	B.Ed.	I.B.M.
	NB	RSA	SBC		N.B.	R.S.A.	S.B.C.

CONTINUATION SHEETS

Many organisations have printed continuation sheets which are used for second and subsequent pages of business letters. Printed continuation sheets may show simply the company's name and logo, as in these examples:

 Shirley Taylor Training and Consultancy   *Continuation*

When printed continuation sheets are not used you should use plain white paper of the same quality as the letterheaded paper.

It is important to include certain details at the top of second or subsequent pages just in case the pages should become separated.

Remember that when using fully blocked style you should maintain consistency by ensuring that all the headings on continuation sheets also begin at the left margin, as in the example shown here.

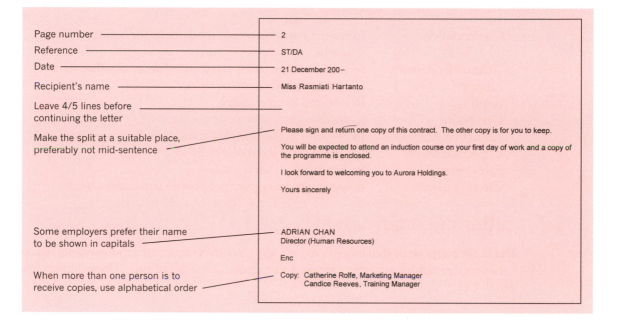

Page number ———————————————— 2

Reference ———————————————— ST/DA

Date ———————————————— 21 December 200–

Recipient's name ———————————————— Miss Rasmiati Hartanto

Leave 4/5 lines before
continuing the letter ————————

Make the split at a suitable place,
preferably not mid-sentence ———— Please sign and return one copy of this contract. The other copy is for you to keep.

You will be expected to attend an induction course on your first day of work and a copy of the programme is enclosed.

I look forward to welcoming you to Aurora Holdings.

Yours sincerely

Some employers prefer their name
to be shown in capitals ———————— ADRIAN CHAN
Director (Human Resources)

Enc

When more than one person is to
receive copies, use alphabetical order ———— Copy: Catherine Rolfe, Marketing Manager
                Candice Reeves, Training Manager

When using a continuation sheet remember these guidelines:

- Do not include 'continued' or 'Cont.' at the foot of the first page. It will be obvious that there is another page if there is no closing section or signature.
- Always take over at least three or four lines of text to a second or subsequent page.
- Try to start a new page with a new paragraph. It does not look good to leave one line of a paragraph at the foot of one page or at the top of the next.

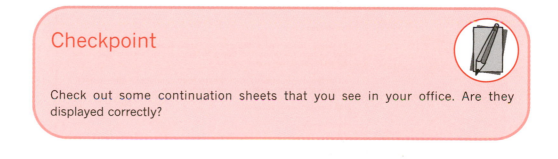

Checkpoint

Check out some continuation sheets that you see in your office. Are they displayed correctly?

CATEGORIES OF BUSINESS LETTER

There are many different categories of business letters. In this section we will look at some very basic letters. A sample letter is shown in each category and then you can practise writing some for yourself.

Some of the main categories of business letter are:

	Aim
Confirmation	To confirm arrangements made between sender and recipient
Acknowledgement	To acknowledge receipt of a letter, order or other item
Enquiry	To request information or prices
Reply	To respond to an enquiry
Complaint	To criticise poor service or goods
Adjustment	To respond to the complaint and hopefully make amends
Collection letters	To obtain settlement of a debt
Sales letters	To sell goods or services
Circular letters	To reach a certain group of people (customers/staff)

Letter of confirmation

The main purpose of this letter is to provide a written record of arrangements made between the sender and the recipient in person or by telephone. These letters are usually very short.

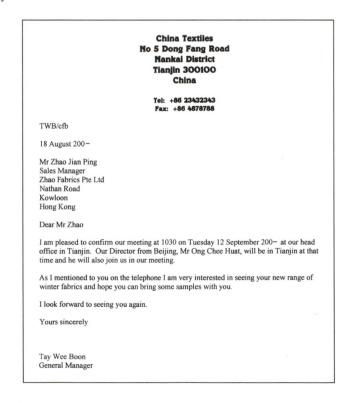

China Textiles
No 5 Dong Fang Road
Nankai District
Tianjin 300100
China

Tel: +86 23432343
Fax: +86 4878788

TWB/cfb

18 August 200−

Mr Zhao Jian Ping
Sales Manager
Zhao Fabrics Pte Ltd
Nathan Road
Kowloon
Hong Kong

Dear Mr Zhao

I am pleased to confirm our meeting at 1030 on Tuesday 12 September 200− at our head office in Tianjin. Our Director from Beijing, Mr Ong Chee Huat, will be in Tianjin at that time and he will also join us in our meeting.

As I mentioned to you on the telephone I am very interested in seeing your new range of winter fabrics and hope you can bring some samples with you.

I look forward to seeing you again.

Yours sincerely

Tay Wee Boon
General Manager

Acknowledgement

This letter is sent to acknowledge receipt of something when a written record is appropriate. An acknowledgement may also be sent to acknowledge receipt of another letter or document which requires further attention. As such you would clearly state that you will look into the matter and reply in more detail at a later date.

✹ Stardust Photo Studio

Rm 9B No 3 Building
1234 Yu Yao Road
Shanghai 200040
China

Telephone +86-21-878787   Fax +86-21-878788

HMY/lk

25 May 200–

Mr Chia Lye Ann
3001 Caobao Road
Xuhui District
Shanghai 234399

Dear Mr Chia

Thank you for your letter of 22 May addressed to our General Manager, Mrs Ho Mei Ying.

Mrs Ho is overseas on business and will not be in the office again until 4 June. I shall be in contact with Mrs Ho and shall inform her about your letter, which I am sure will receive her prompt attention.

Please let me know if I can be of any help.

Yours sincerely

Henrietta Chew (ms)
PA to Ho Xiao Hong
General Manager

Some organisations use printed cards for this purpose, which can be completed easily.

Jonathan Ross & Partners, Solicitors, 45 Queen Street, London SW1 ERT

_____

We acknowledge with thanks the receipt of

which will receive careful attention.

_____

Telephone 0207 456 7890   Fax 0207 432 8765

Enquiry

Enquiries for information about goods or services are sent and received in business all the time. In your letter remember to state clearly exactly what you want – information? a catalogue? a price list? a quotation? Keep your enquiry brief and to the point.

The sender's personal address looks good balanced at the top right

34 Windsor Avenue
Beecher
Chesterfield
S44 2JL

When you write your own personal letters a reference is not necessary, just a date

20 January 200–

Nautilus Cruises plc
Nautilus House
Temple Street
London
SE1 4LL

When writing to a company use the salutation 'Dear Sirs'

Dear Sirs

Introduction

My neighbour, Mr Roland Keating, has recently recommended your luxury cruises to me. He and his wife have often taken a Nautilus cruise and speak very highly about them.

Details

My wife and I are thinking of celebrating our 25th wedding anniversary in August with a special holiday.

Response required

Please send me a copy of your current brochure showing the cost of your cruises together with departure dates.

I hope to hear from you soon.

Close

Yours faithfully

Match the complimentary close with the salutation

MARK FARRELLY

Reply to enquiry

Enquiries mean potential business so they must be acknowledged promptly. If the letter is from an established customer, say how much you appreciate it. If it is from a prospective customer, thank them for their enquiry, give all the relevant information and express the hope of good business relations.

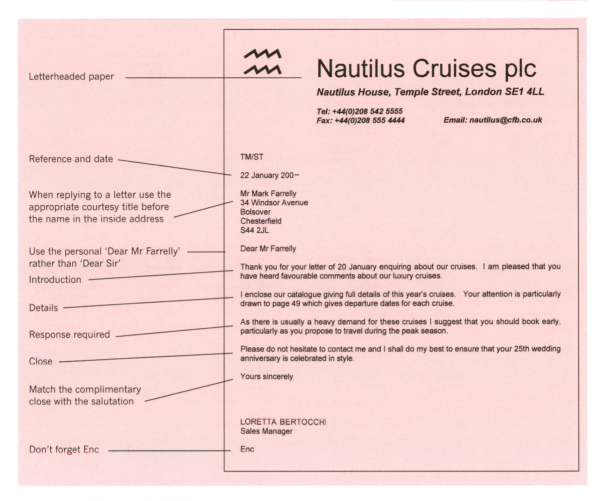

Letterheaded paper

Reference and date

When replying to a letter use the appropriate courtesy title before the name in the inside address

Use the personal 'Dear Mr Farrelly' rather than 'Dear Sir'

Introduction

Details

Response required

Close

Match the complimentary close with the salutation

Don't forget Enc

Nautilus Cruises plc

Nautilus House, Temple Street, London SE1 4LL

Tel: +44(0)208 542 5555
Fax: +44(0)208 555 4444   Email: nautilus@cfb.co.uk

TM/ST

22 January 200–

Mr Mark Farrelly
34 Windsor Avenue
Bolsover
Chesterfield
S44 2JL

Dear Mr Farrelly

Thank you for your letter of 20 January enquiring about our cruises. I am pleased that you have heard favourable comments about our luxury cruises.

I enclose our catalogue giving full details of this year's cruises.   Your attention is particularly drawn to page 49 which gives departure dates for each cruise.

As there is usually a heavy demand for these cruises I suggest that you should book early, particularly as you propose to travel during the peak season.

Please do not hesitate to contact me and I shall do my best to ensure that your 25th wedding anniversary is celebrated in style.

Yours sincerely

LORETTA BERTOCCHI
Sales Manager

Enc

Complaint

There are bound to be occasions in business when you have to make a complaint, or deal with one. When you have a genuine complaint you will feel angry but remember that the other party may not be to blame. They may have a perfectly good defence. Therefore, your letter should be confined to a statement of the facts followed by an enquiry about what the company will do about it or a suggestion of how you expect the matter to be dealt with. At all costs avoid rudeness or sarcasm. This will only cause ill-feeling.

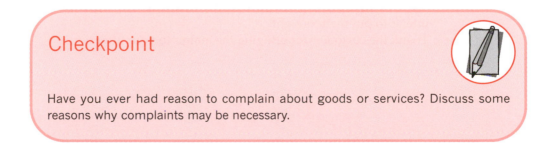

Checkpoint

Have you ever had reason to complain about goods or services? Discuss some reasons why complaints may be necessary.

Note that a telephone number is included with the sender's address

25 Finch Avenue
Marlborough
Leeds
LS20 2JT

0113 4328432

15 June 200–

Mr Steven Foster
Foster's Master Builders Ltd
21 Lodge Lane
Sheffield
S31 3ES

Dear Mr Foster

BUNGALOW AT 1 CRESCENT ROAD, MARLBOROUGH, LEEDS

Introduction and reason for writing – tone is firm but courteous

I signed the contract for the building of this property in September 1999. At that time you estimated that the work would be completed and the bungalow ready for occupation in about 8 months' time. That was 9 months ago and the work is still only half finished.

Inconvenience is emphasised

The delay is causing a great deal of inconvenience not only to me but also to the buyer of my present home. Obviously I cannot transfer until the bungalow at Crescent Road is finished.

Action expected

I hope you can proceed with this work without any further delay. Please let me know when you expect it to be finished.

Yours sincerely

RON MARSHALL

Reply to complaint

Most companies will wish to hear if customers have cause to complain. It gives them an opportunity to investigate, to explain and to put things right. Goodwill can be preserved instead of business being taken elsewhere. Here are some general rules for dealing with complaints:

- The customer is not always right, but it is good practice to assume that the customer may be right.
- Acknowledge a complaint promptly. If you are unable to reply fully give an explanation and reply in full as soon as possible.
- Be polite and try not to offend, even if the complaint is unreasonable.
- Admit blame readily if appropriate, then express regret and state how you intend to put matters right.
- Thank the customer for bringing the matter to your attention.

Foster's Master Builders Ltd
21 Lodge Lane
Sheffield
S31 3ES

Tel: 0114 2872222

GH/ST

17 June 200–

Mr Ron Marshall
25 Finch Avenue
Marlborough
Leeds
LS20 2JT

Dear Mr Marshall

BUNGALOW AT 1 CRESCENT ROAD, MARLBOROUGH, LEEDS

Acknowledge letter and express regret ——— Thank you for your letter of 15 June. I am sorry that the estimated period for completion of your bungalow has already been exceeded. I realise how much inconvenience this delay must be causing you.

Circumstances are explained fully ——— I would, however, ask you to remember that we have had an exceptionally severe winter. This made work on the site extremely difficult during several periods of heavy snow. Secondly there was a nationwide shortage of building materials earlier this year, from which the trade is only now recovering. Had it not been for these two unforeseen difficulties, the estimated completion period of 8 months would have been met.

Assurance that the situation will improve ——— Fortunately the weather has improved a lot in recent weeks and as such work on your bungalow is now proceeding smoothly. Unless there are any other unforeseen delays I can safely guarantee that the bungalow will be ready for you by the end of August.

Courteous close ——— Please do not hesitate to telephone me if you have any further questions.

Yours sincerely

STEVEN FOSTER
Manager

Collection letters

Collection letters are those sent to customers who do not pay accounts promptly. In such letters tone is very important. The way you write such letters will depend on such factors as the age of the debt, whether the customer is habitually late in settling accounts and any previous reminders issued.

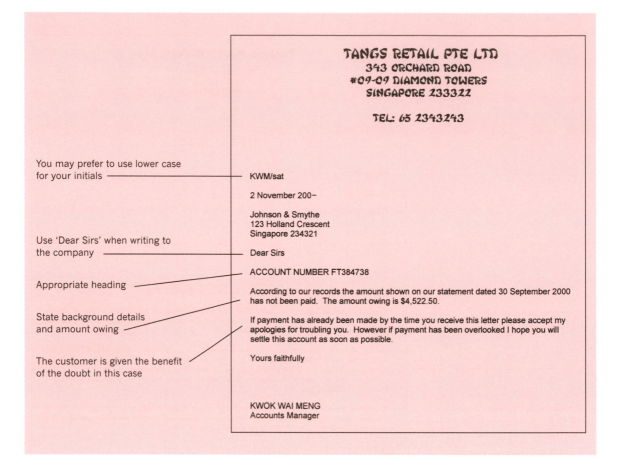

You may prefer to use lower case for your initials ————

Use 'Dear Sirs' when writing to the company ————

Appropriate heading ————

State background details and amount owing ————

The customer is given the benefit of the doubt in this case

TANGS RETAIL PTE LTD
343 ORCHARD ROAD
#09-09 DIAMOND TOWERS
SINGAPORE 233322

TEL: 65 2343243

KWM/sat

2 November 200–

Johnson & Smythe
123 Holland Crescent
Singapore 234321

Dear Sirs

ACCOUNT NUMBER FT384738

According to our records the amount shown on our statement dated 30 September 2000 has not been paid. The amount owing is $4,522.50.

If payment has already been made by the time you receive this letter please accept my apologies for troubling you. However if payment has been overlooked I hope you will settle this account as soon as possible.

Yours faithfully

KWOK WAI MENG
Accounts Manager

If a polite letter like this fails to produce a response, a firmer letter will be sent.

TANGS RETAIL PTE LTD
343 ORCHARD ROAD
#09-09 DIAMOND TOWERS
SINGAPORE 233322

TEL: 65 2343243

KWM/sat

20 November 200—

Johnson & Smythe
123 Holland Crescent
Singapore 234321

Dear Sirs

ACCOUNT NUMBER FT384738

Give background details again and repeat sum due ——— On 2 November we wrote to remind you that our September statement showed a balance of $4,522.50 outstanding and due for payment.

The tone is firmer here ——— Settlement of this account is now almost 2 months overdue. Therefore we must ask you either to send us your payment without delay or at least let us know the reason for this delay.

A prompt reply will be appreciated.

Yours faithfully

KWOK WAI MENG
Accounts Manager

Checkpoint

If another polite letter does not receive any response a letter should be sent stating that legal proceedings will be begun if payment is not made within a specified period. Discuss how you think such a letter would be worded, and make a copy for your files.

OTHER TYPES OF BUSINESS LETTER

There are many different types of business letters. In this unit we have only looked at some of the more routine letters. Unit 5 gives more advice on the rules of good writing with some practical work for you to do. Unit 6 looks at all the letters and other documents associated with applying for a job. Unit 12 looks at more advanced letters in the form of circulars and sales letters.

Remember, there will be many occasions when you will need to write a letter which does not fall into any specific category. In these situations you must remember the general rules of good business writing and plan your letter carefully so that its objectives are met.

STRUCTURE

Many business letters, like the ones we have looked at in this unit, are short and routine. They can be written without any special preparation. Other letters require more careful thought and planning. This four-point plan provides a simple framework for structuring all business communications. The following diagram illustrates the four basic sections (the four-point plan) that will make up all your business communications.

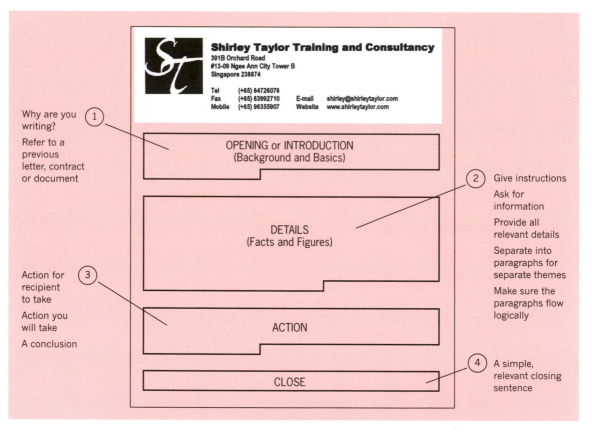

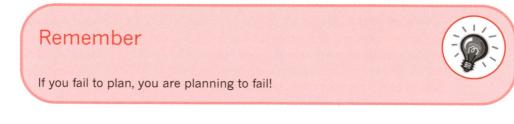

The four-point plan

1 Opening or introduction

The first paragraph of your message could refer to a meeting or previous contact, perhaps to a letter or e-mail received. Otherwise it should introduce the subject that you want to discuss in the message itself. For example:

Thank you for your letter dated . . .
It was great to meet you yesterday.
Thank you for calling me this morning.
It was good to speak to you today.
ST International will be holding a conference for secretaries in April 200–.

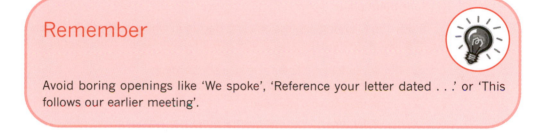

Remember

Avoid boring openings like 'We spoke', 'Reference your letter dated . . .' or 'This follows our earlier meeting'.

2 Details

Here is where you give all the 'meat' – all the facts and figures. This is where you will give information, in a logical order, with separate paragraphs where appropriate. Make sure you include all the key points in a logical order.

3 Action

Here is where you tell the reader what action you want him/her to take as a result of your message. Or alternatively it may be action that you will take after all the points you have mentioned. For example:

I hope you will investigate this and let me have your comments soon.
Please complete the enclosed reply form and return it to me by . . .

4 Close

Finish with a simple one-line close – a relevant one-liner. For example:

I hope to hear from you soon.
Your prompt reply would be appreciated.
Please call me at . . . if you have any questions.

Remember

Avoid incomplete or boring closes such as 'Looking forward to hear from you' or 'Please revert soonest'.

Checkpoint

Four-point plan

Study the following expressions and decide in which part of a business letter you might find them. Write 1, 2, 3 or 4 using the four-point plan as your guide:

1 Thank you for your letter of 4 August regarding Miss Tania Kaur's application for a post in your company. ☐

2 I hope to hear from you soon. ☐

3 Please let me know as soon as the order is ready for collection. ☐

4 I am pleased to inform you that our Crown Prince Suite is available on these dates. ☐

5 Our latest catalogue is enclosed. ☐

6 Our prices for the goods you require are as follows: ☐

7 Thank you for any assistance you are able to provide. ☐

8 Your company has been recommended to me by my colleague, Janine Chew. ☐

9 I hope to see you at the conference next month. ☐

10 Your letter of 15 July has been passed to me by Michael Green, our Customer Relations Manager. ☐

11 We are interested in holding our Annual Dinner and Dance at your hotel in November. ☐

12 Further to your letter of 29 March I am pleased to confirm reservation of our Peninsular Suite for your wedding. ☐

13 A discount of 10% will be allowed on all orders. ☐

14 These goods are in stock and can be delivered within one week of your order. ☐

15 Please do not hesitate to contact me if you require any further information. ☐

16 I can recommend Miss Harriet Tan highly and without hesitation. ☐

17 Unfortunately I am unable to accept your invitation due to a prior commitment. ☐

18 Mr Jonathan Lee has applied to us for the post of Credit Control Manager. ☐

19 I hope you will visit us at stand 26 of this exciting exhibition where we will be revealing our new range of portable computers. ☐

20 This special function will take place on Monday 26 March 200– ☐

Checkpoint

Rearrange the letter

Here are cut-up pads of a business letter. Decide the correct order and rewrite the letter correctly for your files.

a Copy Michael Norton, Divisional Manager, Singapore

b Yours sincerely

c 29 July 200–

d Dear Mr Leong

e I am pleased to say that I planned to visit Hong Kong, Malaysia and Singapore later this year, so in view of your invitation I shall schedule my Singapore visit so that I can attend your celebrations.

f Sally Turner (Mrs)
   Sales and Marketing Director

g Thank you for inviting me to attend your company's 20th Anniversary Celebrations at the Singapore Pagoda Hotel on Friday 15 October 200–.

h

ST International plc

Aurora House
Temple Street
London SE1 4LL

Tel   0207 345375
Fax   0207 453678   E-mail   shirley@shirleytaylor.com
Mobile 09890 333444   Website   www.shirleytaylor.com

i I look forward to meeting you again.

j VISIT TO SINGAPORE

k I hope it will also be possible to meet you at your offices to discuss your proposal to become our agent in Singapore. I have asked our Divisional Manager, Michael Norton, to contact you to arrange a convenient appointment.

l Mr John Leong
   Managing Director
   International Holdings Sdn Bhd
   12th floor Wisma Genting
   Jalan Rajah Laut
   50245 Kuala Lumpur
   West Malaysia

m ST/bp

Checkpoint

Composition

1 Enquiry and reply

The letter below is an enquiry. On the following page is the reply. On the lines provided complete the missing information by matching corresponding parts of each letter.

WESSEX HOTEL GROUP

#21–10 Raffles Tower

Singapore 234929

Telephone +65 2342344 Fax +64 2344244

____ /LYL

21 October 200–

_____

Ward Cutlery Ltd
Richmond Street
Sheffield
United Kingdom
S20 2BJ

Dear _____

A colleague visited England recently and passed on your catalogue to me. We are very interested in purchasing new cutlery for our chain of hotels in South East Asia. Please send us your_____ and price list, and also let us know details of any_____ you are able to offer. Information about _____ would also be appreciated.   .

_____

Yours _____

SANDRA KOH (_____)
Food and Beverage Manager

Checkpoint *continued*

WARD CUTLERY LTD
Richmond Street
Sheffield _____
Telephone +44 114 245145   Fax +44 114 245555

____/PJ
1 November 200–

AIRMAIL

Mrs Sandra Koh

_____

Wessex Hotel Group
#21–10 Raffles Tower
Wessex Road
Singapore 234929

Dear_____

_____ 21 October asking for details of our cutlery.
I have pleasure in enclosing our current catalogue which also contains all
_____ and an order form.
On orders of £500 or more we offer a 20% discount. _____
are usually sent by air freight within 2 weeks of receipt of order.
I hope you find our _____ agreeable but if you have any
queries please _____
_____

Yours sincerely

WILLIAM CHEONG
Manager

---

2 Letter of enquiry

You work for Mr Leslie Lim, Training Manager of Turner Communications, #03–03 Sapphire Building, 215 Lorong Ragu, Kuala Lumpur, Malaysia. Mr Lim has received recommendations for business and secretarial courses at Aurora Training Centre, 21 Exeter Road, #07–04 Grange Tower, Eastern Avenue, Kuala Lumpur, Malaysia. He asks you to compose a letter for him saying that he is considering upgrading some staff. Ask for details of part-time courses available at the college including the examinations which they lead to. You also need to know the dates of the next intakes. Remember to plan your letter first in accordance with the four-point plan.

3 Reply to enquiry

Compose a reply from the Principal of Aurora Training Centre giving details of the courses available at your own college. Plan it first, using a four-point plan, and make sure you include all the necessary points. Include an invitation for Mr

Checkpoint *continued*

Lim to visit your college to view the facilities and discuss their training needs further.

4 Letter of complaint

Your boss asked you to order a new dinner service (cups, saucers, plates, etc.) for the directors dining room. You ordered one that has gold coloured edging. The set was delivered while you were out for lunch, so your colleague signed for it without checking the contents. When you opened the package you noticed that on various items the gold coloured edging is tarnished and flawed. You cannot accept the goods in this condition. Write a letter (or e-mail) to the company and ask them to arrange for a replacement. You have an important meeting in a few days time so this is now urgent.

(When you have finished this assignment, compose a suitable reply from the company.)

Weblink

http://www.business-letter-writing.com/

Tips on effective business letters.

Checkpoint

Many mistakes are made in starting and ending letters and e-mails. Discuss what is wrong with these examples and then rewrite them appropriately.

Opening paragraphs

1 With reference to your letter of 12th June 200–.

_____

2 I refer to your letter regarding the above-mentioned conference.

_____

3 We have received your letter complaining about the above order.

_____

Checkpoint *continued*

4 As spoken in our telecon this morning.

_____

5 It was a pleasure meeting you today and thank you for your lunch.

_____

Closing handshakes

1 Looking forward to hear from you.

_____

2 Anything further, please call.

_____

3 Should you require any further clarifications, please do not hesitate to contact the under-mentioned.

_____

4 Please revert to me on this matter soonest.

_____

5 Thank you.

_____

Remember

If you *must* say thank you at the end of a message, please make it into a full sentence and say thank you for something. For example:

• Thank you for your help.
• Thank you for your support.
• Thank you for your patience.
• Thank you for your understanding.

Checkpoint

Can you add to this list with some more sentences to close a message, starting with 'Thank you . . . .'?

What's wrong?

When writing a letter of complaint it is important to get your tone and approach right. Your letter is more likely to, achieve its objective if you sound hurt rather than infuriated. It is best to assume that your grievance is an oversight on the part of the company concerned rather than inefficiency.

Discuss what is wrong with this letter of complaint and then rewrite it more appropriately.

Dear Sir or Madam

I am speechless at such incompetence! You obviously don't care at all about your customers otherwise you would take more care to avoid the time and trouble your inefficiency has cost me, not to mention the expense!

In my household we pay an extra fee to have two separate entries in the local phone book – one for my wife and one for myself. As it is you have ignored my specific instructions to enter our names as we wished. The entry of E James is totally useless. Look at the book and see for yourself how many more E James there are in Sheffield! I wanted my first name including for obvious reasons of clarity, but you just ignored my request. As if that wasn't bad enough, you even printed the wrong number! For goodness sake, how much more wrong can you get?

I demand an immediate explanation and formal apology.

Yours faithfully

Elton James

Elton James

Checkpoint

In groups, discuss how you think the company would reply to this letter from Elton James. Draft a suitable response.

PRESENTING BUSINESS LETTERS – KEY POINTS TO REMEMBER

1 Use fully-blocked style with open punctuation consistently.
2 Leave one blank line between each section of the letter and between each paragraph.
3 The only big space on your letter should be for the sender's signature.
4 Display your subject heading in capitals and bold to make it stand out.
5 Structure your message according to the four-point plan – with an introduction, details, action and close.
6 Make sure the information in your central section flows logically from point to point. Restructure if necessary.
7 Take special care with your opening and closing paragraphs.
8 Include appropriate headings at the top of continuation pages.
9 Proofread your message carefully, and consider whether it is structured appropriately.
10 Read through your message as if you were the reader. Ask yourself how the reader will feel when it is received.

A–Z OF BLOOPERS AND BLUNDERS, COMMON ERRORS AND CLICHÉS: C

Clarification

I often see sentences like 'Please contact me if you require any further clarifications'. The word should be 'clarification', it becomes countable when you are talking about specific pieces of clarification you need. In most cases you will mean the act of clarifying something, so use the word as an uncountable noun – 'clarification'.

NB: It would be much better to say 'Please give me a call at xxxx if you have any questions.'

Clichés

Clichés (or platitudes) are things that have lost their sparkle, and often their meaning, through overuse. Examples of writing clichés are those old-fashioned terms like 'above-mentioned', 'enclosed herewith', 'please be advised', I am writing to inform you. And there are many more!

Clothing

Another uncountable noun, this word does not need an 's' on the end. Even though you can count the number of pieces of clothing, you should still use the word clothing without the 's'.

Compare to/compare with

When comparing things that are dissimilar, use 'compare to'. When comparing things that are similar, use 'compare with'. Examples:

My life has been compared to a soap opera.
US Congress may be compared with the British Parliament.

Comprise

We should not use the word 'of' to follow 'comprise' or 'comprises'. The word literally means 'to consist of', so when using comprise we don't need the word 'of', otherwise we would be saying 'to consist of of'.

Contact on/contact at

Both of these expressions are correct. 'Contact me on xxxx' is British English and 'Contact me at xxxx' is American English.

IN THE BIN: C

commonly
current
currently

HELP YOURSELF

Identify and correct the errors in these sentences.

1 Please make sure you have fill in all the pricing details.
2 Is there anymore figures to include in this list?
3 We will keep you inform once this has completed.
4 Kindly let me know if you will attend latest by 11/04/06.

5 I have drafted the below information for the new catalogue.
6 I believe there are some new materials that's just been sent.
7 I have created a file for you to input the key details as and when there is any updates.
8 I just spoke to Michael, he is quite please with the situation.
9 Looking forward to your quick response.
10 Below are the information you need.

TEST YOURSELF

1 You are Administrative Assistant (AA) to Anu Morar, Personnel Manager of First State Bank of India, 97–94 High Street, New Delhi, India. Mrs Morar is in a meeting. Carry out the instructions in this note from Mrs Morar. (City & Guilds EFBC1)

AA
Please look at staff record card attached and then fill in standard letter form for me to send in reply.
Thanks.
Anu

Martin's Bank
112–116 High Street
NEW DELHI
India
Tel: 009111 2926136
Fax: 009111 2926137

Request for Reference

Miss Usher Patel has applied for the position of Senior Correspondence Clerk with our bank. We understand she is currently employed by you and would therefore appreciate receipt of a reference. Please confirm her starting date and current position. Comments on her performance and attendance and any other relevant information you are able to give would be much appreciated.

Yours sincerely

Mr Dura Bangura
Human Resources Manager
Martin's Bank

STAFF RECORD CARD		
NAME:	Usher Patel	
POSITION:	Correspondence Clerk	
START DATE:	17 May 1990	

Attendance	Standard of Work	Suitability for Promotion
Above satisfactory	Above satisfactory	**Recommended –**
~~Satisfactory~~	~~Satisfactory~~	**no position available**
~~Poor~~	~~Poor~~	**at present**

Other comments: Usher belongs to the bank's Dance Society and has performed to raise money for various charities.

First State Bank of India

67–94 High Street, NEW DELHI, India

Telephone: 009111 289478 Fax: 009111 289479

To: ....   Date: ....

....   Ref: ....

....

....

Dear ....

Reference for ....

This person has worked for us since .... in the position of

....

Whilst in our service ....

....

....

....

....

....

Yours ....

Mrs Anu Morar
Personnel Manager
First State Bank of India

---

2   You are Administrative Assistant (AA) to Anu Morar, Personnel Manager of First State Bank of India, 97–94 High Street, new Delhi, India. Mrs Morar is in a meeting. Carry out the instructions in this note from Mrs Morar. (City & Guilds EFBC1)

AA
Please draft a letter for me to send to Ms Burgess. Tell her we might be interested in junior staff willing to work here for 6–12 months. We'll need:
* details of her clients' experience
* information about her clients' qualifications
* salary expectations
* advice from Nathan's on how much commission they charge
* to know who arranges accommodation

I'll sign the letter this afternoon.

Thanks
Anu

Nathan's Employment Agency
17 Tower Hill, LONDON, EC1A 9DD UK
Tel: 0207 623 9442
Fax: 0207 623 9444

FAX TRANSMISSION HEADER

To: Mrs Anu Morar – Personnel Manager
Company: First State Bank of India
Fax Number: 009111 289479
From: Claire Burgess – Consultant

Date: RECEIVED

No. of sheets (including header sheet): 1
Message:

We have many clients with banking qualifications who are anxious to gain experience of working overseas. Should you be interested, we would be delighted to supply further details.

Unit 5

Rules of good writing

LEARNING OUTCOMES

After studying this unit you should be able to:

- Understand the key rules of writing relating to all business documents

- Identify and correct examples of poor business writing

- Give examples of poor terminology used in business writing and their modern-day equivalents

- Explain the general guidelines to be used in composing business letters

- Compose a variety of business letters

- Understand the principles of effective proofreading

- State the main points to remember about composing business letters

MODERN BUSINESS COMMUNICATION

Business communications can be written in a much more relaxed style than they were decades ago. Old-fashioned, long-winded jargon is out. You should aim to put across your message naturally, in a friendly, informal style. The secret of good writing is to use plain language as if you are having a conversation. This unit looks at some simple rules you should follow in order to ensure all your communications are effective.

It was good to see you last week. Thank you for a lovely lunch at Pete's place. We must do it again soon.

FIVE KEY RULES OF GOOD WRITING FOR THE TWENTY-FIRST CENTURY

1 Come straight to the point

Busy business people haven't got time to read long-winded documents. They welcome letters that are direct and to the point – but at the same time courteous. Save your reader's time by keeping your sentences short and simple. Shorten these sentences:

- Please be informed that our monthly management meeting will be held on Tuesday 28 August 200– in Training Room A.
- Please note that the fire alarms throughout the company will be tested next Tuesday 14 July 200–.
- I wish to advise you that Mrs Joanna Green is no longer with this department.
- Would you be so kind as to let me know when these goods can be delivered.
- I would like to remind you that petty cash claims should now be submitted to Alvin in Accounts Department.
- I am writing to inform you that our company's Annual Dinner and Dance will be held on Friday 28 December 200–.

2 Remember the KISS principle

Keep it short and simple – that means short sentences and simple words. Don't try to impress your reader with big words – they will not be impressed – they will just have to reach for the dictionary. Choose short words instead of these, and choose one word instead of these phrases:

commence	_____
utilise	_____
terminate	_____
purchase	_____
despatch	_____
ascertain	_____
come to a decision	_____
in the event that	_____
give consideration to	_____
under separate cover	_____
despite the fact that	_____
in the near future	_____
at the present moment in time	_____

Checkpoint

Split into groups and make a list of some more long words that are commonly used in today's business writing – and then decide on their modern-day equivalent.

Did you know?

The Plain English Campaign has a great website at www.plainenglish.co.uk. They have given me permission to reproduce their A–Z of Alternative Words and you can find the full list in the Appendix on page 399.

3 Use active not passive voice

'Voice' refers to the relationship of a verb to its subject.

Active voice means that the subject of the sentence does the action of the sentence. Passive voice means that the subject of the sentence receives the action. For example:

Passive	The study was completed by the marketing director.
Active	The marketing director completed the study.
Passive	Separate requisitions should be prepared by each buyer.
Active	Each buyer should prepare separate requisitions.

Change these sentences from passive to active voice:

1   Your goods will be sent by us within the next 14 days.

   _____

2   The violin was played by Tim.

   _____

3   The faulty wiring was fixed by the electrician.

   _____

4   The business writing workshop will be conducted by Shirley Taylor.

   _____

5   The investigation has been concluded by our client, and the paperwork has been signed.

   _____

Remember

Use active voice in your writing. This is more alive, more focused, more personal – much more interesting and clear.

Is passive voice ever appropriate?
   Yes, there are some occasions when passive voice would be more appropriate.

• It may be better to make a particularly important noun the subject of the sentence, thus giving it extra emphasis. For example it would be better to say:

   Our restaurant has been recommended by all the leading hotels in Singapore.

   This emphasises 'our restaurant', rather than:

   All the leading hotels in Singapore recommend our service.

• When you want to place the focus on the action, not the actor. For example:

   The noise was heard all over the island.

   Here, the emphasis is on the noise, not the people who made the noise.

• When you want to hide something or when tact is important. For example:

   An unfortunate mistake was made.

4 Use the right tone

You alter the tone of your voice to convey messages in a different way. Similarly written communications may be worded so that they sound polite, friendly, firm, bossy, sarcastic, condescending, even rude. If you use the wrong tone in a written communication you could cause real offence to your reader.

Even if you feel angry or frustrated, try not to vent your emotions in writing. Your objectives will be achieved only with carefully considered and appropriate wording.

Study the following expressions and choose an alternative way of saying the same things more tactfully.

You have deliberately failed to reply to my letter.	✗	(too emotive)
.... ✓		
We cannot do anything about your problem. Try calling a plumber.	✗	(too abrupt)
.... ✓		
Your interview will be held on Wednesday 28 August at 1400.	✗	(too bossy)
.... ✓		
The problem would not have happened if you had connected the wires properly in the first place.	✗	(too condescending)
.... ✓		
Your computer's guarantee has expired so you will have to pay for it to be repaired.	✗	(too blunt)
.... ✓		
It's not our fault that your curtains faded. You obviously didn't read the instructions about dry cleaning only.	✗	(too sarcastic)
.... ✓		

5 Use modern language

The main rule of writing today is to write as you speak. If you find yourself writing something that you would not say to the person if you were having a conversation, then you should not be writing it either.

Replace these sentences with modern business language:

1   The above-mentioned goods will be despatched to you today.

2   Please find enclosed herewith a copy of our new catalogue.

3   Following my telecon with your goodself this morning.

4   I should be grateful if you would be good enough to advise me …

5   I am afraid that we are unable to accede to your request due to the fact that your contract has lapsed.

Weblink

http://www.write101.com
Articles on all aspects of writing.

---

www.shirleytaylor.com

Great-grandfather is *dead*!

In my workshops I always joke about 'great-grandfather writing' and wonder why so many young people still use so many old-fashioned expressions. I tell people regularly that we should keep our business writing simple (KISS) and use everyday language that everyone understands.

www.shirleytaylor.com *continued*

The reason for this was brought home to me recently when a friend sent me this e-mail that he had received from his accountants:

Dear Mr Johnson

Thank you for your e-mail of even date.

For the audit of Turner Communications Pte Ltd, kindly furnish us a copy of the company's Balance Sheet, Expenses statements and all the invoices/bills (incorporation and legal fees, etc.) paid by the holding company to our office at the earliest.

We will revert to you on the treatment of the Intangible Asset and the financials of Turner Communications Inc. as soon as possible.

Should you have any queries, please do not hesitate to contact us.

Best regards
Bernard Williams

What a load of gobbledegook and long-winded jargon! I knew people were still writing in an old-fashioned way, but it seems some people take this a little further than most – and this message just proves it!

In twenty-first century business language, this message should read:

Dear Mr Johnson

Thank you for your e-mail today.

For the audit of Turner Communications Pte Ltd, we will need a copy of the company's Balance Sheet, Expenses statements and all the invoices/bills (incorporation and legal fees, etc.) paid by the holding company. Please send these to me as soon as possible.

I will be in touch with you soon on the treatment of the Intangible Asset and the financials of Turner Communications Inc.

Please give me a call on xxxx if you have any questions.

Bernard Williams

What's wrong?

Discuss the following letter in groups. Identify all the old-fashioned boring clichés, then rewrite the letter to keep in your files. Use simple modern business language, with short and concise sentences. Use twenty-first century business writing.

Dear Sirs,

We have received your letter ~~dated~~ 27th March 200-.

unfortunately

We are ~~extremely~~ distressed to learn that an error was made pertaining to your esteemed order. Please be informed that the cause of your complaint has been investigated and it actually appears that the error occurred in our packing section and it was not discerned before this order ~~was despatched to your goodself.~~ *you,*

Arrangements have been made for a repeat order to be despatched to you immediately and this should leave our warehouse later today. It is our sincere hope that you will have no cause for further complaint with this replacement order.

this is not nescecarry

Once again we offer our ~~humblest~~ apologies for the unnecessary inconvenience that you have been caused in this instance.

Please find enclosed herewith a copy of our new catalogue for your reference and perusal.

Kindly contact the undersigned if you require any further clarifications.

yours sincerely

~~Very truly yours,~~

Zachariah Creep & Partners

Remember

When you are writing, ask yourself whether you would say this if you were speaking. Eliminate useless jargon by writing as you would speak.

JARGON OR GOBBLEDEGOOK

Jargon can seriously get in the way of business if no-one understands what people are talking about, or what they are writing about! I'm sure you have often come across messages that leave you feeling very confused, right? This problem happens when people use pompous or long-winded wording and phrasing to try to impress rather than to communicate. Yet really, the end result is that they do neither of these things!

Abbreviations are another thing. I read an article about someone who was making a speech and he mentioned HE (Higher Education). A member of the audience (a qualified engineer) asked 'Why are you talking about High Explosives?' Sure, the context often helps to explain the correct meaning of such abbreviations, but it shouldn't be relied on. So as a general rule, always explain abbreviations when you first use them.

Using jargon can result in one of two things – the reader will get bored and stop reading, or will spend a great deal of time trying to figure out what you meant four sentences ago!

Do you know any writers who sometimes concentrate so hard on what they want to say that they become absorbed in their impressive flow of wonderful words instead of talking in everyday language that the reader will understand? Take a look at these before and after examples found on the www.plainenglish.co.uk website:

Before   If there are any points on which you require explanation or further particulars we shall be glad to furnish such additional details as may be required by telephone.

After   If you have any questions please call.

Before   High-quality learning environments are a necessary precondition for facilitation and enhancement of the ongoing learning process.

After   Children need good schools if they are to learn properly.

Before   It is important that you shall read the notes, advice and information detailed opposite then complete the form overleaf (all sections) prior to its immediate return to the Council by way of the envelope provided.

After   Please read the notes opposite before you fill in the form. Then send it back to us as soon as possible in the envelope provided.

Weblink

http://www.weaselwords.com.au/index3.htm

Weaselwords. An interesting site discussing contemporary clichés and management jargon.

www.shirleytaylor.com

Effective proofreading

Have you ever proofread a letter, leaflet or information sheet 20 times, then printed out 10,000 copies . . . only for someone to look at it and point out a glaring error? Yes, I guess we've all been there, done that! If you are responsible for proofreading important documents (and aren't *all* documents important?) then here are my tips for effective proofreading:

1 Avoid distractions. It's best to proofread in a quiet environment, with no disturbances such as phones, background conversation, etc.

2 Read the work out loud. Using proper intonation will help you to spot faulty sentence construction and bad punctuation and grammar.

3 Concentrate on reading one word at a time. This takes practice. It's fairly common to skim over the words when we read normally. Try to make a conscious effort to stare at each word in turn. This isn't as slow as it sounds – it's just a different reading technique.

4 Be methodical – read one line at a time. Use a ruler to guide your eyes so that you don't miss the odd line.

5 Take a break occasionally. Especially with longer documents, you need a break now and again. Everyone loses concentration after a while, so set a time limit and then take a break.

6 Remember to look also for inconsistencies in style and presentation, such as headings that suddenly switch from capitals to lower case, or a change in font or spacing.

7 Leave a decent period of time between writing and proofreading the work. Reading with a fresh approach will help you to spot more mistakes.

8 Print out a hard copy for the final proofreading. Somehow we always manage to miss a few errors if we rely on proofreading on screen.

9 Keep your knowledge of punctuation and grammar up-to-date. Unless you know what is correct, you cannot spot mistakes.

10 Ask someone else to do a final check of important documents – we tend to be able to find other people's mistakes much more easily than our own!

What's wrong?

Read the following assignment and then study the answer given. It is not satisfactory for several reasons. Discuss the faults and then rewrite the answer correctly.

You work for Mr Michael Harrison, Sales Director of Eastwood Electrical Pte Ltd, 22 Orchard Road, #03–11 Lucky Towers, Singapore 343234. The company sells a wide range of electrical equipment. Mr Harrison received a letter from Mr Gordon

What's wrong? *continued*

Paterson of 21 Bukit Sedap Road, Singapore 104928 complaining that a DVD recorder which he bought last month is not working properly. Mr Harrison talks to you about this matter. He says:

'We'd better reply to Mr Paterson's letter. It's the DVD20 Deluxe that he's complaining about. I think we'd better send one of our Technicians round to his place to check out the machine. Speak to Brian would you, and see what's the best time for him to go round some time next week. Tell Mr Paterson that I find the failure of the machine most disturbing. Something like this really shouldn't happen you know, when the products we sell are thoroughly checked out before they leave the shop. Then again, we can never be sure they've followed the instructions in the booklet correctly can we? Remember Mrs Cheong last month? It turned out that she hadn't connected the wires properly! Anyway Brian will sort it out for him when he calls and see if it's something simple which he can fix on the spot. If it really is defective, we'll give the customer a replacement immediately of course. You'd better ask him to call Brian if the appointment isn't good for him, and quote his extension number. Finish with the hope that it's resolved all right, but tell him to contact me if there's any further problem.'

What's wrong with the answer?

EASTWOOD ELECTRICAL PTE LTD

22 Orchard Road
#03-11 Lucky Towers
Singapore

MH/by

Gordon Patterson
21 Bukit Sedap Road
Singapore 104928

Dear Mr Gordon

Your letter complaining about your faulty DVD20 was received by us today. We will be sending one of our technicians, Brian Lee to check out the fault next Wednesday afternoon.

The failure of the machine is very disturbing. This really shouldn't happen when our machines are checked before they leave our shop. I wonder if you've followed the instructions in the book properly?

Anyway Brian will see if it's something which can be fixed on the spot or if it's defective we'll replace you with a new DVD.

Hope it's resolved satisfactorily but if not please give me a call.

Yours faithfully

Michael Harrison
Sales Director

Checkpoint

Decide whether the following statements are true or false. When a statement is false, discuss what is correct.

1 Long words should be used in letter-writing. True/False

2 'Yours sincerely' should be used when beginning 'Dear Sir'. True/False

3 AB/FTR is a postal code in the UK. True/False

4 Continuation sheets should show the page number. True/False

5 Unnecessary information should not be included in business letters. True/False

6 Long sentences are preferable because they make things clearer. True/False

7 A letter that begins 'Dear Mary' will end 'Yours faithfully'. True/False

8 pp is used when you forget something and have to add it at the end of a letter. True/False

9 Ms is used when you are writing to more than one woman. True/False

10 cc means carbon copy. True/False

What's wrong?

Study the following assignment and the answer given. Discuss what is wrong with the answer shown and then rewrite it correctly.

The Personnel Officer of Design and Production Ltd, Olympia Works, Cirencester, CR2 3BW, has received a letter from the Careers Adviser, Ash Tree Upper School, Ash Lane, Gloucester GL1 2JQ requesting assistance in arranging periods of work experience for sixth form students following a course in Business Studies.

You have been asked to draft the letter which the personnel officer will send in reply to this request. Using the notes given below, draft the letter:

Regret not possible at present.

Management recognises importance of work experience; MD investigating suggestions put forward by Personnel Dept; if scheme can be worked out, it will be implemented asap.

List of schools and colleges wishing to be included being compiled –

Ash Tree Upper to be included; unlikely that everybody can be accommodated this year.

What's wrong with the answer?

DESIGN AND PRODUCTION LTD
Olympia Works
Cirencester CR2 3BW

21 September

Careers Adviser
Ash Tree Upper School
Gloucester
GL1 2JQ

Dear Sir/Madam

ASSISTANCE IN PROVIDING PERIODS OF WORK EXPERIENCE

I regret it is not possible at the moment to acede to your request.

The management of this company recognises the importance of work experience
and the Managing Director is investigating suggestions put forward by me. If a
scheme can be worked out, we will implement it soon. Lists of schools and colleges
wishing to be included is presently being compiled – Ash Tree Upper to be included.

It is unlikely everybody can be acommodated this year though.

Please let me know if you have any queries.

Yours faithfully

MRS LUCINDA TUMALE
Personnel manager

COMPOSING LETTERS – KEY POINTS TO REMEMBER

1 Use short sentences

Short sentences will keep your meaning clear and ensure easier understanding.

2 Choose simple words

Simple words will convey your message more clearly. The use of unaffected
language will help you to achieve the right tone.

3 Avoid wordiness

Choose words with care and be economical while remembering the need for courtesy.

4 Use an appropriate tone

Choose a tone to suit the reader and the subject matter. You can be firm or friendly, persuasive or conciliatory – it depends on the impression you wish to convey. Failure to adopt an appropriate tone will mean that the reader's attention is attracted more to how it is worded than to what is being said.

5 Be precise

Your letter should be long enough to serve its purpose, but no longer.

6 Ensure accuracy

Double check all figures, dates, numbers and prices, as well as spellings, punctuation, tenses, word endings, etc.

7 Check consistency

Ensure consistency of presentation (fully-blocked style with open punctuation) as well as consistency of expression (I, We, etc.).

8 Use your initiative

Ensure the reader knows everything. Instead of 'next week', state a day and date. If an overseas visit is planned give the time of arrival and flight number.

9 Use active not passive voice

Active voice makes your writing more alive and interesting, more specific and clear, and it also makes your sentences shorter.

10 Write as you would speak

Use everyday language as if you were having a conversation.

A–Z OF BLOOPERS AND BLUNDERS, COMMON ERRORS AND CLICHÉS: D

Dated

When replying to a letter, do not say 'Thank you for your letter dated on . . .'. The correct expression is 'Thank you for your letter dated . . .' or 'Thank you for your letter of . . .'. We should not say 'dated on'.

Discuss

It is not grammatically correct to say 'I want to discuss about . . .'. The word *discuss* means *to talk about*, so if you say *discuss about*, you are really saying *talk about about*. The same applies when you use the word *mention*. Say 'Mary mentioned the poor weather recently'. Cut out the about!

Due to the fact that

This is a wordy expression and can simply be replaced by 'As' or 'Since' or 'Because'.

IN THE BIN: D

during the period from
duly

HELP YOURSELF

Identify and correct the errors in these sentences.

1 The new catalogue, that was published last month, shows details of all our new models.
2 Mr John Tan, our Sales Manager will visit you next Monday.
3 We have five different models all with their own special features.
4 Although I agree with your points in general, but there are a few points I would like you to explain.
5 I would like to see you, however I am busy in meetings tomorrow.
6 Thank you for your lunch yesterday, it was great to see you again.
7 As per our discussion I would need 15 minutes for my presentation.
8 Susan King, who has recently been appointed as new CEO will address the conference next week.
9 We need to improve the corporate image, therefore we are employing special consultants for advice.
10 The company has decided to change it's corporate logo.

TEST YOURSELF

1 Keep it short and simple

   (a) Choose a simple way of saying:
      expedite
      ascertain
      individuals
      locality
      kindly
      transmit
      insufficiency
      advise
      materialise
      the above-mentioned

   (b) Choose one word instead of these phrases:
      at an early date
      until such time as
      during the course of
      in connection with
      despite the fact that
      for the purpose of
      on the occasion of
      in the very near future
      on the grounds that
      prior to, previous to

   (c) Choose one word instead of these repetitious phrases:
      absolutely complete
      enclosed herewith
      basic fundamentals
      repeat again
      visible to the eye
      first and foremost
      future plans
      collect together
      reduce down
      actual truth

2 You work as an assistant to Mr Fadzil Malakoff, the Manager of *JEG Products*, a manufacturing company in Kuala Lumpur, Malaysia. Mr Malakoff has shown you this letter he has just received.

METROVILLE COLLEGE
Lorong Mambong
Kuala Lumpur
Malaysia

The Manager   (yesterday's date)
JEG Products
57 Jalan Kuning
Kuala Lumpur
Malaysia

Dear Sir or Madam

I am a student in the Department of Business Studies and I am doing a project on local businesses.

I would be very grateful if I could visit your company. I am interested in finding out such things as:

- the size of the company (number of employees)
- the market in which you operate
- your range of products
- your pricing strategy
- your plans for the future

I am free every afternoon next week.
Thank you for your help.

Yours faithfully

Anita Lai

Anita Lai

Mr Malakoff says this to you:

Yes, I don't mind meeting this student. I like to maintain a good contact with Metroville College – some of our best employees have studied there.

I can certainly say something about our size, our products and our market. I'm sure the students will realise that I can't say much about our pricing strategy and our plans for the future, as this is confidential. You could suggest that they might like to visit our new website (www.jegprod.com) as a lot of information is there.

Please check my diary and see which afternoons I am free next week. Choose one free time and ask them to come along to our main reception at 2 o'clock.

This is Mr Malakoff's diary for the afternoons next week.

Monday	Free
Tuesday	Operations Committee Meeting
Wednesday	Interviews – new Production Staff
Thursday	Free
Friday	Meeting with Finance Director

Task

Write a letter to the student in Mr Malakoff's name. (LCCIEB EFB1 style)

3   You work for Mr Rashid Hassan, Office Manager of Langland Manufacturing, Freeman Industrial Estate, Pitt Lane, Portsmouth, Hampshire PO13 7JJ. The company makes household furniture. (LCCIEB EFB2 style)

Mr Hassan has just recieved this letter and has asked you to draft a reply to it.

MANTLES STORES
261 Milburn Road
Heaton
Newcastle upon Tyne
NE6 SKA

Telephone: 0191 444 7656   Fax: 0191 444 7777

KJ/PL/702   25 June 200–

Mr Rashid Hassan
Office Manager
Langland Manufacturing plc
Freeman Industrial Estate
Pitt Lane
Portsmouth
Hampshire PO13 7JJ

Dear Mr Hassan

As you may know, we are one of the largest chains of furniture stores in the North of England. We are now planning to expand and open a number of stores in the South of England, including one in the Portsmouth area.

We usually try to buy our furniture from local suppliers and I thought it would be useful for both of our companies if we could meet to consider whether you could supply us with some of our furniture, particularly dining tables, chairs and carpets.

I shall be visiting the South of England soon. I shall be in London on 19 July and shall be staying there overnight. If it is convenient I would like to come down to Portsmouth on the 20th to meet you and visit your factory.

I hope to hear from you soon.

Yours sincerely

Keith James

Keith James
Chief Buyer

Mr Hassan says to you:

Please prepare a reply to Mr James and tell him we'd be delighted to meet him and show him our factory. Please ask him how he is going to travel from London to Portsmouth on 20 July. If he's coming by train we can arrange for someone to meet him at the railway station. If he's driving here we will send him a map so that he will be able to find us. If he can arrive mid-morning he can visit the factory and see what we make. We can then talk about a deal over lunch. Let him know that we make a wide range of dining tables, chairs and cabinets and send him our latest catalogue. Say how pleased we were to hear from him.

4   Cedars Hospital opened 50 years ago and the management of the hospital is organising a special anniversary celebration. On 20 December this year the Minister of Health from the national government will visit the hospital to open the new children's ward, and many people who were involved when the hospital opened 50 years ago have been invited.

When the hospital opened, the Chief Nursing Officer was Miss Freda Stills. Miss Stills did a great deal to help set up the excellent nursing department, for which the hospital has become famous.

Miss Stills died many years ago, and had no children of her own. In fact, she does not seem to have any surviving family. However, a man in the area has given the hospital the name and address of someone who now lives in the United States of America. He says this woman is a relative of Miss Stills; he thinks it is her great-niece.

The Hospital Manager, Mr Ashid Khan, has asked you to write to this person. He says he would be delighted if she could attend the celebration in December. The local newspaper would be prepared to pay for her travel expenses if she will give them an interview about Miss Stills.

Mr Khan has asked you to check that she is a relative of Miss Stills and say how much he would like her to attend the celebration.

The name and address of the person who is believed to be Miss Stills's great-niece is:

Mrs Carmen Ramez, 416 Lincoln Highway, Lancaster, Pennsylvania 17311, USA.

Cedars Hospital address is Western Road, Newtown.

Task

Write the letter to Mrs Ramez. (LCCIEB EFB2 style)

5   You are employed in the offices of a shop, *Central Stores*, which sells household items. The shop manager, Mrs Theresa Jerome, shows you this letter she has just received from one of the shop's suppliers.

You investigate this complaint and find that this order was delivered as Mr Chen has said. There was a mix-up in the Finance Department and the letter should have gone to a company called *Brighton Pans*, about their order BP/46/5 a – that order has not been delivered.

Mrs Jerome tells you to write to Mr Chen to apologise for the confusion. She asks you to thank him for reliable service and assure him that this mistake will not happen again.

Task

Write the letter. (LCCIEB EFB2 style)

BRIGHTER PANS
Mandela Boulevard
BRIDGETON

Ref: CH/SK/9
Date: (date)

Mrs T Jerome
Manager
Central Stores
Western Way
River City

Dear Mrs Jerome

ORDER NUMBER BP 47/4a

I was very surprised and disappointed to receive your recent letter, in which you claim that we have not delivered the latest order of non-stick saucepans (order number BP 47/4a). In fact, this order was delivered two weeks ago and was signed for in your Goods Received Department by Mr Paul Dean.

We have been pleased to supply you with our top quality saucepans for many years and we pride ourselves on our prompt delivery. Please confirm you have received this order.

Yours sincerely

Chen Lee Hong

Chen Lee Hong
Sales Manager

Unit 6

Recruitment correspondence

After studying this unit you should be able to:

- **State all the documents involved in the process of recruiting staff**

- **Compose realistic business documents that may be used in the recruitment process:**

  Application letter
  CV
  Invitation to interview
  References
  Testimonials
  Offer of employment
  Job description
  Letter of acceptance
  Letter of resignation

I have often received valuable feedback from readers saying that the information in this unit is very useful in covering a wide range of business documents in a realistic, practical way. For that reason I am keeping this unit in much the same format, but with a few minor amendments. Some readers will merely take a cursory glance at these documents, while others will be able to study them in much more detail.

THE RECRUITMENT PROCESS

Various letters and documents are involved in the process of applying for a job. In this unit we will look at the most common documents from both viewpoints – the applicant's and the employer's.

First of all reorganise this list into the most logical order using the skeleton diagram shown:

Letter to referee

Curriculum vitae

Invitation to interview

Job description

Testimonial from present company

Letter of acceptance

Contract of employment

Letter of resignation

Offer of employment

Reference

Letter of rejection to unsuitable applicants

Letter of application

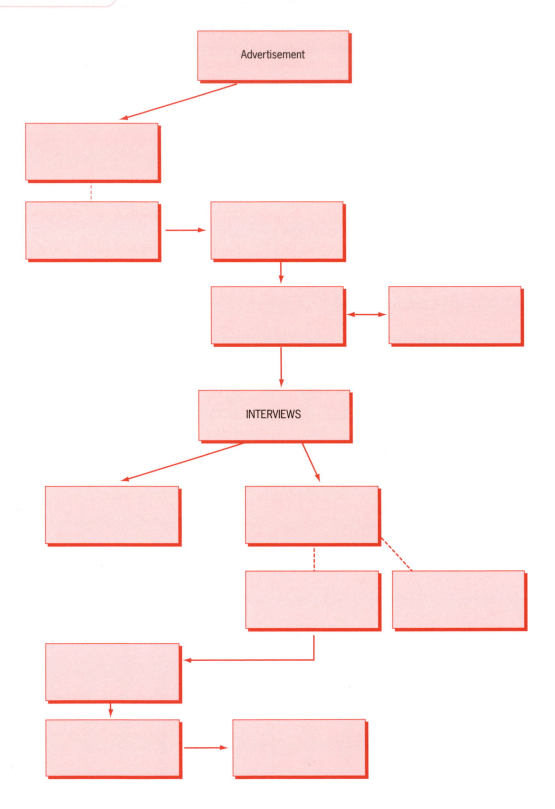

APPLICATION LETTER

When you see an advertisement that attracts your attention, check carefully to note whether applications should be hand-written. If it is not stated, you may type your letter. Keep your application letter short and concise, with your main particulars listed in a curriculum vitae (sometimes called a resumé). This avoids your letter becoming very long and bogged down with unnecessary information.

> Things not to say on an application letter:
>
> 'Let's meet so you can ooh and aah over my experience'
>
> 'You'll want me to be Head Honcho in no time.'

Application Form — **Private & Confidential**

PLEASE PRINT CLEARLY

PLEASE PRINT CLEARLY IN BLACK INK

- Complete this form fully
- Answer all questions honestly and truthfully
- Read the declaration and Data Protection Act consent
- Sign and date the form

Post Applied For ▶

Where did you hear about this vacancy?

When would you be available to start?

Would you work full time? ☐ Yes ☐ No

If part time, state preferred days/hours

If offered this position will you continue to have any other employment? ☐ Yes ☐ No

If yes please give details

Are you willing to travel, if required as part of your employment? ☐ Yes ☐ No

Do you smoke? ☐ Yes ☐ No

Have you ever previously worked for us? ☐ Yes ☐ No

If yes when and in what capacity

Personal Details ▶

Title ☐ Forename(s) ☐ Surname/Family Name ☐

Home address

Postcode

Home telephone Work telephone

Date of birth DD MM YY National Insurance no.

Are you legally eligible for employment in the UK in accordance with the Asylum and Immigration Act 1996 (see notes) ☐ Yes ☐ No

Do you have proof of eligibility to work in the UK? ☐ Yes ☐ No

Do you require a Work Permit to work in the UK? ☐ Yes ☐ No If so please give Work Permit number

Do you need to register under the Workers Registration Scheme? ☐ Yes ☐ No

Are there any restrictions (restrictive covenants) from your current/previous employer which will affect your ability to work for the company?

☐ Yes ☐ No If yes please provide copies.

Note: To comply with The Asylum & Immigration Act 1996, if you are invited to attend an interview, you must bring with you the following items of evidence of your eligibility to work in the UK, namely your passport, ID card or other relevant travel document or, if none of these are available, two separate documents such as your full UK birth certificate and a document giving your National Insurance Number, such as a P45, P46, P60 or a pay slip. No offer of employment will be made unless such evidence has been produced.

FORM 101

Employment History ▶

Please list below present and past employment, beginning with your most recent. You may attach further sheets to the form if required.

page 3

Name & Address of present or most recent Employer

Tel No.   Type of business

From   DD   MM   YY   To   DD   MM   YY   Notice Period

Starting wage/salary   Leaving wage/salary   Full or Part Time

Temporary or Permanent   Job title

Describe your key duties and responsibilities

Reason for leaving/wishing to leave

Name & Address of Employer

Tel No.   Type of business

From   DD   MM   YY   To   DD   MM   YY   Notice Period

Starting wage/salary   Leaving wage/salary   Full or Part Time

Temporary or Permanent   Job title

Describe your key duties and responsibilities

Reason for leaving

Name & Address of Employer

Tel No.   Type of business

From   DD   MM   YY   To   DD   MM   YY   Notice Period

Starting wage/salary   Leaving wage/salary   Full or Part Time

Temporary or Permanent   Job title

Describe your key duties and responsibilities

Reason for leaving

Reproduced for educational purposes only courtesy of Waterlow Business Supplies Limited

Some advertisements specify that you should write in to request an application form, in which case just send a simple letter requesting the standard form. Application forms are often preferred by larger organisations because by giving specific headings the company can be assured of obtaining the same information about each applicant.

Your personal address ———————————————

49 Broome Avenue
Nottingham
NG2 3PJ

Tel: 0115 987654

2 June 200–

Address to person named in ———
the advertisement

Mrs Louise Dunscombe
Human Relations Manager
ST International plc
Aurora House
Temple Street
London
SE1 4LL

Dear Mrs Dunscombe

Use job title as the heading ———

TELEPHONE EXECUTIVE (MARKETING)

I am interested in applying for this post as advertised in today's Nottingham Post.

Give some brief details of ———
what you are doing now

I have been employed as part-time Administration Assistant in Nottingham Technical College for the last 6 months while studying there on a Business Administration course. My course finishes very soon and I am keen to join a progressive company such as Aurora Holdings.

Enclose your CV ———

My full particulars are shown on my enclosed Curriculum Vitae.

I shall be happy to attend an interview at any time, and look forward to hearing from you soon.

Yours sincerely

Adrienne Langston

ADRIENNE LANGSTON (Miss)

Don't forget Enc ———

Enc

CURRICULUM VITAE

Curriculum vitae is Latin, literally meaning 'the course of one's life'. A curriculum vitae (CV) sets out your personal details, education, qualifications and working experience. Make sure you organise all the information logically under headings and use columns where appropriate. All your details can then be found at a glance.

Emphasise the heading
(you may prefer to use resumé)

Appropriate personal details
(you may add race, citizenship,
I/C number or others)

Summarise your main
selling points

Tabulate your education in three
columns (chronological order)

Be specific and list all your
qualifications (not just
'3 O levels')

Present job first, working
backwards

Hobbies/sports you
enjoy/special achievements/
results awaited?

A previous employer?
A teacher?
Youth club leader?

Month and year only

CURRICULUM VITAE

Name
Address
Telephone
Nationality
Date of Birth
Marital Status

PROFILE

EDUCATION

DATES	SCHOOL/COLLEGE	COURSE

QUALIFICATIONS

DATES	EXAMINING BODY	SUBJECT

WORKING EXPERIENCE

DATES	EMPLOYER	POSITION/DUTIES

ADDITIONAL INFORMATION

REFEREES

1	2

Date

INVITATION TO INTERVIEW

A letter inviting shortlisted applicants to attend all interview should be fairly short,
simply thanking the person for his/her application and giving a day/date/time for
the interview.

Interview

The interview is an essential stage in the recruitment process. Unit 2 gives full guidelines on how to prepare for interviews. Perhaps you can arrange for some mock interviews to be held in your class?

ST International plc
Aurora House
Temple Street
London SE1 4LL

Tel   0207 345375
Fax   0207 453678   E-mail   shirley@shirleytaylor.com
Mobile   09890 333444   Website   www.shirleytaylor.com

LD/ST

8 June 200–

Miss Adrienne Langston
49 Broome Avenue
Nottingham
NG2 3PJ

Dear Miss Langston

TELEPHONE EXECUTIVE (MARKETING)

Thank you for your recent letter applying for the above post.

I hope you can attend an interview at 1030 on Friday 16 June.

If this appointment is inconvenient please telephone my secretary to make alternative arrangements.

Yours sincerely

Louise Dunscombe

LOUISE DUNSCOMBE (Mrs)
Human Relations Manager

Annotations:
- Don't forget to include the courtesy title
- Personalised salutation
- Acknowledge the letter
- State date and time for interview
- Suggest how alternative arrangements can be made

REFERENCES

Before a candidate is offered a job the company will usually take up references. It is a good idea to take along to the interview copies of some testimonials which former employers have written about you. However, companies may still prefer to telephone or write to referees asking for comments on the character, personal qualities and work performance of the person they have singled out to be offered the job. If you have not yet started work you could give as a referee your teacher or someone who has known you for several years (not a relative).

ST International plc
Aurora House
Temple Street
London SE1 4LL

Tel   0207 345375
Fax   0207 453678   E-mail   shirley@shirleytaylor.com
Mobile   09890 333444   Website   www.shirleytaylor.com

LD/ST

10 June 200–

Miss Pamela Rashidah
48 The Limes
Carlton
Nottingham
NG31 2BP

Dear Miss Rashidah

APPLICATION FROM MISS ADRIENNE LANGSTON
FOR THE POST OF TELEPHONE EXECUTIVE (MARKETING)

Background details ——— Miss Adrienne Langston has applied for this post and has given your name as a referee.

State the information you require ——— Miss Langston says she has known you for several years, recently as her tutor on a course at Nottingham Technical College. I should be grateful for any information you can give me about her competence, reliability and general character.

Give a little information about the post ——— This post involves a great deal of customer contact so a friendly and courteous telephone manner is essential. There will also be some administrative duties involved in this post.

Ensure confidentiality ——— All information provided will be treated in strictest confidence.

Yours sincerely

Louise Dunscombe

LOUISE DUNSCOMBE (Mrs)
Human Relations Manager

Some writers prefer to centre their personal address and telephone number

48 The Limes
Carlton
Nottingham
NG31 2BP

Telephone: 0115 221221

11 June 200–

Use full name, title, company name and address as shown on letterhead

Mrs Louise Dunscombe
ST International plc
Aurora Holdings plc
Aurora House
Temple Street
London
SE1 4LL

Dear Mrs Dunscombe

Same heading as the incoming letter

APPLICATION FROM MISS ADRIENNE LANGSTON
FOR THE POST OF TELEPHONE EXECUTIVE (MARKETING)

Refer to the letter received

Thank you for your letter of 10 June regarding Miss Adrienne Langston.

State how long you have known the applicant and in what capacity

Give some background information

I have known Miss Langston for the past 10 years as she is the daughter of a personal friend. Since September 1998 she has been attending a Business Administration course at Nottingham Technical College. She gained many NVQ qualifications as well as Pitman, RSA and LCCIEB qualifications. During the past six months she worked part-time in the administration office here at the college carrying out general office duties.

Give details about the applicant's work performance, attitude and character

Miss Langston has been a conscientious student who always participated fully in class discussions and produced excellent work within the given time frame. She worked very hard to compile an excellent portfolio of assignments and project work which contributed to her NVQ qualifications. Comments on her part-time work in the administration office have been very favourable and I know that her supervisors consider her to be very helpful and hard-working.

Mention some personal qualities

Miss Langston is a pleasant, sociable, courteous young lady who has a lot of ambition for the future.

Give a recommendation

I am sure that she will be able to carry out the duties involved in this post to your satisfaction. I have no hesitation in recommending her highly.

Yours sincerely

Pamela Rashidah

PAMELA RASHIDAH (Miss)

OFFER OF EMPLOYMENT

After all the interviews have been conducted a shortlist may be drawn up and second interviews held. Once a decision has been made on the successful candidate, a formal offer of employment will be sent ot the successful applicant. Depending on the size of the organisation, a separate contract of employment may be drawn up. Here we will deal with a simple offer letter enclosing a job description.

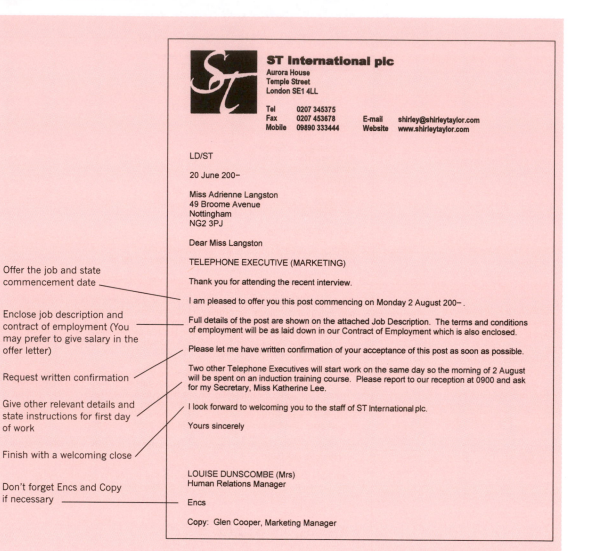

Offer the job and state commencement date

Enclose job description and contract of employment (You may prefer to give salary in the offer letter)

Request written confirmation

Give other relevant details and state instructions for first day of work

Finish with a welcoming close

Don't forget Encs and Copy if necessary

ST International plc
Aurora House
Temple Street
London SE1 4LL

Tel   0207 345375
Fax   0207 453678   E-mail   shirley@shirleytaylor.com
Mobile   09890 333444   Website   www.shirleytaylor.com

LD/ST

20 June 200–

Miss Adrienne Langston
49 Broome Avenue
Nottingham
NG2 3PJ

Dear Miss Langston

TELEPHONE EXECUTIVE (MARKETING)

Thank you for attending the recent interview.

I am pleased to offer you this post commencing on Monday 2 August 200–.

Full details of the post are shown on the attached Job Description. The terms and conditions of employment will be as laid down in our Contract of Employment which is also enclosed.

Please let me have written confirmation of your acceptance of this post as soon as possible.

Two other Telephone Executives will start work on the same day so the morning of 2 August will be spent on an induction training course. Please report to our reception at 0900 and ask for my Secretary, Miss Katherine Lee.

I look forward to welcoming you to the staff of ST International plc.

Yours sincerely

LOUISE DUNSCOMBE (Mrs)
Human Relations Manager

Encs

Copy: Glen Cooper, Marketing Manager

Checkpoint

Does your company issue a formal contract of employment?

What issues are covered in this?

JOB DESCRIPTION

A lob description states the title of the post and to whom the person reports, as well as giving full details of the duties and responsibilities involved.

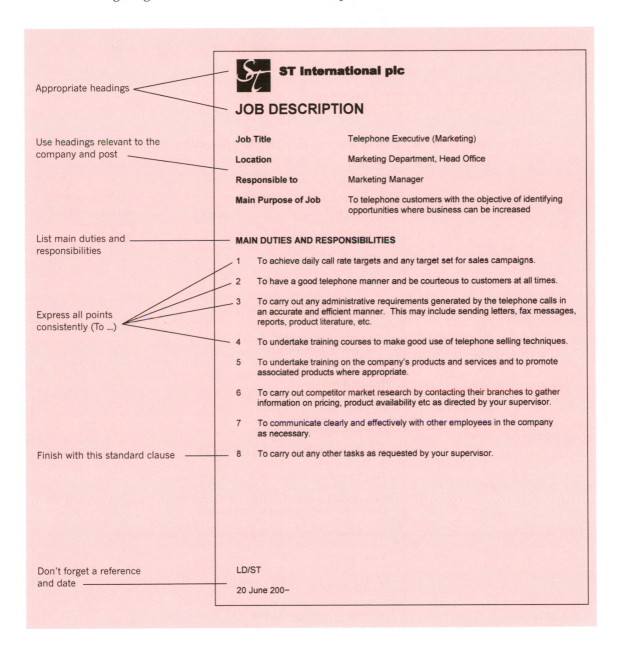

Appropriate headings

Use headings relevant to the company and post

List main duties and responsibilities

Express all points consistently (To ...)

Finish with this standard clause

Don't forget a reference and date

ST International plc

JOB DESCRIPTION

Job Title	Telephone Executive (Marketing)
Location	Marketing Department, Head Office
Responsible to	Marketing Manager
Main Purpose of Job	To telephone customers with the objective of identifying opportunities where business can be increased

MAIN DUTIES AND RESPONSIBILITIES

1   To achieve daily call rate targets and any target set for sales campaigns.

2   To have a good telephone manner and be courteous to customers at all times.

3   To carry out any administrative requirements generated by the telephone calls in an accurate and efficient manner. This may include sending letters, fax messages, reports, product literature, etc.

4   To undertake training courses to make good use of telephone selling techniques.

5   To undertake training on the company's products and services and to promote associated products where appropriate.

6   To carry out competitor market research by contacting their branches to gather information on pricing, product availability etc as directed by your supervisor.

7   To communicate clearly and effectively with other employees in the company as necessary.

8   To carry out any other tasks as requested by your supervisor.

LD/ST

20 June 200–

Checkpoint

Ask your Business Administration teacher to discuss the difference between a job description and a job specification.

LETTER OF ACCEPTANCE

It is usual to write a formal letter to the company accepting the post. Keep it simple.

49 Broome Avenue
Nottingham
NG2 3PJ

25 June 200–

Mrs Louise Dunscombe
Human Relations Manager
ST International plc
Aurora House
Temple Street
London
SE1 4LL

Be consistent – display all
your letters in the same style ———— Dear Mrs Dunscombe

TELEPHONE EXECUTIVE (MARKETING)

Thank you for your letter of 20 June 2000.

I am pleased to confirm my acceptance of this post as detailed in the Job
Description and Contract of Employment.

Finish appropriately ———— I shall look forward to joining the staff of ST International plc.

Yours sincerely

Adrienne Langston

ADRIENNE LANGSTON (Miss)

LETTER OF RESIGNATION

When you have been in employment and wish to leave for whatever reason, it is usual to write a formal letter resigning from your post.

49 Broome Avenue
Nottingham
NG2 3PJ

25 June 200–

Mrs Helen Bradley
Administration Manager
Nottingham Technical College
123 Bridge Avenue
West Bridgford
Nottingham
NG9 7GJ

Dear Mrs Bradley

Express regret and state last day of work ——

Further to our discussion today I regret to inform you that I wish to give one month's notice of my resignation from the company. My last day of work will be Friday 30 July.

Explain tactfully and courteously ——

I have been very happy working here and found my work very varied and enjoyable. I have gained a lot of experience in many areas which I am sure I shall find useful in future employment.

Give thanks ——

Thank you for your help and guidance.

Yours sincerely

Adrienne Langston

ADRIENNE LANGSTON (Miss)

TESTIMONIAL (LETTER OF RECOMMENDATION)

It is useful to ask previous employers for testimonials as these will be useful when applying for future posts.

NOTTINGHAM TECHNICAL COLLEGE

123 Bridge Avenue
West Bridgford
Nottingham NG9 7GJ

Telephone: 0115 876789
Fax: 0115 876889

HB/GB

28 June 200–

Use this heading in place of an inside address ——

TO WHOM IT MAY CONCERN

State position and duration of employment ——

Miss Adrienne Langston has been part-time Administration Assistant in our General Office from 24 May 1999 to 28 June 2000. We asked her to join us on a permanent part-time basis after she had been with us for several short periods of work experience during her Business Administration course.

Mention the duties performed ——

Miss Langston carried out a wide range of general office duties including opening and distributing mail, photocopying, filing, dealing with general telephone and walk-in enquiries and entering data into our computer systems.

State the employee's working attitude and how work was carried out ——

A conscientious, hard-working and reliable employee, Miss Langston set herself very high standards in her work. She had a pleasant telephone manner and was always courteous when dealing with her colleagues and external contacts. She was a good time-keeper and had a good attendance record.

Mention personal qualities ——

Miss Langston has a friendly, outgoing personality, a good sense of humour and she works well as part of a team.

Give a recommendation ——

I feel sure that Miss Langston will be an asset to any organisation.

No salutation and complimentary close are necessary ——

Helen Bradley

Helen Bradley (Mrs)
Administration Manager

Remember

To see more examples of testimonials take a look at *Model Business Letters, E-mails and Other Business Documents*, 6th edition, by Shirley Taylor.

A–Z OF BLOOPERS AND BLUNDERS, COMMON ERRORS AND CLICHÉS: E

Enclosed herewith please find

The only word we really need in this cliché is 'Enclosed'. 'Herewith' is so unnecessary – if it's not herewith, where the heck is it? 'Please find' implies it's like a game asking the reader to find something that's hidden. For twenty-first century writing, throw out all the unnecessary wording and simply say:

> I enclose my November report.
> Enclosed is my November report.
> I am enclosing my November report.

Enquiry/inquiry

'Enquiry' is British English and 'Inquiry' is American English.

Equipment

The word equipment is an uncountable noun and it should never end with an 's'. For example:

> We need some extra equipment for our new offices.
> All the new equipment has arrived. (use a singular verb)
> This equipment – the LCD, OHP and DVD – is needed in the Training Room.

Similar mistakes are made with words like luggage, baggage, furniture, information, clarification.

Emphasise

Emphasise means to stress or to place emphasis on something. We do not say 'emphasise on'. Cut out the 'on'.

Everyday/every day

'Everyday' is an adverb. 'Every day' are adjective and noun. For example:

> Making your bed is an everyday chore.
> I get the bus to work every day.
> Having to write e-mails every day is an everyday task.

NB: See also Anytime/any time.

IN THE BIN: E

each and every one
essentially
extremely

HELP YOURSELF

Choose the correct word from those shown in brackets.

1   Making your bed is an ……………………. chore.
    (every day/everyday)

2   Please ………………. me the book when you come to class tomorrow.
    (bring/fetch)

3   Mark handed the cheque to …………….. today.
    (myself/me)

4   Will you please …………….. me to the airport for my flight tonight?
    (send/take)

5   The manager asked his secretary to ……………. the report from his office.
    (send/take)

6   Every morning on my way to work, I …………… my children to school.
    (send/take)

7   Caroline and …………… will be attending the exhibition.
    (me/I/myself)

8   Do you have ……………………. tomorrow to discuss this?
    (some time/sometime)

9   I will give you a call ………………………. next week.
    (some time/sometime)

10 Any equipment ……………. is faulty should be returned promptly.
    (that/which)

TEST YOURSELF

In this assignment you are going to follow the recruitment process all the way through, looking at it from the point of view of both the employer and the applicant. As you complete each stage, make sure you refer back to the specimens shown in this unit so that you display your documents correctly and consistently. Use an appropriate date on each document and keep all the documents neatly in a folder.

This advertisement will be your starting point.

ST International plc

Aurora Holdings is one of the busiest retailers on the high street today. We currently have a number of vacancies at our head office.

PERSONAL ASSISTANT
TO PROJECT DEVELOPMENT MANAGER

Applicants should be suitably qualified, experienced and computer literate.

ADMINISTRATION ASSISTANT

HUMAN RELATIONS DEPARTMENT

Applicants must have good communication and organisational skills and be able to work under pressure.

WORD PROCESSING OPERATORS

ADMINISTRATION DEPARTMENT

Applicants must have excellent word processing qualifications and an ability to work well as a member of a team in this busy department.

IT ASSISTANT

Applicants must have relevant experience to join the IT team which provides IT support to 150 technical and administrative staff.

Applications with full CV should be sent to:

Jake Williamson
Personnel Manager
ST International plc
Aurora House
Temple Street
London SE1 4LL

1   Apply for one of the posts.

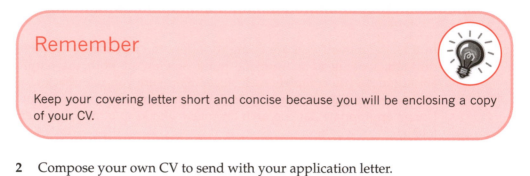

Remember

Keep your covering letter short and concise because you will be enclosing a copy of your CV.

2   Compose your own CV to send with your application letter.

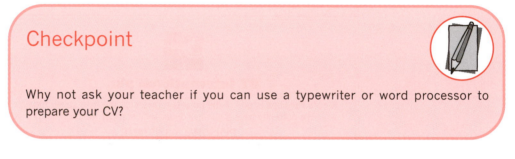

Checkpoint

Why not ask your teacher if you can use a typewriter or word processor to prepare your CV?

3   Compose a letter from the company inviting you to attend an interview. Give a suitable date and time.

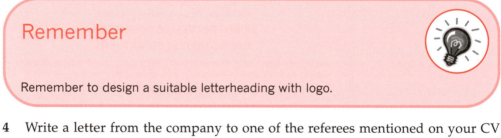

Remember

Remember to design a suitable letterheading with logo.

4   Write a letter from the company to one of the referees mentioned on your CV asking for details about your work performance, character and ability.
5   What would you like to think that your referee will say about you? Write a suitable (but believable!) reference from your referee to the company.
6   Compose a letter offering you the post at ST International plc.
7   Discuss the duties which you would expect to perform in this job.
     Compose a suitable job description.

Checkpoint

Perhaps you can discuss this assignment in your Business Administration lesson? Your teacher will be happy to give you some help.

8 Write a short letter accepting this post.

9 Write a letter that ST International plc can send to all the unsuccessful applicants.

10 As you have accepted the post at ST International plc, you must resign from your present post. Make up suitable details and compose a letter of resignation.

11 You have asked your current employer for a testimonial which you may keep. Compose a testimonial from your present company giving details of your duration of employment, the post(s) you held, your responsibilities, your work performance and any other appropriate details.

Did you know?

Model Business Letters, E-mails and Other Business Documents, 6th edition contains lots of different references and other business documents.

Telecommunications

Unit 7

Fax messages

LEARNING OUTCOMES

After studying this unit you should be able to:

- List the different documents that may be sent via fax

- Describe the procedure to follow in sending a fax message

- Design fax headed paper including all essential components

- Compose fax messages

- State the main points to remember when dealing with fax messages

FAX MESSAGES

A fax machine is a relatively inexpensive – and most would agree essential – item of equipment for any business. Fax transmits and receives any kind of message – handwritten, printed, word-processed; maps, messages, diagrams, photographs. It takes only seconds to transmit a fax message, depending on the length of the document.

Sending messages by fax is a popular choice today due to its versatility and speed. Fax is often used between divisions or branches of the same company instead of telephone or memos. Business letters are frequently either sent by fax or replaced by fax messages.

Most companies use a special fax letterhead for fax messages. This fax headed paper is often used with just a brief covering note explaining an accompanying document. The salutation and complimentary close are normally omitted but the message will generally be signed.

ST International plc

Facsimile message

To:	Classified Ads, Daily News	**Fax:**	3371917
From:	Tarandeep Kaur	**Date:**	19 August 2000
Subject:	Advertisement for Secretary	**Pages:**	2
Copy:	---		

☑ Urgent   ☐ For Review   ☐ Please Comment   ☐ Please Reply   ☐ Please Recycle

Further to our telephone conversation, I would like the attached advertisement to be placed in 'Secretarial Vacancies' on 29 August.

Please fax proof for approval as soon as possible.

Tarandeep

ST International plc
Aurora House, Temple Street, London SE1 4LL

Tel   0207 345375
Fax   0207 453678   E-mail   shirley@shirleytaylor.com
Mobile 09890 333444   Website www.shirleytaylor.com

Checkpoint

Bring in some of your organisation's fax headed paper to show to your fellow students.

If you have to compile your own fax headings, the following layout is suggested:

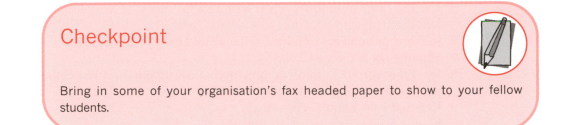

Use letterheaded paper

ST International plc
Aurora House
Temple Street
London SE1 4LL

Tel   0207 345375
Fax   0207 453678   E-mail   shirley@shirleytaylor.com
Mobile   09890 333444   Website   www.shirleytaylor.com

Insert main heading 'FAX MESSAGE'

FAX MESSAGE

The details here are important so use these standard headings

To	Iris Tan, Regional Manager
Company	Aurora International (Asia) Ltd
Fax No	00 65 25330099
From	Michael Ng, Director - Conferences
Ref	MN/ST
Date	15 June 200–
No of Pages	2

Remember to include the number of pages being sent

A salutation may be included before the heading if preferred

VISIT TO SINGAPORE/MALAYSIA

Sophia Lee, Director of Asia Training Enterprises, has invited me to chair the 10th Annual Malaysian Secretaries Conference at the Mandarin International Hotel in Kuala Lumpur on 11/12 August.

Structure the body exactly as you would a business letter

I am therefore rearranging the schedule for my forthcoming trip to Singapore so that I spend a few days in Malaysia before flying down to Singapore on Monday 14 August. My flights are confirmed and a copy of my itinerary is enclosed.

A complimentary close is not necessary

I hope all the arrangements for the Regional Conference in Singapore are going smoothly. Please let me see a copy of your proposed programme soon together with a list of materials you want me to bring from London.

DEALING WITH FAX MESSAGES – KEY POINTS TO REMEMBER

1 Use fax to send a printed copy of any document, especially diagrams and illustrations.
2 Prepare the message on the company's standard fax template where one exists.
3 Make up a fax letterhead if necessary, including headings like To/From/Date/ Fax Number/No. of pages/Copy to/Date.
4 Do not use a salutation or complimentary close on fax messages.

5   Use the same techniques when writing a fax message as you would a business letter.

6   Remember numbers or bullets if this would help your display.

7   Sign the fax in the usual way.

8   Send a cover fax with an accompanying document, and remember to indicate the number of pages being sent in total.

9   Key in the fax number correctly.

10 Keep a copy of important documents.

Weblink

http://www.writerswrite.com/buscomm/

Writers Write.

Articles and resources on business writing.

A–Z OF BLOOPERS AND BLUNDERS, COMMON ERRORS AND CLICHÉS: F,G

Fetch

See Bring and fetch, p. 64.

Fewer/less

Fewer relates to number. Less relates to quantity. For example:

My friend Joe has much less hair than Douglas.
Joe has fewer carpets than Douglas.

Fill up

To fill up means filling up something that is empty with something else, like filling up a glass with water. If you are referring to a form, you fill in a form (British English) or fill out a form (American English).

Gobbledegook

Gobbledegook is writing that is bombastic, pretentious, stuffy and long-winded. It is writing that attempts to sound official or formal. Take a look at this letter from an accountant – it is full of gobbledegook. All the long-winded words and phrases are highlighted in red:

Dear Mr Johnson

We have received your e-mail of even date.

For the audit of Turner Communications Pte Ltd, kindly furnish us with a copy of the company's balance sheet, expenses statements and all the invoices/bills paid by the holding company at your earliest convenience.

We will revert to you on the treatment of the intangible assets and the financials of Turner Communications Inc as soon as possible.

Should you have any queries, please do not hesitate to contact us.

Best regards
Bernard Williams

Goodself

This is so old-fashioned. Please do not use this word in your writing.

Grammar

Too many people still spell this word as grammer. There is no such word as grammer – it's grammar.

IN THE BIN: F, G

for all intents and purposes
for my part
frankly

give this matter your attention
going forward

HELP YOURSELF

Identify and correct the errors in these sentences.

1 When you go to Robinsons, will you please return back this blouse for me.
2 The workshop will be held between 9 am to 5.30 pm.
3 Sherran said she was very boring in the lecture.
4 My luggages are in the boot of John's car.
5 All the new equipments are being delivered tomorrow.
6 Either of the applicants are suitable for this new position.
7 Looking forward to see you at next week's meeting.

8 The company's football team are playing well this season.
9 Although I didn't think it was possible, but I still passed my exam.
10 Running to catch the bus, the car hit me.

TEST YOURSELF

1 You work for Kwik-Print plc and have received instructions to print business cards for Miss Fouzia Suki, Personnel Manager at Trendsetter Training College. The artwork has been prepared but you need to obtain approval from Miss Suki. Compose a fax, leaving space for the business card to be illustrated. Include a simple form at the foot which Miss Suki may sign and fax back to you if the design is approved.

2 You work for the managing director of Stanfield Engineering who is presently visiting clients of your company in the Caribbean. During his absence you receive two important quotations for major office renovations. You know that your employer wants work to commence urgently on these renovations but he is not expected back for some time. Send him a fax message at his hotel, enclosing the quotations, and ask for his instructions.

3 You are Administrative Assistant (AA) to Anu Morar, Personnel Manager of First State Bank of India, 67–94 High Street, New Delhi, India. Mrs Morar has meetings throughout the day and she has left some work for you. Follow her instructions in this note. (City & Guilds EFBC1)

> AA
> I've received this memo from Ravi Singh. Please send a fax to our usual recruitment agency (their card is attached) asking them to find 3 suitable candidates we can interview – give them full details of Ravi's requirements.
>
>   Thanks
>   Anu

> **Message:**
> As you know, our very reliable, long-serving Accounts Clerk, Mrs Minhas, is retiring at the end of the month. We need a replacement as soon as possible – preferably before she leaves so she can train the new person. The basic requirements of the job are:
> * good mathematical skills
> * good IT skills
> * ability to communicate with a range of people
>
> **it would also be desirable for her replacement to**
> * speak good English
> * be prepared to work some evenings and weekends

4   You are Personal Assistant (PA) to Tim Variant, General Manager of Creative Gifts, Preston Road, Cork, Eire. Follow the instructions in this note from Mr Variant. (City & Guilds EFBC2)

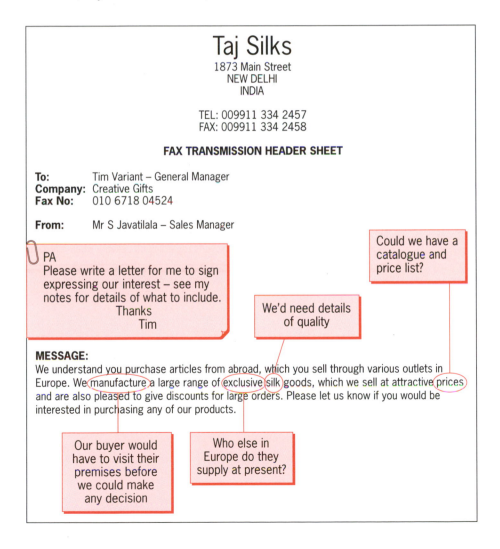

5 You are Personal Assistant (PA) to Tim Variant, General Manager of Creative Gifts, Preston Road, Cork, Eire. Follow the instructions in this note from Mr Variant. (City & Guilds EFBC2)

PA
Please send an urgent fax in reply – some of the goods were eventually to be delivered to England anyway, so suggest they now take container to a depot with a dry warehouse in Bristol where we could arrange for UK goods to be taken out. We'd have to send one of our warehousemen over to supervise this. He could then arrange UK deliveries and then remaining goods could come on here on next week's ship. Obviously, we'd expect them to cover the cost of warehouse facilities and our employee's flights. Express our disappointment with
Tim

Spania plc
Riverview House
Woolwich
LONDON
SE8 6EN
UK
TEL: 010 850 0145
FAX: 010 850 0146

FAX TRANSMISSION HEADER SHEET

To: Tim Variant – General Manager – Creative Gifts
Fax No: 010 6718 04524
From: Jeremy Brewer – Shipping Manager
Date:

RECEIVED

No. of sheets: (including header sheet): 1

Message:

Re: Container CTNU 634978 – loaded with woollen goods from New Zealand.

We very much regret to inform you that the above mentioned container has been unloaded in Bristol, England in error. We realise that you were expecting it in Cork, Eire tomorrow, but will not be able to ship it to Eire until next week. Please accept our apologies and let us know if you have any special instructions regarding its delivery when it arrives in Cork.

Electronic mail

After studying this unit you should be able to:

- **State the advantages of using e-mail**

- **List some pitfalls encountered with e-mail**

- **Discuss the main points to consider when composing e-mails**

- **Explain how to create a good rapport through use of e-mail**

- **Compose e-mail messages and replies to e-mails**

- **Discuss the impact that e-mail has had on business**

- **Discuss Internet and Intranet technology**

- **State the main points to remember about using e-mail**

THE EVOLUTION OF E-MAIL

Businesses today operate in a highly competitive market in which high-speed communication and information transfer is essential. Most of the activities in today's offices are electronic, using computer-based technology. Electronic mail, or e-mail as it is commonly known, has evolved as an effective, low-cost and instant method of communication with friends and colleagues all over the world.

With e-mail, messages are keyed into a computer workstation and then transmitted to the recipient. A single message may be sent simultaneously to many recipients.

The following diagram shows how an e-mail message is sent across the world via the Internet.

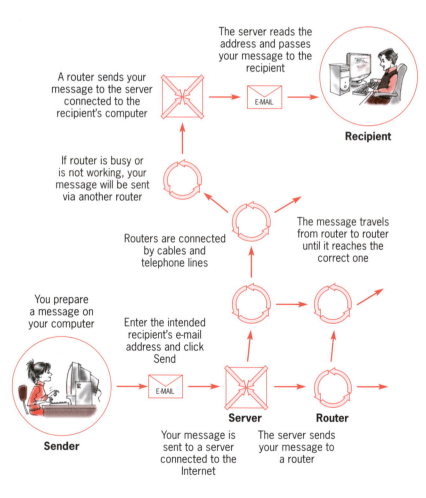

ADVANTAGES OF E-MAIL

E-mail saves a lot of time and effort in producing formal, printed memos, faxes and letters. Many e-mail messages are short and may be deleted after a few days or weeks. With longer or more important messages, they may be retained on the electronic file or printed out as a hard copy.

Some advantages of e-mail are:

- high speed send/receive cycle;
- direct input and retrieval from keyboard;
- virtually instant despatch/retrieval;
- simultaneous circulation to pre-selected groups;
- other files can be attached to e-mails.

Checkpoint

There are also several pitfalls to using e-mail. In groups, make a list of the pitfalls and consider how they can be overcome.

Remember

Once your message is sent, it may be read by the recipient within seconds. Have some respect for your reader and make sure it is *right* before you click 'send'.

E-mail is quick and easy to use, but this should not be an opportunity to forget all the basic rules of good business writing. In business use, try not to use abbreviations which you may use when e-mailing personal friends.

Checkpoint

Many abbreviations like BFN (bye for now) and PCM (please call me) are used in personal e-mail messages. Discuss other abbreviations that you have seen or used.

The way people use e-mail reveals quite a lot about us. People who are open-minded and who welcome new ideas embrace the e-mail culture willingly. They send crisp, clear messages, they reply promptly and they are a pleasure to liaise with. People who are uncreative and full of their own importance tend to sound quite long-winded and pretentious in e-mail messages. They find it hard to adopt the casual, friendly, conversational style that suits e-mail.

Remember

Poor communication skills will be exposed in e-mail messages. As you are most probably thinking and tapping away at the keyboard at the same time, your thought processes are revealed for all to see.

Weblink

www.webfoot.com
A beginner's guide to effective e-mail.

TOP TEN COMPLAINTS ABOUT E-MAIL IN PRACTICE

When I talk to my workshop participants I often ask them what annoys them most about e-mail. Here is my compilation of the top ten complaints about e-mail in practice.

1 Vague subject line

Readers with lots of e-mail every day will not open mail headed 'urgent' or 'hello'. You must compose a SMART subject line that is:

Specific
Meaningful
Appropriate
Relevant
Thoughtful

Remember

What you put in your subject line can often mean the difference between whether your message is read right now, today, next week or never!

2 No greeting

It's just plain courtesy to include a greeting at the beginning of an e-mail. We don't need Dear Mary or Dear Mr Tan, as in letters. In e-mails we can be slightly more informal, with Hi Sally, Hello John. Another reason why I like to see 'Hi Shirley' at the beginning of a message is that this is confirmation to me that the message is to me and not a *cc* or *bcc*.

3 No sign-off

Similarly, it's another sign for me when I see your name at the end of a message – it's a sign that your message is finished. A sign-off should not need to include 'Regards' or 'Kind regards'. Why do we need these boring, useless closes? Just put your name at the end and be done with it!

4 Poor formatting

I hate to receive a message that goes on and on without any blank lines to show new paragraphs. Other people agree that such messages are confusing and boring. Try to think and format in paragraphs when you are composing e-mail messages. Blank lines between paragraphs are a great idea. They not only help you but they help your reader too.

5 Vague messages

Do you receive vague messages? These are messages where you read and read but you cannot see what the writer is trying to say, and you have no idea what the writer expects of you. Many people complain about this. Do yourself and your reader a favour by thinking in paragraphs, remembering appropriate structure, and being clear in your writing.

6 Tell me what to do

This is connected with number 5, in that the writer doesn't tell you what action he or she wants you to take after reading the message. Remember the three Rs – you must guide the *r*eader towards the *r*esponse that is *r*equired – only then will you get the right results.

7 Unfriendly tone

Emotions are hard to convey in e-mails, and some people type out exactly what they would say without thinking of the tone of voice that would be used to signal their emotions. With e-mail you only have words, so without the right tone, misunderstandings could easily happen. You could easily offend or perhaps lose an important business contact. Good writers learn to choose their words carefully, and get the tone just right!

Remember

If you have written a message in anger, leave it in your Drafts folder for an hour. Then go back and look at it again. I really don't think you will send it unless you tone it down a little.

8 CC to the whole world

A friend of mine once said 'Don't send a *cc* to everyone you know. Just send a *cc* to people who need to know!' I agree. It's too easy to send *cc*s nowadays (courtesy copies, not carbon copies!). Please don't contribute to the increasing problem of overflowing inboxes. Send a *cc* only when it is essential.

9 Bad grammar, bad spelling and bad punctuation

As more people use e-mail, sloppy work is becoming a major annoyance. People are receiving poorly formatted messages in one continuous paragraph, poorly structured messages that don't state what response is needed, and poorly written messages with errors in grammar, spelling and punctuation. Remember, your e-mail says something about you and your organisation. Make sure it gives a good impression.

10 Just plain sloppy

Many people comment about the need to reply to e-mails quickly simply because of the urgency of e-mails. In view of this urgency, many people don't take as much care with their writing. Rushed messages are often garbled, unclear, unfocused, with poor structure, poor tone and poor spelling. Readers do not understand such messages, they may be offended by them, and they don't know what they have to do in response.

Remember

The Internet has made it possible for us to communicate with people from all over the world. The only way those people can form an opinion of you is by looking at the way you write. Your credibility could be ruined with one swift click of the 'send' button.

Did you know?

For an interesting website on e-mail, check out
Mary Houton-Kemp's Everything E-mail, on www.everythingemail.net

HOW TO CREATE ELECTRONIC RAPPORT

Here are some techniques you can use to create electronic rapport with your e-mail correspondents:

1 Don't just dive into your message

Try to ease the reader into your message by giving some basic background information. Be warm and friendly in your opening where possible. For example:

- It was good to speak to you this morning. I'm glad we were able to clarify this issue.
- Thanks for calling me today. It was so good to speak to you after all this time.
- Thanks for a great lunch yesterday. Your new project certainly sounds very interesting.
- I'm so sorry to hear about the problem you've experienced with your new LCD projector.

2 Show some feelings

It's too easy just to state the mere facts without showing any concern or feelings. Remember that you can add texture to your message by using emotive and sensory words. Showing some empathy in your message will help you to form a better bond with your readers. For example:

- I appreciate your understanding.
- I certainly see what you mean, and hope we can resolve this problem.
- I am happy to offer you an extra discount of 10%.
- I am pleased to know you will be visiting Mumbai next month.

3 Keep your message positive and focused

Two essential ingredients of e-mail messages are keeping a positive attitude towards your reader and maintaining a focus on their needs. Try to be diplomatic, and never be afraid to apologise if something has gone wrong.

4 Tailor the tone of your message

The speed of e-mail can lead to inappropriate informality. Be careful to tailor the tone of your message accordingly. Distinguish personal from business e-mails, and avoid using abbreviations, exclamation marks and slang when writing to clients.

5 Be precise and clear

All readers deserve a clear and professional message. Pay attention to what is being asked and respond clearly. If you are not precise this will make more work because a further e-mail will be necessary.

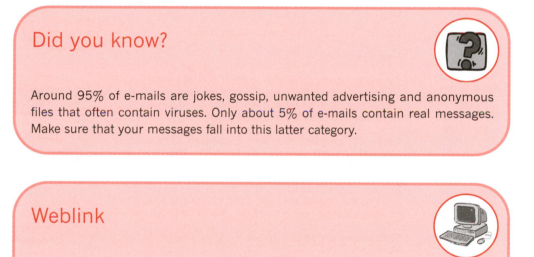

Did you know?

Around 95% of e-mails are jokes, gossip, unwanted advertising and anonymous files that often contain viruses. Only about 5% of e-mails contain real messages. Make sure that your messages fall into this latter category.

Weblink

http://www.albion.com/netiquette/corerules.html
The core rules of netiquette.

SAMPLE E-MAIL MESSAGES

1

To	GinaPorter@GlobalComms.co.uk
From	shirley@shirleytaylor.com (Shirley Taylor)
Date	22.10.04 9.55
Subject	Lunch 28 October

Hello Gina

This is just a reminder that I'm looking forward to meeting you for lunch next Friday 28th. I am glad you've arranged for Jenny Chew to join us too. Can I suggest 12.30 at Hemingways on Orchard Road? I hear this new restaurant is fabulous. My treat of course. Please confirm.

Shirley

Informal greeting

Contractions are OK

Informal, chatty style where appropriate

No formal closing

2

To	MandyWilson@Pioneer.co.sg
From	shirley@shirleytaylor.com (Shirley Taylor)
Date	14.8.04 14:30
Subject	Customer Services Training

Dear Mandy

We are considering sending some of our staff on a training course on Customer Services. Do you have a suitable course available within the next few months? If so please let me have the dates and times plus costs.

If there isn't a regular Pioneer course scheduled, can you tailor-make a course specially for our staff? We could hold it in our conference room.

Perhaps we can arrange to meet to discuss this - are you free next Friday 20 August at 11 am? I could come over to you, or you could come over to my office. Just let me know.

Shirley Taylor
Manager
ST Training and Consultancy
Tel: +65 64726076   Fax: +65 63392710
Mobile: +65 96355907
e-mail: shirley@shirleytaylor.com
http://www.shirleytaylor.com

[This e-mail may be confidential and privileged. Any form of unauthorised use is prohibited. If it has been wrongly sent to you, please delete immediately and notify the sender. Thank you.]

This style is slightly less informal

Short sentences, no padding!

Short paragraphs

Write in a casual style as if you are speaking

A standard 'signature block'

A disclaimer

3 Key e-mail addresses accurately

The time is inserted automatically by your computer

Use an appropriate subject heading

Keep your salutation informal and friendly

E-mail messages are much less formal than other business documents, sometimes more chatty

Finish off informally too

To   Thomas.Sigel@pearson.com
From   Shirley.Taylor@cfb.co.uk
Date   Mon 21 September 200–
Time   12:23:45 +0000
Subject   Communication for Business 4th edition

Hi Thomas

Thanks for your email today. I'm glad you enjoyed your holiday in Canada.

I'm happy to report that I've been able to progress very well with the new edition of Communication for Business. I've received help from some friends and colleagues which has been very valuable. I've also been in touch with lots of big companies who have very kindly given permission for me to use some of their documents in my book.

I should be able to wrap everything up by the end of this month. Would you like to come up and collect the work next week? Shall we say Wednesday 30 September at our usual table in the Red Lion Hotel in Todwick?

Please let me know if this is OK with you.

See you soon.

Shirley

Remember

Once your message is sent, it may be read by the recipient within seconds. You cannot call it back for second thoughts. Proofread it carefully before you click 'send'.

Remember

Have some respect for your reader by checking through your message for grammar, spelling formatting and other errors before you hit 'send'.

www.shirleytaylor.com

Netiquette

In personal relationships the conventions of behaviour are called etiquette. In e-mail we have **netiquette** – a set of rules for e-mail that have evolved from experience. All your emotions and subtleties have to be incorporated into what you write, so misunderstandings are easy to create. Here are my tips for better netiquette:

N ever leave a response too long.
It's common courtesy to respond to a message as quickly as you can – even if you have to say that a detailed response will be sent later.

E -mail addresses must be correct.
Correctly addressed e-mail messages are received within seconds, but it can take a while to receive an error message letting you know that an incorrectly addressed message wasn't delivered. Get your e-mail addresses right first time.

T ake off the caps lock. DON'T SHOUT!
Even though you want to get noticed, please do not use capitals in e-mail messages – this is like shouting – it is rude and will usually be counter-productive. And also ... NEVER RESORT TO EXCESSIVE PUNCTUATION*@!!**?!!!!

I nformality is OK in e-mails.
Replace formal salutations like 'Dear Leslie' with 'Hi Leslie' or even just 'Leslie'. Similarly, replace 'Yours sincerely' with 'Best wishes' or some other informal closing. (Try to avoid the overused 'Regards' and horribly abbreviated things like Tx and Tnks & Rgs!)

Q uestion your subject heading.
People are most likely to read important looking e-mails first. Give your messages a clear and specific subject heading that will get noticed.

U se short sentences and short paragraphs. The shorter your messages, the more likely they will be read and understood. Remember to paragraph just the same as in other business documents.

E numerate with numbers or bullets.
Present your messages attractively. Use numbers, bullets or sub-headings if possible – this will add to the clarity of your message.

T idy up long sentences to eliminate waffle.
Tapping away at the keyboard as you think, it is easy to allow sentences to become too long. Read through your message carefully and improve clarity and understanding.

T ake a pride in your finished message. Make sure your message is accurate, brief and clear as well as attractively presented. In this way it will be understood and will achieve the desired results.

E nsure everything is right before you hit 'send'. You cannot call an e-mail back for second thoughts, so get it right first time!

What's wrong?

In groups, discuss what is wrong with this e-mail message in terms of:

- structure (the four-point plan)
- tone
- format
- language

Re-write it more appropriately.

From	Harry.Lim@presto.co.my
Date	25:7:04 16:06:29
To	shirley@shirleytaylor.com
CC	
Subject	HELLO!

hi Shirley

Hope things r well with u, its good 2 know that u will be back in malaysia again in nov to hold your seminar on effective biz writing. PLS LET ME HAVE SOME FREE DATE while u r over here. some bookstores r interested ina talk cum singing event, I hope u will agree to take part.

tnks & rgs
Harry

THE INTERNET

It was in the late 1980s when the phenomenon known as the World Wide Web took the world by storm. It comprises millions of pages of words, pictures, sounds and graphics stored on computers connected to the Internet. A collection of web pages created by a single organisation is called a website. Every website has its own address, called a URL (Uniform Resource Locator):

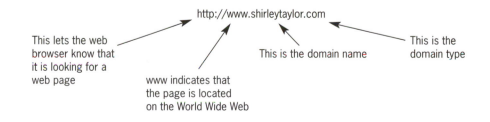

http://www.shirleytaylor.com

This lets the web browser know that it is looking for a web page

www indicates that the page is located on the World Wide Web

This is the domain name

This is the domain type

Weblink

http://www.w3.org/
Learn the latest about the World Wide Web

Did you know?

A domain name is the name of the server to which the message will be sent. The final part of the domain name is called the domain type. This tells you the type of organisation where the server is located. Here are some domain types:

.com or .co	a business or commercial organisation
.org	a non-profit organisation
.edu or .ac	an educational establishment
.gov	a government organisation
.mil	a military organisation
.rec	a recreation or entertainment site
.info	an information services site

Weblink

http://www.webfoot.com/advice/email.domain.html?Email
All about domain names.

SURFING THE NET

A website is a set of interactive pages containing related information. Every website has a home page that lists all the contents of the site, just like the contents page of a book. You can then click on any of the hyperlinks to access the vast amount of information available throughout the site. Here is my home page:

THE IMPACT OF THE INTERNET ON BUSINESS

Digital traffic more than doubles in volume every year. Hundreds of companies are going online every week. Never before has any one development had such an impact on the way business is conducted.

Businesses are increasingly looking towards the Internet as a means of advertising, selling and distributing their services. You can book hotel rooms, flights, hire a car, arrange for flowers to be delivered, order new shoes or clothes, all without leaving your desk and even without picking up a phone. People are regularly shopping online for certain goods, especially books and CDs, even groceries. You can often track the progress of parcels or other deliveries online. There seems no limit to the capabilities of the Internet. It is a host to a wealth of information and services – so whatever you need to find out or order, it is probably on the Internet somewhere.

INTRANETS AND EXTRANETS

Intranets are internal Internets. An intranet is like a company's own internal version of the Internet. A company's intranet can contain a wealth of information about the company, with each department having its own site and information being made available to everyone within the company – but not other people outside the company.

Did you know?

If you need to let all members of a meeting see some notes for reference before a meeting, why not post the notes on your company's intranet and send an e-mail message to all members telling them the exact location of the notes. This saves you having to attach the notes as a separate file, which could jam up their inbox.

Weblink

http://www.ibiztips.com/
Ibiz Tips.
Free tips to help you succeed online.

THE IMPACT OF E-MAIL ON BUSINESS

(Reproduced with permission from *Guide to Effective E-mail* by Shirley Taylor, ISBN 981043879-6)

E-mail is the most popular facility available through the Internet. It has made a lot of changes to the way businesses operate:

- Traditionally secretaries opened their employer's mail and could keep up-to-date on everything. Now that many executives read their own e-mail, a secretary's role could be quite frustrating unless a good understanding has been reached with employers.
- Since many executives read their own mail it is often possible to contact powerful people directly. But remember, not all CEOs are keen to receive information directly from anyone. Just because you know his or her e-mail address, it doesn't always mean that your CEO wants to hear directly from you. Your own line manager may also not be too happy with you if you go over his or her head in such a way.

- Some people get so used to doing everything through e-mail that they forget or don't give as much importance to proper mail. Make sure you check your snail mail at least once a day.
- Some people receive dozens of messages every day, some that are important, others are being sent to them simply for the sake of it when really they don't need to see them. As a result many people find they are spending more than half their time dealing with e-mail. We can all do our part to ease this problem by learning to respect other people's time, and only send mail to people who really need to see it.
- Some people send the same message several times because of errors they spotted after they sent it the first (or second) time. Please correct your mistakes before you hit 'send'. You will give a much better impression to your readers if you get it right first time.
- Very often working with e-mail means you have to develop a good memory. We tend not to print out as many messages as perhaps we should do. Also, may companies implement a system whereby old messages (say 30 days old) may be deleted automatically from your workstation so that the hard disk is not clogged up unnecessarily. Protect yourself by saving paper copies of important messages.

Internal consequences

Traditionally internal communications in business were hierarchical, with messages being passed up and down the chain, often with secretaries acting as a filter between managers and staff. Flatter company structures have changed the whole spectrum of internal communications. A network has now replaced the hierarchical model. With e-mail, every member of staff is able to communicate directly with everyone else – up, down and across the organisation This flatter organisation structure, and the new power of employees to communicate company-wide, means that information can be distributed more efficiently around the organisation. However, because of the relative ease of sending e-mail, messages may sometimes be sent without due thought and consideration.

External consequences

E-mail has undoubtedly helped us to establish and maintain business relationships with branches, clients, suppliers, etc. Relationships with customers and co-workers can be improved and productivity can be enhanced considerably through effective use of e-mail. It used to be said that the business letter was an ambassador for your company, so it should therefore give a very good impression. I believe the same can now be said of e-mail messages. You should take care with all your e-mail messages so that they give a good impression of you and your company.

www.shirleytaylor.com

E-mail your way to the top

E-mail viruses make front-page newspaper headlines. They cost decent computer users a lot of money, they waste our time and energy, and they cause unimaginable distress to people all over the world. Could anything be worse? What about the damage that people are causing to themselves every day by taking e-mail for granted? The familiarity and convenience of e-mail is resulting in sloppy, careless habits that could ruin your business and your reputation just as surely as any e-mail virus.

Electronic mail is having a phenomenal effect on the way we communicate. E-mail is not just a quick, easy and relatively cheap way to keep in touch with family and friends. It has also become an essential tool in business, a fundamental part of the way in which we work. However, the explosive growth of e-mail has created some problems, mainly because there have never been any guidelines on how to compose e-mail messages, no definitive guide to common standards and expectations among writers of e-mail. Consequently systems are being overloaded, communication is rampant, reputations are being damaged, feelings are being hurt and time is being wasted.

One of the main advantages of e-mail is speed, but the pressure of coping with an ever-increasing mailbox is adding to the pressures people already face. This is resulting in messages being sent without much thought or planning, with important details missing, with spelling and punctuation errors, and with abbreviations that some people don't like and others simply don't understand. Some messages look like they are written in code! And people are even neglecting the common courtesies of a greeting and sign-off just for the sake of speed!

High on the list of annoyances when I did some research for my book, *Guide to Effective E-mail*, was **unfriendly tone**. Emotions are hard to convey in e-mails, and some people type out exactly what they would say without thinking of the tone of voice that would be used to signal their emotions. With e-mail all we have are words. Without the right tone misunderstandings could easily happen, or you could offend and perhaps lose an important business contact – or even friend! Good writers learn to choose their words very carefully and get the tone just right.

www.shirleytaylor.com *continued*

E-mail and information overload is another serious problem, with some managers receiving hundreds of messages every day. But if we are suffering from overflowing inboxes, how much of it is self-inflicted? Has it become too easy to send messages to lots of people just because you can? We must learn to use e-mail more thoughtfully by recognising when we should and should not send messages. Do you really need to send all those CC, BCC and FWD copies? If you receive lots of messages that you don't really need to see, tell the authors so that it doesn't happen again. And tell your friends not to send those jokes and personal messages to your work e-mail address. Then there's that prolonged e-mail exchange that lasts for days – wouldn't it be better to pick up the phone? E-mail overload is contributing to a decline in oral communication skills – people send e-mails to the person in the next office rather than walk a few steps! So please remember that it's good to talk and don't let e-mail result in the death of conversation.

As more people use e-mail sloppy work is becoming a major annoyance. People are receiving poorly formatted messages in one continuous paragraph, poorly structured messages that are not specific in the response required, messages written all in capitals (equivalent to SHOUTING) or all in lower case, and, of course, messages with poor grammar, spelling and punctuation.

A friend of mine once said to me:

> "When I receive a message that has lots of mistakes – spelling errors, punctuation, grammar – I think the reader has no respect for me because he/she couldn't take just one minute to check it through before hitting 'send'."
> (Ricky Lien, www.mindsetmedia.com.sg)

I completely agree! The Internet has made it possible for us to communicate with people from all over the world. The only way those people can form an opinion of us is by looking at the way we write! Your credibility could be ruined with one swift click of the 'send' button.

Today's way of conducting business is informal so that's what we should aim for in our business writing too – natural, relaxed, friendly, conversational. The only place for standard boring overused clichés like 'Please find attached herewith', 'I am writing to inform you', 'Please be advised', 'I should be grateful if you would kindly', is the recycle bin! Busy businessmen and women haven't got time to plough through loads of old-fashioned, long-winded jargon. Nor should they be subjected to abbreviated, coded, sloppy messages that are full of errors. We should take just as much care in composing e-mail messages as we should with formal letters, memos or faxes. We should use short words and simple expressions, short sentences and short paragraphs that are clear and concise but still courteous. We should take pride in composing effective messages that are structured logically. Most of all we should identify with our readers, appreciate their feelings, and use words they will understand, written in an appropriate tone.

www.shirleytaylor.com *continued*

If you want to improve your electronic rapport with customers and colleagues, if you want to enhance your credibility and your reputation as well as your productivity, remember – it's not a computer you are talking to, it's a real live human being.

A good writer:
- Carefully words all e-mails
- Always considers tone carefully
- Doesn't use abbreviations in business e-mails
- Sends ccs only when necessary
- Checks all messages carefully before sending
- Always includes a greeting and sign-off
- Never sends sloppy e-mails
- Never uses old-fashioned clichés

What's wrong?

E-mails are often typed and sent very quickly, without paying much thought to appropriate tone. The following e-mail is from an administration executive in accounts department to the manager of the sales department. Read the e-mail and consider how you would feel if you were the recipient. Then rewrite the e-mail in a more appropriate tone.

From	sallyturner@rightway.com
Date	25:7:05 16:06:29
To	johnwong@rightway.com
CC	
Subject	REMINDER!

John

Appreciate if you would consider and bear in mind that I am no longer responsible for dealing with petty cash. Some of your staffs keep bringing their vouchers to me, but this responsibility has been taken over by Martin in Accounts, he is the one who should be contacted henceforth for all petty cash matters

Your co-operation is appreciated in making sure all your staffs know about this.

BRgs/Sally

What's wrong?

Here is an e-mail that has been written quickly and in a tone that is far from courteous.

From	grace.peng@global.co.cn
Date	25:10:05 15:29:45
To	robinzhang@midway.co.cn
CC	
Subject	Your Complaint

Your complaint about your fax machine that you bought from us last year has been past to me for my attn. Please be informed that your policy document shows that you only have a one year guarantee for these products and it ran out on 2nd Sept. So if you want it fixing you will have to pay for it.

Let me know what you want to do.

Rewrite the e-mail in a more appropriate tone.

USING E-MAIL – KEY POINTS TO REMEMBER

1   Compose a SMART subject heading. This will give the recipient a good idea of the contents of the message, and it makes for easier handling.

2   Keep caps lock off. Capitals indicate SHOUTING and can appear threatening. They should never be used in e-mails.

3   Use an appropriate greeting and sign-off. Formality does not read well in e-mails. Replace formal salutations like 'Dear David' with 'Hi David', or even just 'David'. Similarly, 'Yours sincerely' is not appropriate in e-mails. Please don't overuse 'Regards' too. Why not just put your name?

4   Check your syntax. It's easy to allow sentences to become very long and verbose. Keep your sentences short and simple, and check your sentence construction. The more pride you take in composing your message, the more successful you will be in being understood and achieving the desired results.

5   Be sure you hit the right reply button. The message may be addressed just to you or to lots of others, or it may be CC'd or BCC'd to lots of other recipients. Make sure you hit the correct reply key so that the right readers receive your message.

6   Use 'reply to all' wisely. Some writers choose to send an e-mail to lots of people, but it's not always wise or appropriate for every individual reply to be seen by all the same people.

7 Slow down. Every word counts, and one mistake is too many. Because of the speed of e-mail, it's tempting to try to respond quickly. However, speed often creates mistakes. So slow down, take care, focus and get it right.

8 Keep copies. Just as you would keep copies of important letters, it's good practice to print out important e-mails too.

9 Use the right tone. With e-mail all you have are your words. Careful writers learn to choose their words carefully and get the tone just right.

10 Check your message. Re-read your message before you hit 'send'. Proofread means a lot more than spellchecking! Check for accuracy, brevity, clarity, as well as organisation and tone. Also make sure you have attached whatever you have said you will attach.

A–Z OF BLOOPERS AND BLUNDERS, COMMON ERRORS AND CLICHÉS: H

Hereby

Just like *herewith*, this is an old-fashioned cliché that we should not use in the twenty-first century.

However

However – when the meaning is 'nevertheless' – can be used at the beginning, in the middle or at the end of a sentence. It's a good word to help you illustrate a contrast in thought. Note that commas are usually needed. For example:

I rarely work on weekends. However, last weekend was an exception.
I rarely work on weekends. Last weekend, however, was an exception.
I rarely work on weekends. Last weekend was an exception, however.

When you use 'however' to mean 'in whatever way' or 'to whatever extent', note that it is one word, not two:

However you advise her, she will do exactly as she pleases.

IN THE BIN: H

henceforth
howsoever

HELP YOURSELF

Choose the correct word from those shown in brackets.

1 My mother always does the .... on Saturday mornings.
   (marketing/shopping)
2 The new shop will be .... for business next Monday.
   (open/opened)
3 If you are going to increase your shorthand speed, you need to ....
   very hard.
   (practice/practise)
4 Due to the poor economy, it's really not .... to employ any more
   new staff.
   (practical/practicable)
5 Michael wants to .... me to the cinema tomorrow night.
   (take/bring)
6 Please let me know when you have .... free to discuss this project.
   (some time/sometime)
7 We have .... employees this year than we had last year.
   (less/fewer)
8 If we take on the new business, it would .... our present activities.
   (compliment/complement)
9 The person .... chosen as best dressed will win a prize.
   (whose/who's)
10 I hope .... going to be at the party on Friday night.
   (your/you're)

TEST YOURSELF

1   In each of these pairs, choose the SMART subject line:

     1 (a) Results for first quarter of 2005
        (b) Quarterly results up by 20%

     2 (a) Reservation
        (b) Reservation of Juniper Suite

     3 (a) Order ST 678R 24 August
        (b) Problem with our order

     4 (a) Party invitation to all staff
        (b) Invitation to 10th anniversary party

5 (a) Sales Manager Advertisement
   (b) Advertisement needed urgently

6 (a) Report on staff canteen
   (b) Report attached

7 (a) Overseas trip November 2005
   (b) November 2005 Trip to Europe

8 (a) 10% pay increase for all employees
   (b) Directors reject 10% pay increase

2 Place a tick or a cross beside each of these expressions, showing whether they are examples of (✗) old-fashioned writing style or (✓) modern business writing suitable for use in e-mails. Rewrite those that you gave a cross.

(a) Please find attached hereto the documents as per your request.
(b) Please advise me if you concur with this opinion.
(c) I hope to hear from you soon.
(d) Should you require any further clarification please contact the undersigned.
(e) Thank you for your message today.
(f) Please be informed that a departmental meeting will be held next Monday.
(g) Please give me a call on 2874722 if you have any questions.
(h) I am writing to inform you that the annual dinner will be held on 12 November.
(i) The above-mentioned goods will be despatched to you soonest possible.
(j) I am enclosing herewith our remittance in settlement of your account.
(k) Kindly contact me as soon as possible to discuss this matter.
(l) I was pleased to hear about your recent promotion.
(m) I am very sorry to hear about the mistake made with your order.
(n) I am putting in the mail today our latest catalogue for your reference and perusal.
(o) Please note that arrangements have been made for a repeat order to be despatched to you immediately.

3   Study this effective e-mail and then draft a reply. Make up any necessary details.

From	geogiathomas@aurorasuperstores.co.uk
Date	10:7:05 11:35:14
To	lilymcbeal@healthylife.com
CC	richardcage@aurorasuperstores.co.uk
Subject	Eating for Health Campaign

Dear Lily

It was good to meet you again last week. As discussed, I would like to invite you to give the opening speech at the launch of our Healthy Eating Campaign. This will be held at our Leeds superstore on Monday 8 August.

Richard and I are very excited about this campaign. We are hoping it will make the public more aware of the importance of choosing a variety of fresh fruit and vegetables as part of their daily diet.

I am attaching a provisional programme, from which you will see that 10 minutes has been allocated for the opening speech at 9.30 am. We will be happy to arrange your transport to and from our superstore on launch day.

I know that your profile in this industry would bring crowds flocking to this launch. We hope you will decide to join us.

Best wishes

Georgia Thomas
Marketing Manager
Aurora Superstores Ltd
Telephone +44 114 2888724
Mobile +44 7770 2342342
www.aurora.com

4   Discuss what's wrong with this e-mail, and rewrite it more appropriately.

From	EdwardLeong@bettabuy.co.my
Date	9:9:05 14:20:31
To	roger.hardy@stcommunications.co.my
CC	
Subject	Complaint with order

Dear Hardy

We placed the above-mentioned order for 150 CDs on 8/4/05 and it was received by us yesterday. I was shocked to find that 24 of them were badly scratched.

The package containing the goods was in perfect condition and I accepted and signed for the delivery without question, but it was only when I unpack and check the discs that I discovered the damage.

Attached hereto you will find a list of the damaged CDs and should be grateful if you would replace them as soon as possible.

Hoping to hear from you soonest.

Tnks & Rgs

5 Reply to the previous message. Make up the necessary details as you consider appropriate.

6 You work in the Training Department at ST Electronics. Approximately 12 of your staff need to attend a training course on Customer Services. You need to arrange a meeting with Jenny Li, your usual contact at Pioneer Training Services, to discuss this. Send her an e-mail to find out if they have a suitable course available – within the next couple of months would be ideal. If so, ask for relevant details. If not, ask if they could conduct a special course for these staff at your own premises.

7 You are Dave Ikin, Marketing Marketing Manager of ST Electronics. Last week you visited Delia Kwik at Kwik Vision Pte Ltd, a company that specialises in producing corporate videos. Delia showed you around the company's new facilities, which were very impressive. Delia promised to let you have a draft showing her thoughts for a special video celebrating your company's 25th anniversary, a very special landmark in your company's history. The video needs to portray both past, present and future. Delia promised to let you have her outline by the last day of next month. Send an e-mail following up your meeting.

Internal communication

Unit 9

Memos

LEARNING OUTCOMES

After studying this unit you should be able to:

- Explain the purpose of memos

- Design pre-printed memo forms which contain all essential details

- Compose memos from given instructions

WHY MEMOS?

The memorandum (plural memoranda), affectionately called a 'memo', is a written communication from one person to another (or a group of people) within the same organisation. Memos serve a variety of purposes:

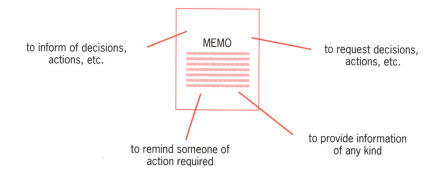

to inform of decisions, actions, etc.

to request decisions, actions, etc.

to remind someone of action required

to provide information of any kind

Just as letterheaded paper is used for letters, many organisations use pre-printed stationery for memos. Here are some examples:

MEMORANDUM   Aurora ☾★

To   Ref

From   Date

✴ **Global Enterprises**   Kuala Lumpur

MEMORANDUM

To   _____

From   _____

Date   _____

Subject   _____

Checkpoint

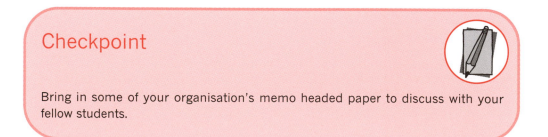

Bring in some of your organisation's memo headed paper to discuss with your fellow students.

It is important that the memo headings show details of sender and recipient as well as reference and date. Courtesy titles (Mr/Mrs/Miss/Ms) are usually not included. If pre-printed memo forms are not used in your organisation, the following headings are suggested.

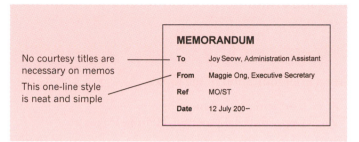

No courtesy titles are necessary on memos

This one-line style is neat and simple

MEMORANDUM

To	Joy Seow, Administration Assistant
From	Maggie Ong, Executive Secretary
Ref	MO/ST
Date	12 July 200–

After these memo headings, continue in the usual fully-blocked style. When more than one topic is dealt with it is good practice to use numbered points and sub-headings. A memo will not include a salutation and complimentary close, but it will usually be signed or initialled depending on the procedure adopted within individual organisations.

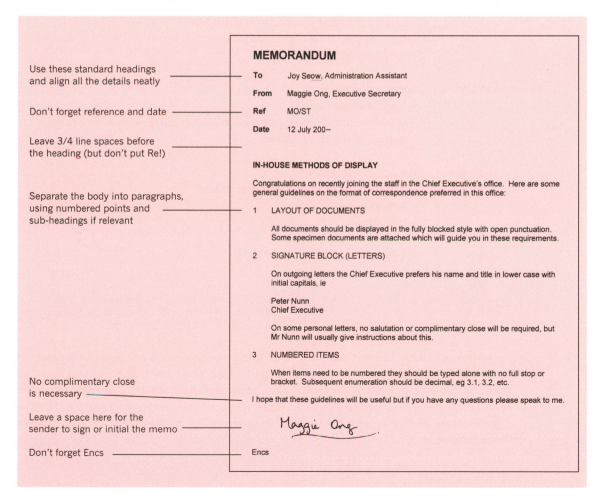

Use these standard headings and align all the details neatly

Don't forget reference and date

Leave 3/4 line spaces before the heading (but don't put Re!)

Separate the body into paragraphs, using numbered points and sub-headings if relevant

No complimentary close is necessary

Leave a space here for the sender to sign or initial the memo

Don't forget Encs

MEMORANDUM

To   Joy Seow, Administration Assistant

From   Maggie Ong, Executive Secretary

Ref   MO/ST

Date   12 July 200–

IN-HOUSE METHODS OF DISPLAY

Congratulations on recently joining the staff in the Chief Executive's office. Here are some general guidelines on the format of correspondence preferred in this office:

1   LAYOUT OF DOCUMENTS

       All documents should be displayed in the fully blocked style with open punctuation. Some specimen documents are attached which will guide you in these requirements.

2   SIGNATURE BLOCK (LETTERS)

       On outgoing letters the Chief Executive prefers his name and title in lower case with initial capitals, ie

       Peter Nunn
       Chief Executive

       On some personal letters, no salutation or complimentary close will be required, but Mr Nunn will usually give instructions about this.

3   NUMBERED ITEMS

       When items need to be numbered they should be typed alone with no full stop or bracket. Subsequent enumeration should be decimal, eg 3.1, 3.2, etc.

I hope that these guidelines will be useful but if you have any questions please speak to me.

Maggie Ong

Encs

STRUCTURE

The four-point plan for structuring all business documents (see page 85) should also be applied to memos.

Subject heading

Give a brief indication of the topic.

✗   Confirmation of meeting
✓   Departmental meeting, 20 June

✗   Letter of complaint
✓   Viva camera model X345

Main body of memo

Introduction	Background information: + briefly give the reason for writing + refer to previous communication + who? what? where? when?
Details	Facts and figures: + logical sequence + separate into paragraphs – each one dealing with a separate aspect of the main theme
Response	An action statement: + action you want the reader to take + action you will take + deadline?
Close	A relevant one-liner

TONE

As you most likely know your recipients fairly well, memos are usually written in an informal style. You should aim to put over your message as concisely as possible while still being courteous, clear, concise and correct. The major consideration in composing memos should be the status of the sender and recipient in the organisation, and of course the topic of the memo. Try to adopt a tone that reflects these factors.

USING LISTS AND BULLETS

Lists can be used in letters, e-mails, fax messages, memos, virtually any document. They are useful to set off important ideas. Your list could be a series of words, names, notes, whatever.

Items could be listed using numbers, letters or bullets. If there are rather a lot of points, numbers are better – then it's easy to refer to item number 3 or whatever. For a simple list of names or words, bullets are better.

Why use lists?

- They help you to organise your thoughts and your points.
- They help focus your reader's attention on important points.
- They help readers find your key points.
- They help to simplify detailed or complicated topics.
- They simplify the skimming process for busy readers.
- They enhance visual impact.

Displaying lists

Make sure you introduce your list appropriately so that your reader knows what to expect. Here are some examples.

Example 1

Be sure that all your list items are parallel in structure. In this example, every point in the list needs to follow the word 'by'.

> You can improve your business writing by:
> 1 adopting a friendly, conversational writing style
> 2 reading your message out loud to check the tone
> 3 keeping to the point and staying focused
> 4 organising your points carefully with my four-point plan
> 5 using language that the reader will understand.

Example 2

Here is a simple list of bullet points. Here all points begin with a verb, to follow the word 'to'.

> When writing a letter of complaint about something you have bought, remember to:
> - describe the item that you bought
> - say where and when you bought the item
> - explain what is wrong and any action you have already taken
> - mention names of anyone you have spoken to and what was discussed
> - state what you expect to be done to rectify the situation.

Example 3

Use sub-headings as a brief cue for readers about what follows. Headings and sub-headings help the reader by fulfilling several functions:

- **Connection** Headings are a visual indication of shifts from one topic to the next. They help readers focus and see the relationship between each section.
- **Attention** Informative headings grab the reader's attention. They also make it easier for readers to find the parts they need to refer to (or indeed skip).
- **Organisation** Headings show the reader at a glance how the information is organised. They sort related information together, and they arrange all the facts into short sections.

What's wrong?

Discuss what's wrong with these lists, and rewrite them more appropriately.

1 The seminar will be held on:

Date	:	26 May, 2005 (Tuesday)
Venue	:	Hilton Hotel, Penang
Time	:	Morning session 9.00 am to 11.30 am
		Afternoon session 1.30 pm to 5.30 pm

2 Here are some tips for presenting your work neatly:

- Make your document interesting and attractive for the reader.
- Too many different typefaces will confuse the reader.
- Visual aids will help to grab the reader's attention.
- Using illustrations or figures will add life to your text.
- There are a number of pre-programmed charts on most computers that will help you display special information.

Remember

Avoid being abrupt or impolite (add 'Please ...').

Avoid over-politeness (do not say 'I should be very grateful ...').

Avoid unnecessary expressions (do not say 'Thank you' or 'Kind regards').

Checkpoint

Here are some memos. The first thing you need to do in each case is to compose a suitable heading. Then follow the instructions in your employer's note and write a suitable reply. Prepare each memo on a separate sheet of paper.

MEMORANDUM

To   Frank Gates, Branch Manager, Leeds

From   Derek Hall, Managing Director

Ref   DH/LPO

Date   20 March 200–

Choose an
appropriate
heading

I will be taking Mr James Hudson, our new Sales Director, to visit all our Northern branches during week commencing 27 April.

Our visit to your branch will be on Monday 27 April and we expect to arrive at 1000.

Please arrange for a brief tour to be conducted in the morning followed by a meeting with you. After lunch Mr Hudson would like to meet all the Sales staff.

Please confirm the above arrangements as soon as possible.

Derek

Please reply – everything's OK for their visit – I'll look forward to mtg JH

FG

Checkpoint *continued*

Choose an
appropriate
heading

MEMORANDUM

To   Ian Henley, Financial Director

From   Michelle Long, Credit Manageress

Ref   ML/SP

Date   14 July 200–

Carter & Co have an overdue account with us in the sum of £25,430 despite 3 reminder letters over the past few weeks.

At this stage I would normally suggest that the matter should be put into the hands of our solicitor. However I know you are a personal friend of Carter's Managing Director and I wondered if you wish to write to him as a final attempt to obtain payment of this debt.

Full details are enclosed for your reference.

Please let me know your decision as soon as possible.

Michelle Long

Enc

Reply – say I've written to Carter's MD today – enc. a copy of my letter. Tell Michelle I'll keep her informed of the outcome.

IH

Checkpoint *continued*

MEMORANDUM

To   All Teachers

From   Pauline Choo, Principal   *Sally Turner* ✓

Ref   PC/BOL

Date   2 November 200–

Choose an appropriate heading

I enclose a draft of a new Lecturer's Record Book which I wish to introduce from the new term in January.

This has been designed to allow space for the following records:

1   SECTION A - CLASSWORK

     Pages are provided for teachers to keep a record of the work covered in each lesson throughout the course.

2   SECTION B - ATTENDANCE

     A register of attendance is provided for individual teachers to keep attendance records for their own subjects. Use of the present class register can be discontinued.

Please let me have your comments on this record book together with any suggestions for amendments or further information pages.

The printer will be coming to finalise the proof on Thursday 15 November so your early reply will be appreciated.

P. Choo.

Enc

Excellent idea — shd be
v. beneficial.
2 additional suggestions:

• In Section A, include small column down r-h side to note Homework issued.

• Suggest extra pages to keep record of marks for class tests, HW, etc.
                                    ST

What's wrong? (1)

Study the reply to the following memo composed from the note shown. Rewrite the memo more appropriately.

M E M O R A N D U M

To   Regional Sales Managers

From   K R Green, Sales Director

Ref   KRG/JKL

Date   4 June 200–

John Bird ✓
(Southern Region)

Choose an appropriate heading ──────────

There will be a meeting of all Regional Sales Managers in the Training Office at Bedford on Tuesday 26 June 2000 from 1000 to 1500.

The main subjects for discussion will be sales planning for the next half year and new promotion campaigns.

Please confirm your attendance and let me know if you have any further items which you would like to be included on the agenda.

Ken Green.

Co. cars for new reps

Please confirm that i'll be able to attend, + mention

What's wrong with the answer?

MEMORANDUM

To Mr KR Green

From Regional Sales Manager

Ref KRG/CF

Date 10 June 200–

I confirm that I can attend the meeting.

I should be grateful if you would include on the agenda discussion of company cars for new reps.

Looking forward to meeting you.

What's wrong? (2)

After reading the following assignment carefully study the answer given. Discuss the errors in the answer shown and then rewrite the memo more appropriately.

You work with Mr Patrick Wayne, Managing Director of Wayne Machinery Pte Ltd, a large manufacturing company. Talking to you today, Mr Wayne says:

> We need to send a memo to all departmental managers about the new car parking arrangements – they'll be in effect in two weeks' time. Tell them that unauthorised parking will create havoc – there are so many large lorries delivering raw materials and collecting goods from our factory. Make a special point to stress this. Attach a copy of the plan to the memo and say all staff must park in the areas indicated on the plan for staff parking. Managers should also pin a copy of the plan on their department's noticeboard.

> All departmental managers will be issued with red permits within the next couple of days. They should be given to staff in their departments with cars. Staff should be instructed to display these permits on their cars at all times. Explain the procedure for visitors too – they should report to the security gate on arrival – they'll get green permits from security, and they'll direct them to the visitors' car park. Department managers should inform their staff to tell the gatehouse in advance when visitors are expected.

Compose a suitable memo.

What's wrong with the answer?

MEMORANDUM

To   Departmental Managers

From   Patrick Wayne

Date   24 June

TO INFORM ABOUT NEW CAR PARK

The new car parking arrangements will come into effect in 2 weeks' time. Your co-operation will be much appreciated in ensuring there is no unauthorised parking, as this will cause inconvenience.

A plan is attached for your information. I would be grateful if you would pin this on your notice board. Please inform all your staff that they should park in the areas indicates on the plan. Red permits will be issued to staff soon for display on their cars.

As for visitors, they will be given a permit when they report to the security gate.

Your co-operation is requested in ensuring that these new arrangements are a success.

Thank you and regards

MEMOS – KEY POINTS TO REMEMBER

1 Make a plan first before writing memos. Group your points together in a logical order.
2 Remember my four-point plan so that you draft your message in a logical structure.
3 Use simple, clear language that the reader will understand.
4 Give your memo an appropriate subject heading.
5 Adopt a tone that reflects the status of the sender and the reader as well as the topic of the memo.
6 Use a variety of presentation methods to enhance the display of your message.
7 Use lists and bullets where appropriate.
8 Avoid unnecessary expressions like 'Thank you' and 'Regards'.
9 Do not include a salutation or complimentary close on memos.
10 Sign your memo in the usual way.

In fact

This is a two-word phrase, just like 'in spite' and 'a lot'. They should not be written as one word.

In order to

This is an old-fashioned wordy phrase that can easily be shortened by removing the first two words. Just say 'to'.

In the event that

These four words can easily be reduced to one word – 'if'.

In view of the fact that

Six words that can easily be reduced to one – 'as', 'since' or 'because'.

Investigate/investigation

Investigate means to look into. We therefore do not follow either of these words with into. For example:

Please investigate this matter and let me have your comments.

-ise or -ize

Many words end in this suffix. Be *consistent* in your use. -ise is often used in British English, -ize in American English.

NB: There are, however, some words that *must* end in -ise whichever spelling convention you follow. Here are just a few:

arise
comprise
compromise
disguise
surprise
supervise

Its/it's

It's is written with an apostrophe only when it is a contraction for 'It is'. For example:

It's very funny when you see a little puppy chasing its tail.

I am writing to inform you

Six words that we can cut out of our writing. Come straight to the point and cut out unnecessary clichés like this from your writing. Other useless phrases include: 'Please be informed that', 'Please be advised that', 'I wish to inform you that'.

IN THE BIN: I, J

I am of the opinion that
I would like to say
in all honesty
in due course
in many instances
in the final analysis
in this connection
in total
in view of the fact that
intrinsically
it goes without saying

HELP YOURSELF

Identify and correct the errors in these sentences.

1   Remember to bring all the clothings you need for a winter holiday.
2   When you speak to Iris, please remember to discuss about last month's sales.
3   Thank you for your letter dated on 27 July.
4   All the furnitures need to be covered when we decorate tomorrow.
5   Please ask Diana to emphasise on image when she talks to new staff.
6   I get the MRT to work everyday, but John takes the bus.
7   Pass this form to Patrick and ask him to fill it up.
8   I normally go to the gym everyday, however today I went straight home.
9   I must read the new book in order to keep up-to-date with modern writing.
10 Remember to buy some fish when you do your marketing later.

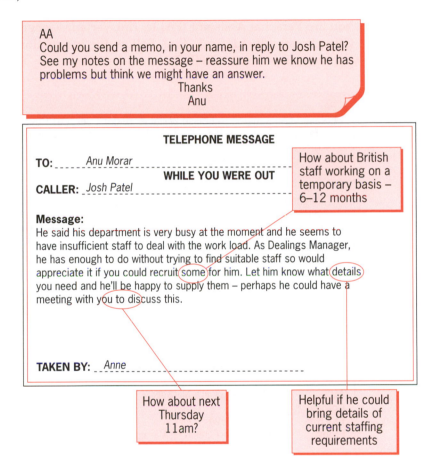

TEST YOURSELF

1   You are Administrative Assistant (AA) to Anu Morar, Personnel Manager of First State Bank of India, 97–94 High Street, New Delhi, India. Mrs Morar is in a meeting. Carry out the instructions in this note from Mrs Morar. (City & Guilds EFBC1)

> AA
> Could you send a memo, in your name, in reply to Josh Patel?
> See my notes on the message – reassure him we know he has problems but think we might have an answer.
>   Thanks
>   Anu

TELEPHONE MESSAGE

TO: _Anu Morar_

WHILE YOU WERE OUT

CALLER: _Josh Patel_

Message:
He said his department is very busy at the moment and he seems to have insufficient staff to deal with the work load. As Dealings Manager, he has enough to do without trying to find suitable staff so would appreciate it if you could recruit some for him. Let him know what details you need and he'll be happy to supply them – perhaps he could have a meeting with you to discuss this.

TAKEN BY: _Anne_

> How about British staff working on a temporary basis – 6–12 months

> How about next Thursday 11am?

> Helpful if he could bring details of current staffing requirements

2   You work in the offices of the *Southern Star Insurance Company*. The company has recently redesigned all its stationery (writing paper, memo pads, invoices, company cards, envelopes, etc.) and these are to be issued to all staff next week.

The Company Manager, Ms Zarina Malik, says this to you:

'Could you send a memo to all staff please? Let them know that we will be sending each department a supply of the new stationery later this week. If any department doesn't get it by Friday afternoon, they should let me know.

'Please remind everyone that they have to use the new materials immediately, even if they still have a lot of the old stationery. I know this means we might have to waste some of the old material, but we could always use it as scrap paper.

'The new material is very well designed and I'm sure all our staff and customers will like it.

'You had better send the memo in my name.'

Task

Write a memo to all staff in the company. A suitable answer is likely to be of 150–200 words. (LCCIEB EFB1 style)

3   You are Personal Assistant (PA) to Tim Variant, General Manager or Creative Gifts, Preston Road, Cork, Eire. Follow the instructions in this note from Mr Variant. (City & Guilds EFBC2)

PA

Please send a memo to Louise Williamson, our Overseas Buyer.
* Tell her we've received a fax from Taj Silks in India offering large range of silk goods.
* Ask if she thinks we have a market for such items.
* Also mention attached fax from Wendy Jones.
* Does Louise have any ideas for supplying Cymru Souvenirs?
* Might it be worth asking Taj Silks if they can make goods to others' designs?

Cymru Souvenirs

Coed Duon Road
FLINT
N.WALES

TEL: 01916 457475
FAX: 01916 4573476

FAX TRANSMISSION HEADER SHEET

To: Tim Variant – General Manager
Company: Creative Gifts
Fax No: 010 6718 04524
From: Wendy Jones – Purchasing Manager

Date: **RECEIVED**

No. of sheets including this one: 1

Message:

We have recently found tourists are becoming far more discerning and now require higher quality goods than ever before. Are you able to supply goods, especially clothes, made of natural fibres eg. wool, cotton or silk? We would be particularly interested if you were able to supply clothes made to our own exclusive designs.

4   You are employed by *HST Products*, a large manufacturing company. You work as an assistant to the General Manager, Mr Julius Muzenda.

Mr Muzenda is Chairman of the company's Operations and Development Committee and the next meeting will take place on Wednesday next week. You have told the members of the committee that the meeting will be in the usual place, Committee Room 4, at the usual time, 1000. A buffet lunch has been arranged for 1230 after the meeting ends.

Today, Mr Muzenda says this to you:

Could you please *send a memo* to all members of the Operation and Developments Committee? The Managing Director, Maria Perez, wants to join us but she can only come in the afternoon. So I've made the arrangements for the meeting to start at one o'clock instead of 10. There will still be lunch provided at 12.30 before the meeting starts.

'Mrs Perez wants to talk about the new Development Plan so it's very important that everyone attends the meeting. You can apologise for the short notice but please stress that everyone should be there.

'Oh yes, we will be in a different room – Committee Room 1. Thanks.'

Task

Write the memo in Mr Mazenda's name. (LCCIEB EFB2 style)

5   You are employed by *Metroville College*, a small college that provides a range of training and education, including Computing, and Information & Communications Technology (ITC). The Head of Department of ITC, Mr Sukhwinder Dhassi, has discovered that on more than one occasion recently a computer virus has been introduced to the computers in the department. He thinks that the viruses have been introduced from computer disks brought in by students. He has decided to introduce a system where all disks used in the department must be checked for a virus before they can be put into the computers.

He says to you, 'I'd like you to *send a memo* in my name to all teachers who use the computer rooms. You'll have to tell them that all disks brought in by students must be checked before they are used. The teachers have to check them carefully, of course. We've got to stop these viruses being introduced before they cause serious problems. Oh yes, remind them to lock up the rooms when they leave. Please tell them to be careful what they say to students; we are not sure which students have introduced the virus so we should not upset them all.'

Task

Write the memo. (LCCIEB EFB2 style)

Unit 10

Reports

LEARNING OUTCOMES

After studying this unit you should be able to:

- Explain the purpose of reports

- Describe some routine reports that may be written in business

- Explain the differences between formal and informal reports

- Describe the different formats for presenting reports

- Discuss the writing skills needed for compiling reports

- State some reasons why we should write good reports

- Identify and correct inappropriate language used in reports

- Compose a suitable covering memo for a free-standing report

- Compose reports according to given instructions

TYPES OF REPORT

Many reports are written in business. They are a very important method of gaining and giving information. Although many reports are presented orally, for example at a meeting, reports are usually presented in writing.

Examples of some reports submitted in business follow.

Routine reports

- representatives' reports on sales visits
- managers' reports on the work of their departments
- equipment and maintenance report
- progress report
- safety report
- accident report.

Special reports

- reports written in response to requests for specific information
- reports made on a special topic after research and investigation
- report regarding a change of policy
- market research report.

The ultimate purpose of any report is to provide the foundation for decisions to be made and action taken.

Some reports consist of no more than a simple statement recording an event, a visit or some circumstances with a note of action taken. Other reports include detailed explanations of facts, conclusions, and perhaps recommendations for future action.

More detailed reports demand research which may involve interviews, visits questionnaires, investigations. The information may be presented in tabular or graphic form and the writer would need to produce clear conclusions and recommendations.

Remember

Take a look at Unit 18 which discusses the techniques for designing question-naires which may be used for gathering information for the purpose of compiling a report.

Whatever their purpose and length, all reports require the following special writing skills:

- the ability to record facts clearly and objectively
- the ability to interpret information and make conclusions
- the ability to present suggestions on ways in which a situation may be improved.

Checkpoint

What reports are submitted regularly in your organisation?

Is a standard form used for the reports? Perhaps you can bring in some copies for your colleagues to look at.

FORMAL REPORTS

Formal reports are usually written by a committee or group of people after fairly detailed investigation or research. They are often presented under the following prescribed series of headings:

Headings

There should be two headings to a report: the name of the company; the report heading (Report on ...).

Terms of reference

This section should state exactly why the report is being written. Why are you writing the report? What was requested? Who requested it? When were you asked to do it? A useful pattern for this section is:

To report on ... (subject) ... as requested by ... (name and title) on ... (date) ...

Procedure

Give a brief description of the methods used to collect the information. Perhaps interviews were held, visits made, questionnaires issued? Use numbered points if appropriate.

Findings

This will be the longest section of the report. Go through the procedure point by point and use numbers and sub-headings for this section. Under each heading state what information was gathered at each stage.

Conclusions

No new facts must be introduced in this section. You must look at the findings and state the logical implications of them. What can you infer or conclude from the findings?

Recommendations (if requested)

Again no new facts must be introduced here. On the basis of information presented in Findings and Conclusions, make some suggestions for action. Remember that the writer of a report cannot make decisions – he or she can only suggest what action should be taken.

Closing section

A report should be signed and there should be a name and title shown at the foot, plus the date the report was written.

Example of a formal report

Company's name and report title (be specific)

Who asked for the report? What was requested? When was it requested?

List the steps taken to gather the information (past tense)

Present the information obtained through each step mentioned in 'Procedure'

Use numbered points and sub-headings for clarity

AURORA HOLDINGS

REPORT ON COMPLAINTS ABOUT POOR SERVICE AND FOOD PROVIDED IN THE STAFF RESTAURANT

TERMS OF REFERENCE

To investigate complaints about poor service and food provided in the staff restaurant and to make recommendations, as requested by Mr Michael Lee, Administration Director, on 14 April 200–.

PROCEDURE

1   An interview was held with Mrs Alice Newton, Restaurant Manageress, on 15 April.

2   Interviews were held with a cross-section of staff (48) who used the restaurant between 15 and 20 April.

FINDINGS

1   INTERVIEW WITH RESTAURANT MANAGERESS

    1.1   STAFFING

        Mrs Newton has 3 full-time assistants. The youngest, Miss Lily Ng, attends day-release classes at Southpoint College on Monday, Wednesday and Friday each week. She works 1400–1700 on those days.

    1.2   EQUIPMENT

        A schedule of current equipment and their year of purchase is attached. No problems were reported. However Mrs Newton said that additional equipment would be useful:

        1 microwave oven
        1 slow cooker
        1 rice cooker

2   INTERVIEWS WITH STAFF

    20 staff from the 1200–1300 lunch sitting were interviewed, and 28 from the 1300–1400 sitting.

    2.1   CHOICE

        The food available is shown on the attached schedule. 60% of the staff interviewed said they would prefer some cold meals to be provided. They said they may make alternative lunch arrangements if the variety did not improve.

Include the page number at
the top left margin ———————— 2

2.2   QUEUEING

70% of staff took lunch from 1200 to 1300 hours as opposed to 30% from
1300 to 1400. This resulted in large queues forming at the first lunch sitting.

What are the logical implications
from the 'Findings'? ———————— **CONCLUSIONS**

1   There are insufficient assistants to cope with the preparation of food in the morning
       and with the popular first lunch sitting.

2   The present equipment is insufficient.

3   The selection of meals is not wide enough to cater for staff requirements.

4   The ratio of staff to each sitting is not balanced.

What action do you suggest
should be taken, based on ———————— **RECOMMENDATIONS**
Findings and Conclusions?

1   A new assistant should be recruited to work 0900-1400 hours on Monday, Wednesday
       and Friday.

2   Mrs Newton should be asked to look into prices and availability of the new equipment
       required.

3   Mrs Newton should be asked to devise some new dishes which also include cold
       choices.

4   The number of staff attending each sitting should be reviewed so that a more even
       balance can be achieved.

Leave a space for the
writer to sign ————————

Name and title of writer ———————— TAN LAY HONG (Miss)
                                    Business Administration Officer

                                    ML/tlh

Reference and date ———————— 24 April 200–

Remember

Reports should be objective, impersonal and factual. Write in full sentences using
third person and reported speech. Do not use I/We/You.

Other formats for formal reports

It is sometimes felt that the format discussed above is suitable only for lengthy reports which stretch to many pages. Many writers are often uncomfortable with writing reports using this five-part structured format. The decision on how to present a report very often depends on the purpose of the report and the nature of the information it contains, also the preference of the writer. Look at these examples:

1 You are asked to discuss the arguments for and against a certain matter and make some recommendations:
   - Introduction
   - Advantages
   - Disadvantages
   - Conclusions
   - Recommendations

2 You are asked to analyse some comment forms received from clients at a large hotel and make some recommendations
   - Introduction
   - Standard of service
   - Facilities
   - Eating places
   - Conclusions
   - Recommendations

The system of using a different structure and composing your own headings specific to the subject matter is illustrated here.

Company's name
Report title
Introduction (who? what? why?)
List steps taken to gather information

Findings
• use sub-headings to classify the information logically
• use enumeration consistently
• remember to use reported/ impersonal speech

Conclusions
• state the logical implication of the findings

Recommendations
• if requested, recommend action

name/title/reference/date

COVERING MEMO

Whenever a free-standing report is issued, don't just issue the report on its own or leave it on someone's desk. It is courteous to attach a brief covering memo which explains it. Here is an example of a short covering memo.

MEMORANDUM

To   Michael Lee, Administration Director

From   Tan Lay Hong, Business Administration Officer

Ref   ML/TLH

Date   24 April 200—

**REPORT ON COMPLAINTS ABOUT POOR SERVICE
AND FOOD PROVIDED IN THE STAFF RESTAURANT**

Further to your recent instructions I have completed my investigations into this matter.
My report is attached.

If you have any queries please let me know.

Tan Lay Hong.

Enc

INFORMAL REPORTS

An informal report may be presented in the previously discussed format (with your own composed headings) or as a memorandum. Here is a short memorandum report.

Names/titles of
sender/recipient

Date report was written

Heading – specific
and clear

Introduction
- In a memo first person
  can be used here
- Mention date report was
  requested
- State steps taken to
  gather the information

Findings
- Use sub-headings and
  numbered points for clarity
- State results of your
  investigations
- Use past tense, reported
  speech

Conclusions
- State the logical implications
  of the findings

Recommendations
- If requested, suggest action

Final paragraph goes back to first
person with suitable close

MEMORANDUM

To   John McIver, Office Manager

From   Ian Fisher, Administrative Assistant

Ref   JM/IF

Date   5 August 200–

REPORT ON POOR TIME-KEEPING OF GENERAL OFFICE STAFF

Further to our meeting on 20 June I have investigated the complaints about time-keeping of
staff in the general office. An interview was held with each of the 12 employees concerned.
Their times of arrival over a 2-week period were noted.

1   PRIVATE TRANSPORT

       Four members of staff travel to work by car. These employees were usually punctual
       and no problems were noted.

2   PUBLIC TRANSPORT

       2.1   Eight members of staff travel to work on public transport, using the A25 bus from
              the town centre. These staff were often up to 15 minutes late, arriving at work
              around 0915.

       2.2   The A25 bus should stop outside the office at 0855 but it was quite erratic in this
              respect. Its arrival varied from 0900 to 0910. The previous A25 bus from town
              arrived outside the office between 0830 and 0840.

3   CONCLUSIONS

       The staff relying on public transport cannot be blamed for the late arrival of the A25 bus
       from town. They also cannot be expected to arrive 30 minutes early each day to avoid
       being a few minutes late for work. However changes in the office routine could help
       the problem.

4   RECOMMENDATIONS

       The staff who use public transport should be given the option of starting work at 0845
       and finishing 15 minutes earlier than usual.

I hope you find this report satisfactory. If you have any questions please let me know.

Ian Fisher

Remember

Again note that the central section of the report uses reported speech and third
person. The first and final paragraph use 'I' and 'me' as this is appropriate in a
memo report.

Another example of a short formal report follows

LANGLAND MANUFACTURING plc

REPORT ON POSSIBLE SUPPORT FOR STAFF FOOTBALL TEAM

TERMS OF REFERENCE

To report on the possibility of the company supporting the staff football team to play in a local league, as requested by Mr Rashid Hassan, Office Manager, on 8 August 200–

PROCEDURE

25 members of staff and 10 keen football players were interviewed to ask for their opinion

POSITIVE FEEDBACK

1   There is a lot of general staff support for the football team
2   The players would like the company to supply the football strips for the team. This would not be expensive as it was felt that a good rate could be obtained from a supplier. The company name and logo would appear on the shirts. This would be good advertising.
3   The team would not expect the company to be involved in running the football team. A committee would be appointed to select the team and organise the football games. This could achieve good publicity if successful.

PROBLEMS

4   Problems could be encountered if other sports fans asked for similar support.
5   Some female staff felt that supporting a men-only team is unfair to women.
6   The company must consider the consequences of footballers being injured and unable to work.

CONCLUSIONS

Although supporting the football team could cause some problems, the company would receive good publicity.

RECOMMENDATIONS

It is recommended that support be given to a company-sponsored football team for one year, at the end of which it should be reviewed.

SHARON TAN (Miss)
Administration Officer

RH/ST
25 August 200–

Checkpoint

Wording in reports

These expressions are not suitable for including in a report. The language may be inappropriate, details may be missing or they may be vague. Express the statements in appropriate, businesslike report language. The first one has been done for you.

1   Rachel Jones is the best person for the job.

Rachel Jones is considered the most suitable applicant for the post of beauty salon manager.

2   Most staff are negative about the proposal but some would like to try it for a while.

_____
_____
_____

3   The planning department said we should have no problem in getting permission for this new project.

_____
_____
_____

4   Bob saw no reason why we shouldn't use some of the club, funds to purchase new equipment.

_____
_____
_____

5   We could take advantage of Aurora's special offer on office furniture.

_____
_____

CHECKLIST FOR COMPILING REPORTS

1   *State the facts*
    Reports set forward a series of facts obtained through study or investigation. Someone may be required to make a decision based on the information provided. Reports should be complete with nothing of relevance omitted and nothing irrelevant included.

2   *Be objective*
    Keep your own opinions and preferences out of the report, unless they have been requested. Instead, you must act like a camera, impartially recording only what it sees.

3   *Be logical*
    Classify the findings under headings and sub-headings, using numbered points. How you classify the material will depend on your brief and the subject matter.

4   *Be consistent*
    Make sure all sentences in a series consistently follow the same grammatical pattern. Similarly, make sure that you use the same spacing throughout the report and that the headings and sub-headings are presented consistently. Attention to these points will make your report clear and will give a good impression.

5   *Be concise*
    Avoid long explanations and keep to the point. Check that all the information is accurate and all the reasoning valid.

6   *Be clear*
    Use a simple, easy to read style and presentation which will help the reader to understand the content easily.

Remember

A report should be understandable, without the need to ask further questions, by someone with no specialised knowledge of the subject.

Checkpoint

Rearrange a report
Here are the terms of reference and procedure, for a report, together with cut-up sections of the rest of the report, Rewrite the report correctly for your files. You will need to compose appropriate headings, sub-headings and numbering. Sign the report as if you have written It, and decide on a suitable title. Don't forget to include an appropriate reference and date at the foot.

Terms of reference
To report on the unrest amongst factory workers and make recommendations, as requested by Mr Richard Fish, Works Manager, on 21 April 200–.

Procedure

1   The three supervisors were interviewed.

2   A meeting was held with all (25) factory workers to gather details of grievances.

3   10 factory workers, selected at random, were interviewed personally.

(a) The human resource manager should hold a meeting of all factory staff and explain the findings of this report.

(b) Safety regulations were being ignored by some members of staff. Protective guards had been removed from many machines.

Checkpoint *continued*

(c) A table showing rates of pay at this company and at other companies is attached.

(d) Rules laid down in the company handbook were being contravened, with some workers leaving machines dirty after use.

(e) The company's rates of pay compare favourably with those paid to apprentices at other companies in this area. Grievances might stop if our staff were made aware of this.

(f) Supervisors reported that many staff were generally un-cooperative and not working to their usual standards.

(g) Supervisors should be reminded of the importance of ensuring that all staff comply with the company's rules and safety regulations.

(h) A widespread unrest and resentment was noted in view of what is considered to be low rates of pay.

(i) Removal of safety guards from machines is an offence against the Factories Act.

(j) A training scheme should be compiled that will ensure balanced experience in all areas of the factory as well as adequate supervision.

(k) Supervisors are not enforcing compliance with rules laid down in the company handbook.

What's wrong? (1)

Read the following assignment and then study the answer given. Decide what is wrong with it before reading the comments provided.

You work at the head office of a large group which has several branches in your area. Eighty per cent of employees from head office and branches are members of the group's sports and social club. Various social activities are arranged, including fortnightly get-togethers for younger employees which have proved very popular. Your chairman has asked you to look into whether it would be viable to buy a hi-fi system so that discos could be organised. Prepare your report, making suitable recommendations.

What's wrong with the answer?

MEMORANDUM

To   Chairman   From   Sharon Tan

Referring to our conversation last week. I can
now give details about the question of purchasing
a music system for the sports and social club.

1   Questionaire issued to members.
All questionaires returned said it would be a good
idea to have regular discos. Rock and contemporary
music was preferred rather than any other music
types.

2   Interviewed treasurer re financial situation.
He saw no reason why some money shouldn't be spent
on new equipment.

3   I visited several department stores re cost of
equipments.

The best equipment was Supersound. The most
suitable being:

Sony – $3, 000
Technics – $2, 750

4   Although it would prove very popular to hold regular
discos, but members felt they should be alternated –
one fortnight a disco, the next fortnight a quiz night or
other event.

5   I recommend the following:

(a) The Sony music system should be purchased, and
with Supersound's special sale now it's obviously
the best deal. The Technics system referred to above
does not have a CD, whereas the Sony systemon special
offer comprises CD as well as record deck, not to
mention cassette deck, radio andspeakers.

(b) We could also take advantage of Supersound's
special offer where we could buy 10 cassettes and
50 singles at half price.

(c) Howard Chew, a long standing member, should be
offered the job of DJ, as he has previous experience
and has expressed an interest.

If you need any more information please let me
know.

What's wrong? (2)

Discuss the faults in the answer to the following question, and then rewrite the report correctly.

You are a member of Aurora Music Society, a large amateur group that gives several public concerts each year usually in a local church hall or school. The Music Society used to enjoy strong support from local people but during the last 2 years the attendance figures for its six concerts have been:

400 (full house) 340 280 180 150

It has been suggested that there could be several reasons why attendance figures are declining: the type of music performed may not appeal to popular taste; the quality of the music may have fallen; there may be insufficient rehearsal time; the arrangement whereby each member of the Music Society tries to sell tickets may not be working well; publicity could be at fault; seat prices may be too high.

The Chairman of the Society, Mr Andrew Webber-Floyd, has asked you to look into the problem carefully. Prepare a formal report with your recommendations for action. You may invent any other minor details as required.

What's wrong with the answer?

MEMORANDUM

To   Mr Andrew Webber-Floyd

From   Timothy Reece

Subject   PUBLIC CONCERTS

Further to your request for me to look into the above-captioned. I have investigated the declining attendance figures by issuing a questionaire to all people attending church last Sunday. Personal calls were also made by me to private houses in the area. The band members were also interviewed.

1   QUESTIONAIRES

         Concerts have been held on unpopular evenings, and the majority of people felt the timing was not suitable.

         The public did not really like the music performed.

         Everyone complained about seat prices.

         No-one had seen any advertising of our concerts. Alot of people were not aware that we held concerts and would have liked to attend.

2   DISCUSSIONS WITH BAND

         Most members were not fond of the type of music they were playing.

         Some members cannot attend rehearsals on the designated evening, as they are members of a local sports club which they attend on the same evening.

         Members don't have enough spare time to visit private houses personally to sell tickets.

3   CONCLUSIONS

         The day and time of the concerts are not suitable.
         The music performed is not popular.
         Seat prices are too high and publicity is no good.
         The rehearsal nights need changing.

4   RECOMMENDATIONS

         4.1   All future concerts will be held on Saturday nights, which the public prefer.
                They will start at 8.00 pm instead of at 7 pm as at present.

         4.2   Posters will be placed in music shop windows to advertise the concerts.

         4.3   Rehearsals should be held on a different night.

         4.4   Popular music should be incorporated in future concerts to satisfy both
                the public and the band.

www.shirleytaylor.com

Report writing – reasons to do it well

(This article was contributed to my website by Tim North. My thanks to Tim for allowing me to reproduce it here.)

You probably don't have a burning desire to write reports. Nonetheless, you've ended up having to write them. There's a natural tendency to want to get the darn things written and off your desk as soon as possible. There are all sorts of reasons for this:

- Writing can be a pain in the behind.
- You didn't take this job to become a writer.
- You've got a dozen other 'real jobs' that need doing.
- You're just having one of those days (or weeks or months).
- It's Friday afternoon.

etc.

We can all identify with these feelings. Still, to use a cliché, if something's worth doing, it's worth doing *well*. Now that's not just hollow sentiment. There are good reasons for taking your writing responsibilities seriously. Here are a few of them.

Reputation

Over time, what you write – and the way you write it – will be remembered, for better or worse. If you succumb to the 'just get it done' or the 'near enough is good enough' schools of thought then, over time, the people you write for will start to judge you accordingly.

Conversely, if you go the extra yards and do a good job on your reports, letters and memos, that too will be remembered; and it will influence your reputation accordingly.

Remember: you are what you write.

Credibility

The reputation that we just discussed has a flow-on effect: it influences your credibility. Consider two staff members:

Person A doesn't like writing. She has a reputation for writing reports that have to be sent back or fixed. They don't always answer all of the things they were supposed to; facts sometimes contain errors; material is inappropriately cut and pasted from earlier reports without change; the layout isn't in the approved style, etc.

www.shirleytaylor.com *continued*

Person B also doesn't like writing. Still, she has a reputation for writing reports that don't need to be sent back or fixed; they answer all of the things they were supposed to; the facts presented are well checked; her reports are well written and well presented, etc.

An incident occurs, and each person provides a different written version of events. Which account will have the greater credibility? Regardless as to who is *right* in this particular case, it's human nature that a person with a reputation for well-written, accurate reporting will have his or her written statement awarded a greater level of credibility. This credibility may not just be extended to his or her written work. People may come to judge your character and work ethic on the basis of a history of well-written submissions.

Reciprocity

When you write reports (or letters or memos), you're often doing so in response to a specific request. It may often seem that the people who make these requests are completely unaware of how much work it takes for you to write the reports or how inconvenient they can be.

This won't always be the case though. At least some (perhaps most) of the people who ask for such reports do understand that you'll have to work on them. And some (hopefully most) will appreciate the effort you put in to submitting a good report.

One day, you might want something from them.

If you have a history of submitting well written reports that are right the first time, a good manager will recognise this effort. When you next need a favour, hopefully your efforts will be remembered and your request treated in a favourable light.

Bottom line: time spent writing well is not wasted. You get the benefits described here, and your employer gets better reports. It's a win-win situation.

PROPOSALS

A proposal is a special type of report that is designed to present ideas and persuade the reader to accept them. A proposal will analyse a problem, present a solution and suggest an approach to solve the problem.

This proposal is reproduced with permission from *How to Write Proposals and Reports that get Results* by Ros Jay and published by Prentice Hall.

FLEXIBLE WORKING HOURS

An initial study for ABC Ltd

by

Jane Smith

FLEXIBLE WORKING HOURS

An initial study

Objective

To identify the factors involved in introducing flexible working hours, to examine their benefits and disadvantages and to recommend the best approach to take.

Summary

At present, almost all employees of ABC Ltd work from 9.00 to 5.00. A handful work from 9.30 to 5.30.

Many, though not all, staff are unhappy with this and would prefer a more flexible arrangement. Some are working mothers and would like to be able to take their children to and from school. Some, particularly the older employees, have sick or elderly relatives who make demands on their time which do not fit comfortably with their working hours.

For the company itself, this dissatisfaction among staff leads to low morale and reduced productivity. It also makes it harder to attract and retain good staff.

There are three basic options for the future:

1 *Leave things as they are*. This is obviously less demanding on resources than implementing a new system. At least we know it works even if it isn't perfect.
2 *Highly flexible system*. Employees would clock on and clock off anytime within a $12\frac{1}{2}$ hour working day until they have 'clocked up' 35 hours a week. This would be the hardest system to implement.
3 *Limited flexibility*. Staff could start work any time between 8.00 am to 10.00 am and work through for eight hours. This would not solve all employees' problems but it would solve most of them.

Proposal

Introduce a system of limited flexibility for now, retaining the option of increasing flexibility later if this seems appropriate.

Position

The current working hours at ABC Ltd are 9.00 to 5.00 for most employees, with a few working from 9.30 to 5.30.

Problem

Although this works up to a point, it does have certain disadvantages, both for the organisation and for some of the employees.

The organisation: The chief disadvantage of the current system is that many of the staff are dissatisfied with it. This has become such a serious problem that it is becoming harder to attract and retain good staff. Those staff who do join the company and stay with it feel less motivated: this, as research has shown, means they are less productive than they could be.

▶

The employees: Some employees are satisfied with their current working hours, but many of them find the present system restrictive. There are several reasons for this but the employees most strongly in favour of greater flexibility are, in particular:

- parents, especially mothers, who would prefer to be able to take their children to and from school, and to work around this commitment
- employees, many of them in the older age range, who have elderly or sick relatives who they would like to be more available for.

A more flexible approach would make it easier for many staff to fulfil these kinds of demands on their time.

An initial study questioned nearly 140 employees in a cross-section of ages. A large majority were in favour of a more flexible approach, in particular the women and the younger members of the company. It is worth noting that a minority of staff were against the introduction of flexible working hours. Appendix 1 gives the full results of this study.

Possibilities

Since this report is looking at the principle and not the detail of a more flexible approach, the options available fail broadly into three categories: retaining the present system, introducing limited flexibility of working hours, and implementing a highly flexible system.

Retaining the present system. I have already outlined above the problem with leaving things as they are. On the plus side however there are one or two points to make.

Although the system is not perfect, at least we know it works. The staff all signed their contracts on the understanding that the company worked to standard hours of business, and while it may not be ideal for them it is at least manageable. Better the devil you know.

Implementing any new system is bound to incur problems and expense, consequently retaining the present working hours is the least expensive option in terms of direct cost.

Highly flexible system. A highly flexible system would mean keeping the site open from, say, 7.30 am to 8.00 pm. All staff are contracted to work a certain number of hours a week and time clocks are installed. Employees simply clock on and off whenever they enter or leave the building, until they have reached their full number of hours each week.

This system has the obvious benefit that it can accommodate a huge degree of flexibility which should suit the various demands of all employees. They could even elect to work 35 hours a week spread over only three days. A further benefit to the company would be that doctors' appointments and so on would no longer happen 'on company time' as they do at present. This system does have several disadvantages, however:

- Many staff regard occasional time off for such things as doctors' appointments or serious family crises as a natural 'perk' of the job. With this system they would have to make up the hours elsewhere. Not only would they lose the time off, but many would also feel that the company did not trust them. This would obviously be bad for company morale.

- It would be difficult to implement this system fairly. The sales office, for example, must be staffed at least from 9.00 to 5.30 every day. What if all the sales staff want to take Friday off? How do you decide who can and who can't? What if the computer goes down at 4 o'clock in the afternoon and there are no computer staff in until 7.30 the following morning?

Limited flexibility: This would mean asking employees to continue to work an eight hour day but give them a range of, say, ten hours to fit it into. They could start any time between 8.00 and 10.00 in the morning, so they would finish eight hours later – between 4.00 and 6.00.

On the plus side, this would give the employees the co-operation and recognition of their problems that many of them look for, and would therefore increase staff motivation. For some it would provide a way around their other commitments.

On the other hand, this approach still does not allow enough flexibility for some of the working mothers, in particular, who want to be available for their children at both ends of the day.

Proposal

Given the number of staff in favour of more flexible working hours, and the importance of staff motivation, it seems sensible to adopt some kind of flexible approach. But it is probably advisable to find a system that allows the significant minority who prefer to stay as they are to do so.

So which is the best system to choose? It is harder to go backwards than forwards in developing new systems: if the highly flexible approach failed it would be difficult to pull back to a less flexible system (in terms of keeping the staff happy). On the other hand, a limited degree of flexibility could easily be extended later if this seemed appropriate.

So at this stage it seems that the most workable system, which contains most of the benefits required by the employees, is the limited flexibility of working hours.

Appendix I

Table of employee responses to the proposal for flexible working hours

AGE GROUP	MEN Total number consulted	MEN Positive response	MEN Negative response	WOMEN Total number consulted	WOMEN Positive response	WOMEN Negative response
18-30	20	19	1	18	18	0
30-40	23	19	4	29	27	2
40-50	15	8	7	12	8	4
50-60	12	2	10	8	7	1
	70	48	22	67	60	7

Reproduced courtesy of Pearson Education Limited

REPORT WRITING – KEY POINTS TO REMEMBER

1 Business reports help companies to make decisions and solve problems.
2 Proposals present ideas and persuade the reader to accept them.
3 Write reports in third person and reported speech.
4 Keep all the facts and information impartial and impersonal.
5 Use sub-headings to classify the information logically, breaking it down into logical sub-sections.
6 State the steps that were taken to collect the information at the beginning of your report.
7 Present conclusions based on the facts in the findings.
8 Suggest recommendations when they are requested.
9 Compose a covering memo when sending a free-standing report.
10 Remember that a report should be understandable by someone who has no prior knowledge of the subject.

A–Z OF BLOOPERS AND BLUNDERS, COMMON ERRORS AND CLICHÉS: K, L

Kindly

I was on an aeroplane recently when the stewardess announced, 'Ladies and gentlemen, we will shortly be landing at Singapore Changi Airport. Please kindly return to your seat and fasten your seatbelt.'

'Please' and 'Kindly'? We don't need them both – and certainly never in the same sentence.

'Kindly' is definitely a great-grandfather word that we should not be using in the twenty-first century. Use 'please' instead. Avoid phrases like 'I would be grateful if you would' or 'I should appreciate it if you could'. Just say 'Please'.

Learnt/learned

Both are correct. 'Learned' is usually American English, while 'learnt' is British English. The same is true for burnt/burned, leant/leaned, spelt/spelled, spilt/spilled, spoilt/spoiled.

Luggage

Luggage is an uncountable noun. It should not be written as *luggages*. This word should be written with a singular verb. For example:

My luggage was lost when I flew to Bangkok recently.

The same goes for *baggage*, *equipment*, *information* and *furniture*. Can you think of more?

IN THE BIN: K, L

kind of

last but not least

HELP YOURSELF

Identify and correct the errors in these sentences.

1 When you see Melanie later, please don't mention about her hair.
2 Please give Linda or myself a call if you have any questions.
3 I want to reiterate again that this behaviour will not be tolerated.
4 Please revert to me on this matter as soonest possible.
5 The said invoice is 2 months overdue for payment.
6 Will you be able to send me to the airport on Friday night?
7 How have you been effected by the retrenchments?
8 Can you spare me sometime tomorrow to discuss your report?
9 The meeting will start promptly at 12.00 am.
10 Whose to blame for spilling the water all over the table?

TEST YOURSELF

1   You work for Aurora Holdings plc, a large manufacturing company. In a recent board meeting it was decided to review the company's staff benefits. At present they include only a company pension scheme and a subsidised canteen.

The human resource director asks you to research the additional benefits which could be introduced. You should also recommend three benefits which you consider would be most welcomed by all members of staff.

You have made notes about some possible benefits:

Private life assurance scheme – private hospital and medical insurance – loans at low interest rate – sports and social facilities – luncheon vouchers for local shops – arrangements for discounts at local shops – payment of fees to attend courses.

Compile your report.

2   You work for Mrs Ruth Fairless, Manager of the Bateman Hotel, Norland Road, Tenwick, Cumbria C49 8JY. (LCCIEB EFB2 style)

When guests 'sign out' before they leave they are able to make any comments on their feelings about the hotel and the service they have received. You have to write a report each month for Mrs Fairless on the points raised. These are the comments made by guests last month.

'The service in the restaurant was not very good. We often had to wait half an hour between courses.'

'EVERYTHING WAS LOVELY – IT IS A WELL RUN HOTEL.'

'There aren't enough satellite channels on the TV – no movie channels.'

'Very helpful staff – very polite.'

'We had a splendid holiday - but the service in the restaurant could be quicker.'

'The best hotel in Cumbria. Very good value.'

'It was three days before the broken light in my room was repaired.'

'Lovely food – but poor service at meal times. Very slow.'

'The gardens are beautiful.'

'We will definitely come back. The staff are very friendly.'

Write the report.

3   You are Personal Assistant (PA) to Tim Variant, General Manager of Creative Gifts, Preston Road, Cork, Eire. Follow the instructions in this note from Mr Variant. (City & Guilds EFBC2)

PA
The board want a brief (approx. 200 words) informal report to assist with discussions they are currently having on whether we should be buying more clothing than other souvenirs and whether some natural fibres are selling better than others. I've attached some statistics sent over from the Sales Dept. Could you please draft something suitable with any relevant conclusions and recommendations?

Thanks
Tim

4   You work in the Human Resource Department of a company that provides Information Technology software, *Kwikbyte Systems*. Students from the local college sometimes take up work experience placements at the college and recently a Business Studies student, Ingrid Knutsen, spent a month working in various departments. The Human Resource Manager, Mr Martin Graham, likes to keep a record of all students' work, progress, attitude and relationship with other members of staff, so he has asked you to speak to her supervisors and then writer a report on Ingrid's placement. It is possible that Ingrid might apply for a job with Kwikbyte Systems in future so it is important that a good report is produced.

Here are your notes from your conversations with supervisors.

Comments from Head of Finance Department

'Ingrid was very pleasant and got on well with the staff. She was late arriving once or twice – I think she missed the bus – but she has a good head for figures and would do well in this department.'

Comments from Head of Sales and Marketing Department

'I liked Ingrid very much; she was always pleasant and helpful. She got on well with everyone but she is a little shy. If you work in sales you need to be very self-confident and Ingrid was too reserved sometimes. But she worked hard and was quite imaginative.'

Comments from Head of Human Resources

'Well, she wasn't very punctual, I remember. She was late more than once. But she was always very polite and she got on well with the staff. I would say that she needed help with some of the more difficult tasks, but she tried her best and with more experience she will be very good.'

Task

Write the report. (LCCIEB EFB2 style)

5   *Styleways* is a well known store that sells high quality and expensive ladies clothing and other items. One of its more popular departments sells exclusive perfumes. You are employed by the store and one of your jobs is to investigate customer complaints.

Yesterday one of your customers, Mrs Andrea Bellini, returned a bottle of an expensive perfume, *Presique*. Mrs Bellini claimed that when she opened the perfume she found that the bottle contained pure water. Mrs Bellini is a good customer and has never complained before, so you were asked to investigate the complaint.

Here are your notes about the complaint.

Mrs Bellini bought small bottle of *Presique*, cost $75 on (date) and returned it the following day. She claimed that the bottle contained pure water – which she showed us – this was true.

This bottle in a batch delivered 2 weeks ago – 3 other bottles of the batch sold – no one returned any other.

Inspected other bottles in store – 16 bottles – 4 looked as if they had been opened – and contained water. 12 did not look as if they had been opened – I opened one and found it contained genuine perfume.

All staff in perfume department have worked for store for many years – not likely to replace perfume.

Order not checked carefully when delivered – staff have never had problems before.

Possibly bottles were tampered with before delivery. Suggest we replace Mrs Bellini's perfume – very good customer – send letter of apology with box of chocolates or flowers.

The Store Manager, Mr Martin Lee, has asked you to write a report on what has happened, how the problem could have happened, and what the store should do now.

Task

Write the report. (LCCIEB EFB2 style)

Unit 11

Meetings

LEARNING OUTCOMES

After studying this unit you should be able to:

- Explain the purpose of meetings

- Describe the different types of meetings that take place in business

- State the documents that are used in the meetings process

- Discuss the basic presentation requirements of each document

- Compose agenda, chairman's agenda and minutes

MEETINGS IN BUSINESS

Many meetings take place in business and an effective meeting is an efficient tool in the communication process. Meetings enable face-to-face contact of a number of people at the same time. They provide a useful opportunity for sharing information, making suggestions and proposals, taking decision and obtaining instant feedback. Active participation of all members of the meeting is usually encouraged.

Meetings are used for a variety of purposes:

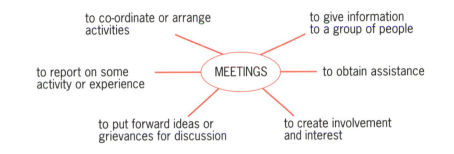

Checkpoint

What meetings are held in your organisation? Who attends these meetings? Discuss the purpose of these meetings.

TYPES OF MEETING

Formal meetings

The rules of conduct of formal meetings are laid down in a company's Articles of Association and/or Constitution or Standing Orders. With such meetings a quorum must be present, i.e. the minimum number of people who should be present in order to validate the meeting. A formal record of these meetings must be kept, usually by the company secretary.

Annual General Meeting (AGM)

AGMs are held once a year to assess the trading of the organisation over the year. All shareholders are invited to attend the AGM but they must be given 21 days' notice.

GLOBAL ENGINEERING PLC

ANNUAL GENERAL MEETING

NOTICE IS HEREBY GIVEN that the Tenth Annual General Meeting of the Company will be held in the Hillview Hall, Hillview Place, Bedford, on Wednesday 25 August 20-- at 1100 hours

A G E N D A

1   To receive and consider the Directors' Report, Accounts and Balance Sheet for the year ended 31 July 20--.

2   To confirm the Preference Dividend paid in May 20-- and the Ordinary Interim Dividend paid in June 20--.

3   To declare an Ordinary Final Dividend.

4   To propose that the name of Mr D Williams be added to the list of authorised signatories to be attached to the Bank Mandates for City Bank plc, Grange Road, London.

5   To transact any other business that may be brought before an Ordinary General Meeting.

G Hope

G HOPE
Secretary

4 July 20--

JR/GH

Statutory meetings

Statutory meetings are called so that the directors and shareholders can communicate and consider special reports. Companies are required by law to hold these statutory meetings.

Board meetings

Board meetings are held as often as individual organisations require. They are attended by all directors and chaired by the chairman of the board.

Informal meetings

Informal meetings are not restricted by the same rules and regulations as formal meetings. Such meetings may take the form of brainstorming or discussion sessions where strict agendas may not be necessary and minutes may not be kept. However, it is usually considered good business practice for an agenda to be issued to all members prior to the meeting so that they can prepare adequately in order to make a valuable contribution.

Management meetings

These meetings are attended by a group of managers who may need to discuss a specific matter, report on progress or receive progress reports. For example, the marketing manager, sales manager, production manager and research and development manager may meet to discuss the launch of a new product being launched soon.

Departmental meetings

These meetings are called by the head of department or manager of a certain section. All staff will be invited to attend so that information can be passed on or reports received from some members of staff regarding a specific project.

Working parties

Working parties may be set up to work together on a specific project or problem. At meetings, progress reports will be given and decisions for further action taken.

Checkpoint

Discuss different situations that may require working parties to be set up. Who would attend such meetings? What matters may be discussed?

ATTENDING MEETINGS

Meetings probably account for 50–60 per cent of a manager's time in business. When they are conducted efficiently, meetings are a very effective way of helping the decision-making process, briefing teams, exchanging information and problem-solving. However, it is a sad fact that many meetings in business are unproductive because of poor management or because of being unsure of each individual's role in meetings.

As a member of any meeting, even if you are not the chairman, there is a lot you can do to help make meetings effective:

1 Understand the purpose of the meeting, as well as your role and what is expected of you.
2 Read all the papers in advance. Make some notes about any input you would like to make. Do your homework, talk to people who you may be representing at the meeting, get other people's views on important topics so that you have fuel for any discussions in the meeting.
3 Don't sit there silently. You are a member of the meeting for a reason, so be sure to give your opinions and take an active part in the meeting wherever possible.
4 Do not interrupt anyone who is speaking. Give everyone a chance to voice their own opinions. At an appropriate moment, give some praise if possible first and then give your own views. If you disagree with something, try to be as constructive as possible.
5 Watch the other members of the meeting and listen to them carefully. Watch body language, gestures, eye contact, movements, nuances and all the unique subtleties happening around the table.

Remember

The success of any meeting depends largely on its leader. If the leader is well prepared, and if the members have been chosen carefully, the meeting should be productive.

NOTICE AND AGENDA

The success of a meeting depends on a variety of essential preparations. An important one is to ensure that all the documentation is dealt with efficiently. The notice and agenda are usually combined in one document. The portion at the top is known as the notice. This gives details of the type, place, day, date and time of the meeting.

The agenda is the middle portion of the document. This is the list of topics to be discussed at the meeting. On the example shown here note that the first three and final two items are known as *ordinary business*. These are items which will be included on every meeting agenda. After the opening items of ordinary, business there will be a list of *special business* – these are special matters to be discussed at this meeting only.

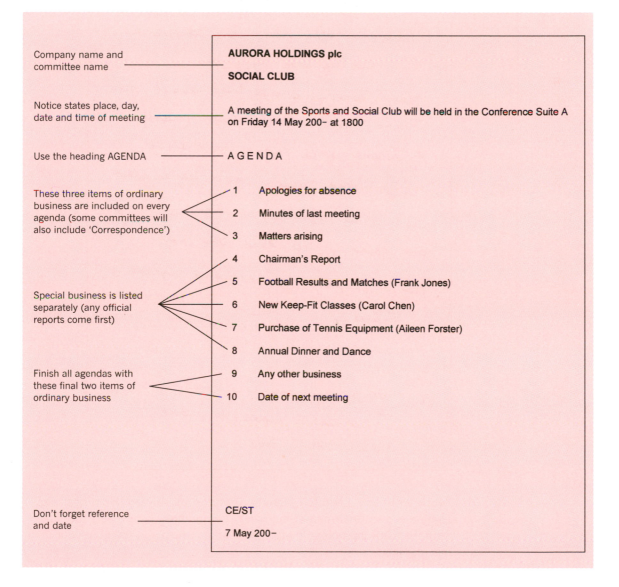

Company name and committee name

Notice states place, day, date and time of meeting

Use the heading AGENDA

These three items of ordinary business are included on every agenda (some committees will also include 'Correspondence')

Special business is listed separately (any official reports come first)

Finish all agendas with these final two items of ordinary business

Don't forget reference and date

AURORA HOLDINGS plc

SOCIAL CLUB

A meeting of the Sports and Social Club will be held in the Conference Suite A on Friday 14 May 200– at 1800

A G E N D A

1   Apologies for absence

2   Minutes of last meeting

3   Matters arising

4   Chairman's Report

5   Football Results and Matches (Frank Jones)

6   New Keep-Fit Classes (Carol Chen)

7   Purchase of Tennis Equipment (Aileen Forster)

8   Annual Dinner and Dance

9   Any other business

10   Date of next meeting

CE/ST

7 May 200–

Checkpoint

1 You work with Jackie Marsden, Personnel Manager of Aurora Holdings plc. Mrs Marsden also acts as Secretary of the company's Social Committee. Deal with the following note which you found in your in-tray this morning:

> I need to arrange a mtg of the Social Committee — Thursday after next. The conference rm shd be free by 7pm.
> Mark Jones wants to talk about the Trivial Pursuits Quiz held recently & Jeremy Price wants to discuss a sponsored swim. We'd better also see how the monthly Musical Evenings are going — I'll deal with that.
> Please prepare the notice & agenda.
> Thanks
> Jackie.
>
> PS   Just saw the Chairman — he has a report to make this time too.

2 You work with Joe Leighton, Safety Director of Aurora Holdings plc. Mr Leighton is also Chairman of the Safety Committee which meets monthly. Deal with the following note and attached memos which you found in your in-tray this morning:

Checkpoint *continued*

MEMORANDUM

To   Candice

From   JL

Date   24 June

Please prepare the notice & agenda for the next mtg of the Safety Committee. Include the usual items plus there are the items mentioned in the attached docs.

Date? Some time towards the end of next wk – late afternoon –

Thanks

JL

MEMORANDUM

To   Joe Leighton, Safety Director

From   Christopher Lim, Company Secretary

Ref   CL/mlw

Date   12 June 200–

SAFETY

It is well over 6 months since our last fire drill was held.

In line with Company policy please arrange for this issue to be discussed at the next meeting of the Safety Committee so that arrangements can be made.

Chris.

Checkpoint *continued*

MEMORANDUM

To   Joe Leighton, Safety Director

From   Terry Aspel, Production Director

Ref   TA/FR

Date   20 June 200–

ADAM WARD'S INDUSTRIAL INJURY - 7 MAY

The delay in reporting this accident has been the cause of a large claim for compensation against the Company.

It is important that measures are taken to improve our present safety procedures within the Company.

Please arrange for this item to be discussed at the next Safety Committee meeting.

Terry .

What's wrong?

Study the agenda written as a result of the following scenario. Rewrite the agenda correctly.

As secretary of the Students' Union Group you have been asked by the Chairman to prepare the agenda for the next meeting. In conversation with the Chairman, she said

'The meeting is next Friday – usual time and place. This time we need to have a discussion on lunch-time queues in the refectory – they're becoming very frustrating. There's also the matter of student lockers to be resolved. The provision is quite inadequate, so we need some more urgently. John should be able to give us his report on the recent disco held for charity. Wasn't it a great night? The Students' Common Room is desperately in need of decorating so we must discuss what should be done and nominate someone to take charge. Apart from the usual other items that's about all.'

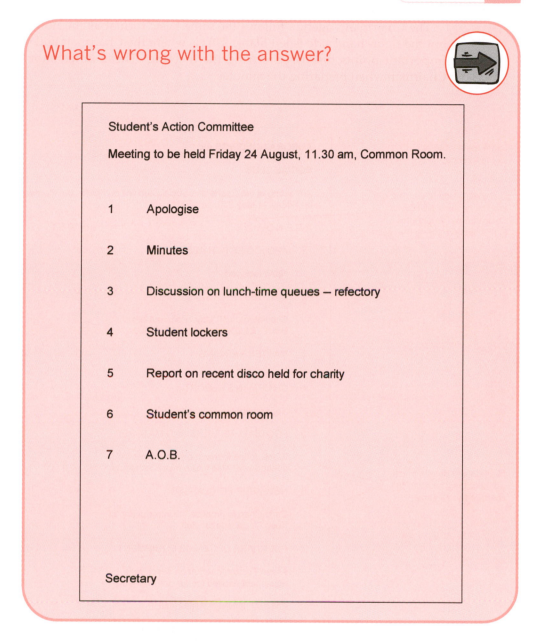

What's wrong with the answer?

Student's Action Committee

Meeting to be held Friday 24 August, 11.30 am, Common Room.

1   Apologise

2   Minutes

3   Discussion on lunch-time queues — refectory

4   Student lockers

5   Report on recent disco held for charity

6   Student's common room

7   A.O.B.

Secretary

CHAIRMAN'S AGENDA

The Chairman has an important responsibility to manage the meeting once it is in progress. He or she must allow everyone equal opportunity to participate in discussions and control the discussion in an orderly way. In order for the Chairman to lead the meeting effectively, he or she may have a special Chairman's agenda which contains extra notes for the Chairman to use when introducing each item.

The Chairman's agenda follows the same basic format as the notice and agenda but the right- hand side is left blank. This is where the Chairman will make notes of important points discussed during the meeting. These notes should assist the Chairman when preparing the minutes.

Same main headings
as the Agenda ——————

Leave right side blank and
use the heading NOTES
Chairman will write notes
in this section during the meeting

Mention any details which
will help the Chairman to
conduct the meeting

Reference and date ——————

AURORA HOLDINGS plc

SOCIAL CLUB

A meeting of the Sports and Social Club will be held in the Conference Suite A on Friday 14 May 200– at 1800

A G E N D A   NOTES

1   APOLOGIES FOR ABSENCE   1

     None received

2   MINUTES OF LAST MEETING   2

     Circulated on 16 May. Point out error
     in 4.1 - £1,200 should read £12,000

3   MATTERS ARISING   3

4   CHAIRMAN'S REPORT   4

     Separate notes attached

5   FOOTBALL RESULTS AND MATCHES   5

     Frank Jones to report on 3 matches held
     during April. Also future match schedule.

6   NEW KEEP-FIT CLASSES   6

     Carol Chen to propose the introduction of
     Keep Fit classes for staff.

7   PURCHASE OF TENNIS EQUIPMENT   7

     Aileen Forster to report on new tennis
     equipment needed for July tournament.

8   ANNUAL DINNER AND DANCE   8

     Discuss date and venue, ideas for
     programme and appoint person in charge.

9   ANY OTHER BUSINESS   9

10   DATE OF NEXT MEETING   10

     Suggest 24 June 200–

CE/ST
12 May 200–

Checkpoint

1   Prepare the Chairman's agenda for the meetings of the social committee and safety committee for which you prepared the notice and agenda earlier in this unit. Make up any necessary details.

2   You work with the managing director of a medium-sized sports equipment manufacturing company. Your employer will shortly be going overseas on a business trip, returning on 14 October. He asks you to make all the preparations for a board meeting to be held on 16 October. The main items for discussion will be next year's budget, salary increases for regional managers and sponsorship.

   (a)   Write the memo you would send to the board members, giving them the necessary details and asking them to submit to you any additional items which they wish to be included on the agenda.

   (b)   Prepare the agenda and Chairman's agenda for the meeting.

What's wrong?

Study the Chairman's agenda written as a result of this assignment. Then rewrite it correctly.

You are secretary to Douglas Michaels, Managing Director of Seagrave Manufacturing Co Ltd. Mr Michaels chairs the management committee meetings which are held during the first week of each month. In a meeting with you this morning he said to you:

'There's a management committee meeting next Thursday so we need to prepare the documents. I must remember the error in item 6 – the figure for microwave ovens should be 42% not 24% as typed. What else is there? Oh yes, Mrs Wright spoke to me yesterday. She's had a request from the Head of Secretarial Studies at Southern Point Technical College asking if we can provide help with work experience placements for their students. John also mentioned that he wants to outline some problems that he's experiencing with the training schemes, so you'd better add that on the agenda too. There are also the problems in Sales to be discussed – Ken will have to announce the Northern Sales Manager's resignation effective at the end of next month – then we must discuss a replacement and decide whether to promote internally or advertise the post. I think that's all. Oh, I almost forgot ... Mike Smith (Production Manager) retires next month after 20 years. We must arrange a presentation for him. That's all. Thanks.'

What's wrong with the answer?

MANAGEMENT COMMITTEE

CHAIRMANS AGENDA

NOTES

1 Apologise for absence   1.

2 Minutes of last meeting   2.

3 Matters arising

   Correct error in item 6 – microwave
   ovens should be 42%.   3.

4 Southern Point Technical College   4.
   To discuss providing help with work
   experience placements.

5 Problems with training schemes.   5.
   John to outline problems.

6 Sales Manager's resignation   6.
   Announcement of Ken's resignation
   at end of next month.
   To discuss recruitment of replacement

7 Mike Smith retires   7.
   20 years in company
   To arrange presentation

8 ANY OTHER BUSINESS   8.

9 DATE OF NEXT MEETING   9.

....

....

MINUTES OF MEETING

An accurate written record of meetings is essential not only for all those who attended the meeting but also for those who were unable to attend.

Verbatim minutes

These are used primarily in court reporting where everything needs to be recorded word for word.

Minutes of resolution

Only the main conclusions that are reached at the meeting are recorded, not a note of the discussions that took place. These are usually used for minutes of AGMs and other statutory meetings. It is important to note the exact wording of any resolutions passed.

---

4   PURCHASE OF PHOTOCOPIER

The Company Secretary submitted a report from the Administration Manager containing full details of the trial of the AEZ Photocopier.

IT WAS RESOLVED THAT the AEZ Photocopier be purchased at a cost of £8,000.

Minutes of narration

These minutes will be a concise summary of all the discussions that took place, reports received, actions to be taken and decisions made.

---

4   PURCHASE OF PHOTOCOPIER

The Company Secretary submitted a report from the Administration Manager containing full details of the trial of the AEZ Photocopier. This machine had been used for a period of 4 weeks in the Printing Room. The machine's many benefits were pointed out, including reduction/enlarging facilities and collating. After discussion it was agreed that such a machine would be extremely valuable to the Company

The Company Secretary was asked to make the necessary arrangements for the photocopier to be purchased at the quoted price of £8,000.

Layout and wording of minutes

Minutes may be displayed in a variety of formats depending on the preference of your employer and organisation. The layout shown in the example is a popular method.

As they are a record of what has taken place, minutes should be written in past tense using third person and reported speech. These minutes have been prepared from the previously shown agenda and Chairman's agenda.

Checkpoint

Go through these minutes and study the wording carefully. Highlight the wording which is written in past tense, reported speech, e.g. '… were received' and 'The Chairman asked …'.

Main heading includes meeting, place, day, date and time

List those present in alphabetical order with Chairman first

This separate ACTION column is a popular way of displaying minutes

The minutes must be corrected if necessary before they can be signed

Break down items if appropriate into separate headings

Insert initials or full names in the ACTION column

AURORA HOLDINGS plc

**MINUTES OF A MEETING OF THE SPORTS & SOCIAL CLUB
HELD IN CONFERENCE SUITE A ON FRIDAY 14 MAY 200– AT 1800**

PRESENT   Mr Chris Evans (Chairman)   Mr Frank Jones
            Miss Carol Chen   Miss Maxine Street
            Miss Aileen Forster   Mrs Wendy Williams

ACTION

1   APOLOGIES FOR ABSENCE

     No apologies were received.

2   MINUTES OF LAST MEETING

     The Chairman asked members to correct an error in item 3.1 where
     the figure £1,200 should read £12,000. After this correction the
     minutes were approved and signed by the Chairman as a correct
     record.

3   MATTERS ARISING

     There were no matters arising.

4   CHAIRMAN'S REPORT

     The Chairman pointed out that membership had fallen by 20%
     over the last 6 months. It was felt that this was due largely to lack of
     publicity during the present year, and also because new employees
     were not sure how to join. Various decisions were reached:

     4.1   CIRCULAR TO STAFF

           A letter would be sent to all employees who were not members
           of the Club outlining its aims and activities. A tear-off slip
           would be included for interested employees to indicate their
           areas of interest.   CE

     4.2   SOCIAL EVENING

           A social evening with refreshments would be organised specifically
           for non-members. Carol Chen agreed to make arrangements.   CC

5   FOOTBALL RESULTS AND MATCHES

     5.1   Frank Jones reported on the results of the 3 football
           matches during April:

           Team A v Victory Enterprises   12 April   Won 4-3
           Team B v Pentagon Supplies   19 April   Lost 3-2
           Team A v Ward Hi-Tech   26 April   Won 5-2

Include the page number at the top left ——————

2

5.2 Future matches were scheduled to be:

Team A v Team B	18 May	1500	Home
Team A v Connolly Industries	25 May	1500	Away

6 NEW KEEP FIT CLASSES

Carol Chen proposed that Keep Fit classes should be held. Sharon Warner from the Fun N Fitness Gym had agreed to conduct such classes on the Company's premises every Wednesday evening 1800–1900.

A discussion was held on a suitable room for the classes, and it was agreed that the Training Office would be suitable. Carol would circulate a notice to all staff announcing the first Keep Fit class on Wednesday 22 May.   CC

7 PURCHASE OF TENNIS EQUIPMENT

Aileen Forster reported that the in-house tennis tournament would start on Monday 4 July. New nets and balls were needed and the tennis courts needed repairing. It was agreed that Aileen should make the necessary arrangements as soon as possible.   AF

8 ANNUAL DINNER AND DANCE

It was agreed that the Annual Dinner and Dance would be held on Saturday 14 September. Wendy Williams agreed to take charge of all the arrangements. She was asked to contact Aston Hall to make preliminary enquiries about their facilities and to report back to the   WW
next meeting. Members were asked to consider ideas for the
programme for discussion at the next meeting.   Members

9 ANY OTHER BUSINESS

There was no other business.

10 DATE OF NEXT MEETING

It was agreed that the next meeting would be held in Conference Suite A on Thursday 24 June 2000 at 1800.

Leave a space for Chairman to sign and date at the next meeting ——————

.... (Chairman)

.... (Date)

CE/ST

16 May 200–

Remember

Remember to use:

was	*not*	is
would be	*not*	will be
had been	*not*	has been
were	*not*	are

Checkpoint

1 When composing minutes, past tense and reported speech must be used consistently. Here are some expressions that are often used in minutes. Can you add to this list with some suggestions of your own as to what could be used instead of '... said ...'?

asked	....	....
reported	....	....
proposed	....	....
agreed	....	....

2 The following are verbatim records of what was actually said at a meeting. Rewrite these as the record would show in the (narrative) minutes:

(a) (The Chairman)

'Miss Jones, will you please arrange for quotations on the recarpeting of the sales office and report back next time.'

_____

_____

_____

Checkpoint *continued*

(b) (Mr Norton)

'I'd like to recommend the purchase of a photocopier for the Personnel Department.'

_____

_____

_____

(c) (Miss Clark)

'The drinks machine on the third level is out of order.'

_____

_____

_____

(d) (Mr Morgan)

'It's been brought to my attention that empty boxes are being left on the stairs next to reception. This is causing a safety hazard.'

_____

_____

_____

(e) (Mrs Newman)

'All arrangements for Quiz Time next Saturday afternoon at 3 o'clock have been made. Four teams have been organised and the questions are being devised by Julie Lee.

_____

_____

_____

(f) (Chairman)

'Arrangements for Saturday morning lecturers are the responsibility of our committee, and I'd like to invite suggestions for speakers.'

_____

_____

_____

(g) (Miss Graham)

'As you can see from these press cuttings, we've received a lot of publicity for our Open House in March.'

_____

_____

_____

What's wrong?

Study the minutes written as a result of the notes made on this agenda by the Chairman, Mr Alan Hill. Discuss the errors and rewrite the minutes correctly:

AURORA HOLDINGS plc

A meeting of the Sports Club Committee will be held in Room 208 on
Monday 29 June 200– at 1800

AGENDA   *Present — DAllen (Treasurer)*
              Green, Armitage, Parker
              Mrs Reeves, Leighton

1   Apologies for absence   *— James, Johnson*

2   Minutes of last meeting   *✓ OK*

3   Matters arising   *— None*

4   Treasurer's report   *PA pleased w. bal in hand £395*
                          — this will be chewed up by exp. bbq soon

5   Hospital visiting (Derek Armitage)   *took flowers recently*
                                          — letter of thanks rec'd
                                          (Northern General Hosp)

6   Barbecue (Steven Green)   *9 Aug 8–11 pm — sub-committee appointed:*
                               (Green, Johnson, Reeves, Parker) to work
                               out details & report back next time

7   Squash tournament (Gary Parker)   *final last Mon. Geoff Jones (Sales)*
                                       won
                                       v. successful — sports highlight of yr.

8   Any other business   *Proposal for amendment to constitution*
                          to be put on agenda next time

9   Date of next meeting   *3 wks — same time — same place!*

AH/ST

16 June 200–

What's wrong with the answer?

MINUTES OF MEETING

Sports Club Committee Meeting – Monday 29 June

Present

Mr Armitage
Mr Parker
Mr Hill
Mr Allen
Mr Green
Mrs Reeves

1   Minutes of last meeting

The minutes were signed as a correct record.

2   Matters arising

None

3   Treasurers Report (Mr Allen)

The Treasure is pleased with the balance in hand. This will be chewed up by the expensive bbq which is coming up soon.

4   Hospital visiting

Mr Armitage took flowers recently and a letter of thanks were received.

4   Barbecue

The bbq will be held on 9 August at 8 to 11 pm. A sub-committee was appointed to report back to the next meeting. Sub-committee are Green, Johnson, Reeves, Parker.

6   Squash

The final was held last Monday with Geoff Jones the winner. It was very successful, and Mr Parker said it was the sports highlight of the year.

7   AOB

A proposal for amendment of the constitution was put. This had been placed on the agenda for the next meeting.

8   Date of next meeting

The next meeting will be held in 3 weeks time in room 208.

Alan Hill (Mr)

MEETINGS – KEY POINTS TO REMEMBER

1 A notice and agenda is sent out to give all members advance notice of the purpose, date, time and venue of a meeting.
2 An agenda is a list of topics to be discussed at a meeting.
3 The agenda should have ordinary business at the beginning and the end – business that is discussed at every meeting.
4 Special business will be included in the central section of the agenda – business that is unique to each meeting.
5 The Chairman may have a special agenda with extra notes to help him manage the meeting.
6 Minutes are a record of a meeting and they are essential for everyone who attended as well as those who were absent.
7 Minutes may be presented in different formats depending on the preference of each company.
8 It is usual to include an 'Action' column stating who is responsible for dealing with each item.
9 The same headings should appear on the minutes as on the agenda.
10 Write minutes in past tense and third person using reported speech.

A–Z OF BLOOPERS AND BLUNDERS, COMMON ERRORS AND CLICHÉS: M

Marketing

In standard English the word 'marketing' is used to describe what companies do when they promote a product. It is not used to describe what we do when we go to the market or supermarket. For example:

My mother does her shopping in Carre Four.
My aunt went to the market to do some shopping.
A lot of money is spent on marketing new products.

Mention

Mention and *mentioned* are not followed by the word about (same as *discuss* and *discussed*). For example:

The teacher mentioned that next Monday is a public holiday.

Myself/I/Me

These words are often misused. Note the correct uses:

Please call John or me/not me if you have any queries.
 (NB: You would not say *Please call I …*)
Ronald and I will be attending the exhibition.
 (NB: You would not say *Me will be attending …*)
Emily loves mahjong, same as I.
Mark handed the cheque to me today.

IN THE BIN: M

maybe
more or less

HELP YOURSELF

Identify and correct the errors in these sentences.

1 You have to convince the interviewer that your the right person for the job.
2 Will you bring these flowers to Mandy when you visit her tonight?
3 Experience will take precedents over age at the interviews.
4 Linda and Gordon said their definitely coming to Singapore this year.
5 I wonder that these figures are really correct?
6 Anyone of the students would be able to do the job.
7 Its a mistake to judge a book by it's cover.
8 I didn't get to sleep till 12pm last night.
9 When you have stamped your card, please precede to level 2.
10 Next time your in Kuala Lumpur, please come and see me.

TEST YOURSELF

1 You work with Mr Robert Branson, Director of Administration. Mr Branson chairs the Human Resource Policy Committee which is held at 1000 on the last Monday of each month in the Board Room. Other members of the committee are Michael Kramer, Marketing Manager, Masrita Hadi, Office Services Manager, Sharon Leng, Human Resource Manager and Mohammed Alaradj, Research and Development Manager.

   Mr Branson asks you to draw up for him an Agenda as well as a Chairman's agenda for next month's meeting. During a discussion with Mr Branson you make the following notes:

Minutes of previous meeting – correct error in 2.1 – name should read Marsha Gold not Sharon Yap.

Two special items – Proposal for new promotion policy and Job Enrichment Schemes.

Present promotion policy = advertise on notice boards and in Aurora News, promote internally. Could be obstacle to progress.

Proposed new policy = advertise in local/national press (and Co. magazine) – need new people, new ideas, wider experience.

Job enrichment schemes – need to increase job satisfaction – ask for suggestions.

Prepare the Agenda for circulation to members and also the Chairman's agenda for Mr Branson to use at the meeting.

2   You work with Martin Lewis, Company Secretary of Aurora Holdings plc who is also Secretary of the company's Social Club. Mr Lewis has made some notes on the agenda of a recent meeting. Compile appropriate minutes.

AURORA LAWN TENNIS CLUB

MEETING HELD ON 21 OCTOBER 200–

AGENDA

1   Apologies for absence   —   Francis Tan (Treasurer)
                                    Joe Summerfield

2   Minutes of last meeting   ✓ OK

3   Matters arising   ✗

4   Report from Social Committee   Report from SC
① Halloween Disco
– great success
– made £200
② New Year's Dance
– prep'ns well in hand
– tickets with printer –
on sale at reception
from next Mon.

5   Indoor Tennis Courts — RW:
① lights defective
– will arrange for repair
② walls very shabby
+ need decorating
RW to check
cost for next time

6   Tennis Nets   JH: Nets very old – poor condition
will find out cost of new
Gate to court 1 defective
– groundsman to be notified + repair

7   Any other business
AGM: 18/11 – 1030

8   Date of next meeting
last Fri in Nov

M Lewis.
Martin Lewis
Secretary

10 October 200–

Present: S Gingell, R Williams
J Hardy   Mary Wilson
George Newman (Chair)   M Lewis

3 The following dialogue is taken from a meeting of the Welfare Committee of Aurora Holdings plc, which was held at 4 pm on Tuesday 21 October 200– in the Chairman's office. Choosing speakers from your class, act out this meeting. Then use narrative style to prepare the minutes.

> *Mrs Taylor (Chairman):* Well it's 4 o'clock and we all appear to be here so shall we get started? Anthony Long won't be joining us as he's attending a business conference this week. Do you all have the last meeting's minutes?
>
> (agreement)
>
> Are there any amendments or can I sign them as a correct record?
>
> (Chairman signs)
>
> Good, matters arising? Anything to report?
>
> *Mr Thomas:* Yes, Georgia and I visited Reneé in hospital on the 16th to deliver our Committee's basket of flowers and our good wishes for a speedy recovery. She hopes to be back at work a week on Monday so she'll be with us again when we next meet.
>
> *Chairman:* That's marvellous news. Right then, let's move on to item 4. John, you were going to talk about the restaurant I believe. Did you bring along the accounts for the half year ending 31 July?
>
> *Mr Cage:* Yes, I have copies for everyone (distributes copies). As you will see, the accounts show that we made a profit of £1,300 over the first 6 months of the year. I'd like to suggest that we utilise some of this by buying a new coffee machine. The present one is rather old and frequently breaks down.
>
> *Chairman:* I think we'd better obtain some estimates first before a decision can be made. Could you ask around please and we'll talk about it more next time?
>
> (Mr Cage agrees)
>
> *Chairman:* Right, we'll move on to Washroom Facilities now. I've received several complaints about the female toilets on the second floor. I've been to see what all the fuss is about and I agree that they do need upgrading.
>
> *Miss McBain:* Yes, these are near my office. Apart from several locks being faulty there are chipped tiles, and the state of decoration is very poor.
>
> *Chairman:* I'd like a volunteer to arrange for some local workmen to look at the washroom and give us an estimate on the cost of the repairs.
>
> *Miss McBain:* I'll gladly do that. Something needs to be done quickly.
>
> *Chairman:* Right, that's something else to continue with next time. Richard, you're next, I believe?
>
> *Mr Fish:* Thank you. Well, as you know, as Training Officer I have a lot of contact with our young trainees. Many of them are attending Cliff College on evening courses which the Company sponsors. Examinations are coming up in December and these people don't have much time to study. I'd like to suggest that they be given two weeks' study leave prior to their exams.

Miss McBain: That's a valid point, Richard. Lesley in my department, bless her, she works very hard for us and I know she goes to college three evenings a week. It would kill me!

Chairman: I can sympathise, but I really don't think it's within our power as a committee to make such a decision. Can I suggest that you write a formal memo to the Board? They have a Board Meeting early in November I believe, so you should ask them to include this item on the agenda. By the time we meet again, we should have an answer from them.

Mr Fish: Yes, I think that will be best. I'll get a memo out tomorrow.

Chairman: Now, the final item. Christmas dinner and dance. Miss Sheppard, did you get some specimen menus from hotels?

Miss Sheppard: Yes, I have some samples for us to look at.

(distributes copies)

Mr Fish: This one looks brilliant – the Marina Hotel – quite reasonably priced too.

Mr Thomas: I agree, it seems far superior to the others.

Miss Sheppard: That's what I thought too. I suggest we should confirm with the Marina, if everyone agrees?

(agreement)

Chairman: Has a date been agreed yet?

Miss Sheppard: No, I suggest the last Saturday before Christmas, the 21st, if that's OK?

(agreement)

Chairman: Right then, Miss Sheppard, can we leave it to you to make all the necessary arrangements?

Miss Sheppard: Oh sure, I'll get in touch with the Marina to confirm with them, and I'll also put up a notice on the staff bulletin board. I hope it will be as successful as last year's.

Chairman: With everything left to you, Miss Sheppard, I'm sure it can't fail to be successful.

Right, moving on, is there anything else anyone wants to discuss? No? Right, then let's decide on a date for the next meeting ... 4 weeks' time as usual? Can I suggest the 20th November then? Same time? Good, OK then, thank you all for attending.

Section 5

Persuasive communication

Many communications in business call for a persuasive approach. Circulars, sales letters, press releases, house magazines, advertisements, notices, leaflets and invitations – they all attempt to influence the reader in some way.

All these documents meet important needs within an organisation's communication system. They are generally easy to produce, effective methods of conveying information to different people.

Composition of persuasive documents is a demanding skill. It depends as much on marketing and sales skills as on language ability. In this section we will look at the specific writing requirements relating to each one of these persuasive communications.

Circulars and sales letters

LEARNING OUTCOMES

After studying this unit you should be able to:

- **Explain why circulars and sales letters may be used**

- **Understand the techniques involved in writing such letters**

- **Explain why tear-off slips are used**

- **Design tear-off slips**

- **Identify poor business writing and make appropriate corrections**

- **Compose circulars and sales letters**

CIRCULAR LETTERS

A circular letter is one that is sent out to many people at the same time. The letter may be prepared once only and then duplicated. With modern technology, however, it is more likely that each letter could be personalised to look like an original. Circular letters may be sent for many reasons:

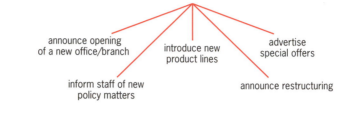

announce opening of a new office/branch

introduce new product lines

advertise special offers

inform staff of new policy matters

announce restructuring

When writing a circular letter remember these important guidelines:

- keep it brief, otherwise it may not be read
- ensure the letter is informative and direct
- use individual terms, e.g. 'you', not 'all of you'.

Reference and date (month and year only) ——————

ST/et

November 200—

Use singular expressions here (not students) ——————

Dear Student

I thought you might like to keep this example showing the correct layout of a circular letter.

A circular may be sent to all customers of a company announcing something new, eg

- a move of premises
- introduction of new goods/services
- a forthcoming sale or special event

Internally a senior executive may send out a circular letter to all employees. This is sometimes called an **Open Letter**.

Use individual expressions in the body, i.e. you NOT 'all of you' or 'you all' ——————

Although a circular letter will be sent to many people, the term ***you*** is used in the body of the letter. Never use the wording ***all of you*** or ***all customers***. Remember that only one person will read each letter so it must be worded in a personal style.

Note that as many copies are required it may take a while to print out all the letters, so only the month and year are shown in the date.

I hope this example is useful to you.

Yours sincerely may be used ——————

Yours sincerely

SHIRLEY TAYLOR
Training Consultant

Checkpoint

Very often circulars are received in the mail. Have you received any circulars recently? Bring them in to class and discuss them.

CIRCULAR WITH TEAR-OFF SLIP

Sometimes when sending out a circular letter a reply is needed. To ensure that you receive the required reply from everyone, a tear-off slip may be included, which may be completed and returned to you. Remember the following points when designing a tear-off slip:

- use a continuous line of dots or hyphens for 'tearing'
- include a return date and address
- use double-spacing where details have to be completed
- leave sufficient space for completion of relevant information.

Line of hyphens and scissors symbol separate main text from tear-off portion	✂ ---
Include date for return and name/address details	Please return by 28 November 200– to Mr Samuel Chan Sales Manager Aurora Holdings (Asia) Pte Ltd Suite 2002 Peak Towers 210 Peak Road Kowloon Hong Kong
Heading will probably be the same as the main document	OPENING OF NEW SHOWROOM – WEDNESDAY 18 DECEMBER 200 –
Keep it simple and precise	I shall/shall not* be able to attend the Cocktail Evening to mark the opening of your new showroom at 1930 on Wednesday 18 December. Signature .... Date ....
Use double spacing for the section to be completed	Name (in capitals) .... Company .... Telephone .... Fax ....
Use this footnote when appropriate	* Please delete where appropriate

REPLY-PAID CARDS

Sometimes a company will enclose a special reply-paid card for you to complete and return. The postage on these cards is pre-paid by the company. A charge will be made by the post office only for the actual cards that are returned.

```
BUSINESS REPLY SERVICE
LICENCE NO NG1211                    2| |


              ST International plc
              Aurora House
              Temple Street
              London
              SE1 4LL
```

Checkpoint

You work for a charity organisation with shops in many major cities around the UK. Your committee wants to help people suffering from the effects of a recent earthquake in China. Write a letter to be printed in a national newspaper appealing for help. Describe the disaster and its effects, the condition of the people and their needs. Ask for urgent help in the form of money that can be donated by returning a tear-off slip (cheques or credit card payments only) or clothes that can be taken to any of your shops.

SALES LETTERS

Sales letters are a very selective form of advertising. They aim to sell a company's goods or services, or they persuade readers to take up special offers. All sales letters must:

- arouse interest
- sound convincing
- create a desire
- encourage action.

In this sales letter Aurora Mobile enclose a newsletter and make everything sound so appealing and attractive.

☪ **Aurora Mobile**

**It's important
to stay**

in touch

Dear Valued Customer

With the introduction of our new **Connect Card**, Aurora Mobile has brought a new era of convenience in mobile communications. With the **Connect Card** you can enjoy all the benefits of Aurora Mobile's leading-edge network without worrying about monthly bills. Find out how in this month's issue of **In Touch**.

In Touch also introduces you to our vastly expanded international roaming services - **Roam-a-round** - which allows you to roam to all corners of the globe. Inside **In Touch** you will find out why no-one covers the world better than Aurora Mobile.

Many more features can be found inside **In Touch** ...

✆ generous savings when you call another Aurora Mobile customer
✆ what's new at our website
✆ see and read about our performance at a recent Communications Exhibition

Inside **In Touch** we have also included an exciting contest for you to win fabulous prizes such as a free subscription to our value-added services, a free **Connect Card** worth £20 and restaurant privileges in leading restaurants.

With your continued support we have become the UK's leading network service provider. Thank you for staying with us.

Yours sincerely

Lesley Bolan

Lesley Bolan (Ms)
Senior Director
Marketing, Sales and Customer Service

☪ *Aurora Mobile, Aurora House, Temple Street, London SE1 4LL
Tel: +44(0)208 542 4444 Fax: +44(0)208 555 4444 Email: auroramobile@cfb.co.uk*

Remember these important principles when writing sales letters:

1 Try to get on the same wavelength as your reader in the opening paragraph.
2 Present the advantages of the product or service showing relevance to the reader.
3 Write in a positive, convincing style without being aggressive.
4 Encourage the reader to respond by placing an order, completing a reply form or card, requesting further details.

5   Use singulars rather than plurals, e.g.

✓ Dear Customer   *not*   Dear Customers   ✗
✓ I know you will appreciate   *not*   I know everyone will appreciate   ✗
    this unique product   this unique product.

Another example of a sales letter follows.

ST Publishing Sdn Bhd
134–138 Leng Wah Street
10930 Kuala Lumpur
Malaysia

Telephone xxxxxxx   Fax xxxxxx

Improve your performance — go out for the day …

to the 200– Executive PA Show

Tailor-made for senior secretaries, this FREE show — produced in association with the Malaysia Times — includes everything from business travel to office technology, conference to recruitment.

With a comprehensive seminar programme, practical careers advice and IT clinics, not to mention a Networking Café, this show is guaranteed to boost the PA's career.

**The Executive PA Show will be held on Friday 8 September 200–
at the exclusive Royal Regent Hotel, Kuala Lumpur**

This show has everything you can expect from the top professional magazine for senior secretaries and Pas. Can you afford to miss it?

Simply complete the coupon below to send off for your FREE ticket.

✂--

Please return to: Jeremy Bonne, Senior Executive, Aurora Publishing plc,
                     134–138 Leng Wah Street, 10930 Kuala Lumpur, Malaysia
                     or fax 3878787.

☐   Yes please, I'd like to register for my FREE Ticket to the Executive PA show.

Name ....

Job title ....

Company ....

Address ....

....

....

Telephone number .... Fax number ....

E-mail address ....

What's wrong?

Study the letter written in answer to this assignment. Discuss what is wrong with the answer and then rewrite the letter correctly.

Aurora Travel arranges package holidays. On 4 February the company was informed that the Paradise Hotel at Montego Bay, which was to be used during the forthcoming season, had been badly damaged by a hurricane and would not therefore be available to accommodate their clients.

Prepare a circular letter from the sales manager to be sent to clients who have already reserved holidays at this hotel. Explain that a limited number of vacancies are available at other hotels, that the holiday price is unchanged and that the same amenities and standards apply. Some hotels are away from the beach – 5 kms from Montego Bay – but they have swimming pools and free transport provided from hotel to coast during the holiday. Twenty per cent discount given if holiday is booked immediately, or money refunded and deposits returned.

What's wrong with the answer?

AURORA TRAVEL
2 Windsor Place
Sheffield
S31 0ES

Telephone 0114 2877777

21 April 200–

Dear Clients

HURRICANE SPOILS HOLIDAY

We are writing to all clients who booked holidays at the Paradise Hotel in Montego Bay with our firm.

This hotel had been badly damaged by a hurricane and we would no longer be able to accommodate our clients at this hotel.

A limited number of vacancies are available at other hotels. The holiday price is unchanged and the hotels will have same amenities and standards, etc. In addition some hotels are away from the beach, 5 miles from Montego Bay, but they do have swimming pools, etc. Free transport will be provided from hotel to coast during your holiday.

A 20% discount will be given if the above-mentioned holidays are booked immediately. However money can be refund to clients who are not satisfied with this new arrangements. Deposits will, of course, be returned.

Hope to hear from you soon.

Yours sincerely

CHLOE BRADLEY
Secretary to Sales Manager

www.shirleytaylor.com

Writing to persuade – the carrot-and-stick strategy

(This article was contributed to my website by Tim North. My thanks to Tim for allowing me to reproduce it here.)

Certain types of writing involve doing your utmost to persuade the reader to accept your recommendations. Business examples of persuasion include:

- arguing for more staff
- assuring the boss of the merits of a new project
- convincing management to continue with a worthwhile programme
- encouraging your manager to investigate a safety hazard
- justifying a budget increase
- promoting your innovative business strategy
- selling a product or service
- supporting your position over that of others

There's a five-step process that I call the carrot-and-stick strategy. It can be very effeive in such situations. The strategy is this: the following five elements should be in *every* attempt to persuade:

1 A clear statement of the reader's problem.
2 A clear statement of the consequences for the reader of not solving the problem.
3 A clear statement of your proposed solution to the problem.
4 A clear statement of the benefits to the reader of solving the problem.
5 A clear request for a specific action, e.g. 'Please sign and return this application'.

Let's look at these five elements in further detail.

1 The problem

If you want to get a sleeping teenager out of bed, simply telling him or her to get up may be only marginally effective. Pointing out that the house is on fire is likely to be far more so. Why? The first approach may be perceived as just another request for compliance. The second, though, presents a problem: their problem.

So, if I want to persuade someone to do something then the first step in the carrot-and-stick strategy is to convince him or her that they have a problem that needs to be solved.

Little other than self-interest motivates some people; others can be paralysed by indecision and only act when compelled. No matter the situation, no matter the person, one of the best ways to put people in the mood to act is to convince them that they have a problem.

In an unsolicited case or proposal this is especially important as the reader may be completely unaware of the existence of the problem, and it will be your job to walk them through it.

www.shirleytaylor.com *continued*

Of course, some cases and proposals will be solicited, in which case the reader presumably already knows that there's a problem that needs solving. In such cases, you may need to spend less time explaining it to them.

Never skip this step, though, as the reader may have forgotten the problem since you last discussed it. Alternately, she or he may be underestimating how severe it is.

2 The consequences

Having demonstrated to the reader (in whatever depth is necessary) that they have a problem, the second step in the carrot-and-stick strategy is to outline the dire consequences to them of not acting.

List and discuss all the problems and threats that are faced if the problem is not addressed: financial, environmental, PR, social, IT, everything. This is the stick element of the carrot-and-stick strategy. You are (figuratively) beating him or her with all the dreadful things that might happen if nothing is done to address the problem.

Not surprisingly, this is a very persuasive technique for putting someone in a frame of mind where they're ready – and probably quite desperate – to find and apply a solution.

3 The solution

Now that the reader is in a receptive frame of mind, you reel them in by describing your solution to their problem.

4 The benefits

Having described your proposed solution, you now dangle the carrot by waxing lyrical about all of the benefits and features that it provides. Describe all of its good points: financial, environmental, PR, social, IT everything.

See what we've done in these first four steps? We have established a need, described the solution to that need, and then lauded the benefits of that solution. This carrot-and-stick strategy is a highly effective way of persuading people to say 'yes'.

5 The closing request for action

Commercials often use phrases such as 'Act now!' and 'For a limited time only'. Used-car salesmen are notorious for phrases such as 'I can only do this deal today'. These are all examples of closes: lines that try to get you to act immediately on the proposal that's in front of you.

The final element of the carrot-and-stick strategy is to close with a specific request for action. You've presented your case, and the reader is motivated to act. It would be a shame to have gone to all this trouble only to waste it now.

www.shirleytaylor.com *continued*

Make a specific request, now, while you've got their interest. For example:

- Please sign and return the attached application form.
- Please alter the budget accordingly.
- Please call Jane at Human Resources and authorise her to place the ad.
- Please phone Bill and express your support for this idea.
- etc.

End with a firm and clear request for some immediate action, or you run the risk that the reader will put your case or proposal to one side. You want them to act now, while it's fresh in their minds, so tell them what you want them to do.

© 2004 Tim North

You'll find many more helpful tips like these in Tim North's much applauded range of e-books. Free sample chapters are available, and all books come with a money-back guarantee. http://www.BetterWritingSkills.com

CIRCULARS AND SALES LETTERS – KEY POINTS TO REMEMBER

1 Circular letters are useful for communicating a message to hundreds, sometimes thousands of people.
2 Circulars may be sent for a variety of reasons – to introduce new products, to advertise special offers, to inform of new policy, etc.
3 Make circulars personal by using 'you' not 'all of you'.
4 Remember that only one person will read each individual letter so this has a bearing on the language used.
5 Sales letters are a special form of advertising, aiming to sell a company's goods or services.
6 Sales letters must arouse interest, sound convincing, create a desire and encourage the reader to take action.
7 Write in a positive, convincing style but don't be aggressive.
8 Present advantages and benefits to the reader.
9 Use the 5 step process in the 'carrot and stick strategy'.
10 Encourage a response from the reader – a phone call, a visit, a reply on an attached form, etc.

A–Z OF BLOOPERS AND BLUNDERS, COMMON ERRORS AND CLICHÉS: N

Needless to say

Three words that should be in the bin! If it's needless to say, then why say it?

Nice

Another overused word with an indistinct meaning. 'I had a nice time.' 'The weather was nice.' Be a bit more descriptive and precise.

Numbers

A couple of decades ago there used to be a rule that the numbers one to ten should always be spelled out in full, but all others could be written as numbers. However, today the rules have relaxed somewhat. Spell out the number one and the first word of a sentence, but all other numbers can be written as numbers. For example:

One person must be nominated to represent each department at the meeting.
There will be 30 people at the workshop next week.

IN THE BIN: N

needless to say
not to mention

HELP YOURSELF

Identify and correct the errors in these sentences.

1 I need your full committment to this project for it to be successful.
2 Has it never occured to you to die your hair blonde?
3 I was really embarrassed when he told John about our date.
4 We will need accomodation for 3 nights in Shanghai.
5 We need to do some advance planning for next year's 10th anniversary.
6 Mark your calender with the important date for next month's meeting.
7 Will you be elligible to apply for the new position in Sales?
8 The difference between the 2 candidates is negligable.
9 Please fill in this questionaire and return it to me.
10 There are 6 of us going to the party, so we will take seperate taxis.

TEST YOURSELF

1   You work for Aurora Enterprises Inc. The company produces a range of magazines and is shortly to introduce a new magazine called 'Sports Monthly'. This will cover all major sports and will include reports, interviews, tactics, famous moments from the past and a range of competitions. The cost will be £3. The Marketing Director, Mr Richard Cliff, asks you to prepare a circular letter to be included in all the other magazines published by Aurora Enterprises. He leaves you this note:

Describe the new mag and give some details of the first issue. This will be sold at a special price of £2 and will include details of a special annual subscription (£30 for 12 issues).

Write the letter. (LCCIEB EFB1 style)

2   You work for *Healthy Life*, a magazine that is published monthly. Write a circular letter to send to all subscribers of the magazine informing that their subscription is due to expire. State the last issue they will receive. These readers can renew their subscription for the special annual subscription price for six bi-monthly issues of only £15.

   If they renew now they will receive an exclusive discount card that entitles them to 10% off selected health farms and supplements available from Healthy Life Health Stores; 15% discount at all Green Cuisine café; 20% off allergy testing at Scanhealth Ltd (further details about this in next month's issue).

   Design a circular including a tear-off portion for readers to send back to you with their subscription. Compose any details you feel are needed. (LCCIEB EFB2 style)

3   You work for Mr Frank Lim, Marketing Manager of Best International plc, a large retail group in the UK. The company will shortly be expanding its operations by opening a chain of furniture superstores throughout the UK. The first one will be open at Bedford in July 2000. Opening times 0900–2000, Monday to Saturday, 0900–1700 Sunday.

   Use these notes from Mr Lim and prepare a letter for his signature:

Store will be of particular interest to the DIY enthusiast.
Special discounts for the first 50 customers. Visitors will be able to see on display a variety of kitchens, bathrooms, dining rooms, bedrooms and lounges. A planning service is available.
Store holds everything which may be needed – paints, wall coverings, tiles, carpets.

Each department supervised by friendly, qualified staff.
Parking for 400 cars or bus 214 stops right outside the store.
Free delivery of orders over £100 otherwise small charge.
Credit facilities available at low interest rates.

(LCCIEB EFB2 style)

Unit 13

Publicity material

PUBLIC RELATIONS

The public relations (PR) function in any organisation is usually carried out by staff who have specialised in this sector. Public relations, as the name suggests, is all about the relationship between the organisation and the general public. One of the aims of PR is to influence the general public through the mass media, e.g. newspapers, television, radio, information services, exhibitions, sponsorship. The job of the PR person in any organisation is to be constantly on the lookout for newsworthy events, products, developments and human interest stories and then turn them into any of the following:

- a news release
- a press conference
- a photo opportunity for newspaper coverage
- corporate material for direct mailing
- briefing packs for potential customers
- briefing packs for special groups of visitors
- free educational packs for schools and colleges.

If you are responsible for helping to produce public relations material, here are some guidelines to follow. Effective PR material will:

- be factual, newsworthy and impartial
- appeal to human interest
- contain up-to-date information
- be appropriately distributed
- be produced professionally.

Here is a section of the corporate brochure produced by Sheffield Wednesday Football Club Ltd. Excellent design, effective layout with headings and bullet points, careful wording and specially selected artwork give this material a very professional, polished finish.

Welcome to
Hillsborough...

Sheffield Wednesday FC are greatly experienced in providing a superior service for all their customers and are keen to welcome new partners and friends to this historic and prestigious stadium.

Whether you are entertaining important clients, looking for brand awareness or simply want an enjoyable day out with friends, family or colleagues the Owls Match Day team will respond to your every need.

Our constant objective is to exceed your expectations providing you with the confidence that your clients are in the most capable hands allowing you to relax and enjoy the day.

At Hillsborough we offer flexibility which allows our experienced Corporate Sales team to match your requirements making the whole Hillsborough occasion unforgettable.

A package can be created to suit most budgets, so whether a daily or seasonal booking is required you can be confident you are receiving value for money.

The personal service and attention to detail we exhibit ensures from the moment you enter Main Reception and are welcomed by a friendly face to taking your padded seat inside the stadium, your Match Day experience at Hillsborough is second to none.

Executive Boxes

Offering fantastic value for ten guests throughout the season.

Come and enjoy our outstanding hospitality and service in the privacy of your own Executive Box at Hillsborough. Executive Boxes can accommodate ten guests and are a first-class facility for entertaining corporate customers.

The package includes:

- Reserved car parking
- Complimentary Match Day programmes
- Three-course meal from our superior Match Day Menu
- Bar allowance
- Your own 10 seated Executive Box with padded balcony seats
- Half & full time refreshments
- Use of your box on Non Match Days for meetings etc.

Seasonal rates start from £15,750+VAT, that's only £68 per person over 23 matches

Day rates start from £850+VAT.

Dooleys Executive Club

A fine dining experience.

This modern Restaurant, situated in the heart of the South Stand, offers you and your guests a fine dining experience whilst enjoying a great Match Day atmosphere. Our dedicated team will be on hand to serve you and your guests and meet your every need.

- Reserved car parking
- Complimentary Match Day programmes
- Three-course meal from the Match Day Menu
- Reserved seats in the South Stand Executive seating area
- Half & full time refreshments

Seasonal rates are £1,260+VAT per person.
A small number of tables are available on a Match-by-Match basis starting from £65+VAT per person

For more details please contact the SWFC Corporate Sales team on: **0114 221 2333**

Your Goals are Our Goals

Summary of available packages at Hillsborough

	MATCH DAY SPONSOR	ASSOCIATE MATCH DAY SPONSOR	MATCH BALL SPONSOR	EXCECUTIVE BOXES	DOOLEYS EXECUTIVE CLUB	THE PRESIDENTS CLUB	THE CHAIRMANS GUESTS	THE CENTENARY LOUNGE	THE RIVERSIDE SUITE
RESERVED CAR PARKING FACILITY	✓	✓	✓	✓	✓	✓	✓	✓	✓
BUCKS FIZZ RECEPTION	✓	✓	✓		✓		✓		
THREE-COURSE MEAL WITH TEA, COFFEE & CHOCOLATES	✓	✓	✓	✓	✓	✓	✓	✓	✓
COMPLEMENTARY HOUSE WINES	✓	✓	✓				✓		
DRINKS ALLOWANCE	✓			✓					
A TOUR OF HILLSBOROUGH STADIUM WITH A COMPLEMENTARY PHOTOGRAPH	✓	✓	✓				✓		
HALF AND FULL TIME REFRESHMENTS	✓	✓	✓	✓	✓	✓	✓	✓	✓
A POST MATCH PRESENTATION TO YOUR CHOSE SHEFFIELD WEDNESDAY FC MAN OF THE MATCH	✓	✓	✓						
COMPANY LOGO IN THE MATCH DAY PROGRAMME	✓	✓	✓				✓		
COMPLIMENTARY MATCH DAY PROGRAMME	✓	✓	✓	✓	✓	✓	✓	✓	✓

For more details please contact the SWFC Corporate Sales team on: **0114 221 2333**

Contact numbers

Switchboard	**0114 221 2121**
Main fax	**0114 221 2122**
Ticket Office	**0114 221 2400**
Ticket Office fax	**0114 221 2401**
Owls Members Club	**0114 221 2407**
Superstore	**0114 221 2345**
Superstore fax	**0114 221 2350**
Sales Department	**0114 221 2333**
Special Events	**0114 221 2460**
Conference & Banq.	**0114 221 2310**

Napoleons Casinos
Club Sponsor

SWFC
Sheffield Wednesday Football Club

DIADORA
Kit Sponsor

www.swfc.co.uk

Sheffield Wednesday Football Club | Hillsborough | Sheffield | S6 1SW
Telephone: (0114) 221 2121 | Fax: (0114) 221 2122

Your Goals are Our Goals

Reproduced courtesy of Sheffield Wednesday Football Club Ltd

Checkpoint

Does your company publish corporate material? Could you bring some in for discussion with your classmates? If you are not working, visit or write to some local companies and ask for copies of their corporate material.

NEWS RELEASES

A news release is an announcement sent to the press and other media about anything considered to be newsworthy. A press release is not an advertisement but it can result in useful publicity for the company issuing the release.

Some reasons why a company may send a news release to the media are:

- relocation of offices
- introduction of new products
- purchase of new buildings
- move to new premises
- changes in top personnel.

Checkpoint

Can you think of any other reasons why a company may issue a press release? Discuss this with your colleagues and make a list.

Checkpoint

Do you deal with news releases in your company? Do you know the person who does? Can you ask if you can see copies of some press releases and perhaps show them to the rest of your class?

In this press release Singapore MRT (Mass Rapid Transit) Ltd announce their new lifestyle hub in Singapore.

SMRT

SMRT Corporation Ltd
251 North Bridge Road
Singapore 179102
Tel : 65 6331 1000
Fax : 65 6339 4229
www.smrt.com.sg

Date of Issue :   23 February 2005

Embargo Date/Time :

Press Release

RAFFLES XCHANGE OPENS

- SMRT transforms Raffles Place MRT station into "lifestyle hub" -

SMRT Corporation Ltd (SMRT) today launched Raffles Xchange, the first of a series of "lifestyle hubs" to offer commuters a shopping experience seamlessly integrated into the travel system. The event reaffirms SMRT's commitment to enhance the lives of the passengers it serves.

Said Ms Saw Phaik Hwa, President & CEO of SMRT: "Besides providing reliable and efficient travel across our network of trains, buses and taxis, we are constantly investing in initiatives to enhance and enrich our commuters' travel experience. The opening of Raffles Xchange will bring within easy reach basic necessities and lifestyle needs through the presence of convenience and specialty retailers."

SMRT marked this milestone amidst much fanfare and a rousing display of lion dance. It culminated in Ms Saw writing the Raffles Xchange *FU* [福] calligraphy to wish commuters, tenants, SMRT's business partners and employees growth and prosperity in the years ahead.

In conjunction with the launch, SMRT and the tenants at Raffles Xchange have jointly organised a series of promotional activities lasting through March 2005. Shoppers can enjoy fabulous discounts from retailers, and participate in the *Raffles Xchange Guess & Win Lucky Draw* by estimating the retail value in a special merchandise display. In addition, they can also take home attractive prizes in the Raffles Xchange sure-win lucky dips.

From 23-25 February 2005, the public can catch performances by homegrown flutist, Colin Yong and a Latin musical performance by Luis Tarraga.

- End-

Media Contacts:

Desmond Ho
Executive, Corporate Communications
Did: 6331 1140
Hp: 9017 4572

Dawn Low
Manager, Corporate Communications
Did: 6331 1137
Hp: 9788 5497

SMRT Trains Ltd SMRT Light Rail Pte Ltd SMRT Road Holdings Ltd SMRT Buses Ltd SMRT Taxis Pte Ltd SMRT Automotive Services Pte Ltd
SMRT Investments Pte Ltd SMRT Engineering Pte Ltd SMRT International Pte Ltd Bus-Plus Services Pte Ltd Singapore Shuttle Bus (Pte) Ltd RFP Investments Pte Ltd

CRN: 200001855H

Reproduced courtesy of Singapore MRT Ltd

Here is the resulting article that appeared in Singapore's *Business Times*.

SMRT looking to expand into retail sector

By **LIZA LIN**

[SINGAPORE] SMRT Corporation is branching into non-core business areas and the sector it is most keen to develop is retail, said its chairman, Choo Chiau Beng.

Mr Choo was speaking yesterday at the launch of Raffles Xchange, a 2,600 sq m retail stretch within Raffles Place MRT station. Adding that he hoped the retail sector would be most profitable, he said: "We are looking for ways to grow our non-fare revenue and give mass transport passengers the lowest fares. We will make use of under-utilised assets, try to reduce costs, increase advertising revenue and grow our fleet of taxis."

Last August, the commercial area inside Raffles Place MRT station underwent $7 million of renovation works which increased retail space from 1,700 sq m to 2,600 sq m and the number of shop units from 35 to 53. The result — Raffles Xchange, one of the 13 "lifestyle hubs" that SMRT is planning to develop by year's end.

Five have already been completed and another eight are earmarked for development. The 13 projects are estimated to cost the company about $20 million. The other four, which offer conveniences such as kiosks and ATM facilities, are located at Marsiling, Yew Tee, Sembawang and Bukit Batok stations, and occupy a total retail area of 8,291 sq m.

According to Mr Choo, this push into the retail sector is part of SMRT's recent foray into non-fare related revenue ventures. They include increasing advertising in its stations and trains, providing engineering services in MRT management, and increasing its current fleet of taxis. He said: "Our current fleet is very small compared with Comfort Delgro, and there is still scope for us to grow our business."

Mr Choo added that the revenue generated from these areas last year helped SMRT cover increasing costs such as rising fuel charges and the 2 per cent GST increase.

Lim Hwee Hua, Minister of State for Finance and Transport and guest of honour at the event, commended SMRT's move to use commercial space within its stations.

"Another benefit of SMRT's hard work is that the additional commercial revenue generated will increase the revenue stream of SMRT and help pay for the operating costs of our public transport system. Such efforts play an important part in holding off more frequent fare increases."

Reproduced courtesy of SPH – The Business Times

Compiling a press release

Editors who receive the press release may publish an edited version, publish it as written or contact the initiator to find out further details. Unfortunately 90% of press releases are thrown in the editor's waste paper basket. Only 5–10% are actually used. To make sure your press releases are in this small percentage, special writing skills are needed:

- *Headline* Compose an appropriate, snappy heading.
- *Opening* A good opening paragraph is essential to grab the editor's (and ultimately the reader's) attention. Give the main essence of the message in this opening.
- *Middle* Central paragraphs should be short and self-contained so that the editor can cut them out if necessary without ruining the sense or the flow.
- *Close* A conclusion or a summary may be appropriate at the close, or a brief repeat of the main message. It is often useful to include a quotation from a key person.

GUIDELINES FOR WRITING NEWS RELEASES

- Use third person. Write as though you are the newspaper editor, talking about your company as an outsider.
- Do not make your press release sound like an advertisement or invitation.
- Write in an interesting, snappy, punchy style with short sentences. Something that may seem an uninteresting event can be made into an effective story by using appropriate wording and innovative angles.
- Try to appeal to human interests where possible.
- Use a style suitable to appear in a newspaper with as few changes as possible.
- Your press release must answer the following questions:

What?	What is happening?
Who?	Who is involved?
Where?	Where is it happening?
When?	When is it happening?
Why?	Why is it newsworthy?

Remember

Remember: a flat, vague, dull, boring, long-winded press release will end up in the editor's wastepaper bin.

What's wrong?

Study the following scenario and discuss what's wrong with the press release that follows. Rewrite the press release more appropriately.

The Principal of your college held a meeting of all staff today and had the following to say:

'I want to hold an Open House on Wednesday September 14th from 10 until 8. It's quite some time since our last Open House and we've made quite a few additions since then, so I'd like to invite people to look around our facilities – we could put on a demonstration of the fax machine, also the new computers.

What's wrong? *continued*

The students have some interesting wall displays so there could be a tour also – that way members of the public can learn more about what we do here. Has anyone any suggestions?'

Kathryn Yeo said 'As there are a few weeks until September 14th, perhaps teachers could encourage students to prepare projects and other exhibits for display?'

Doreen Choo said: 'We could include the new library in the tour to show our up-to-date and wide range of books.'

Sharon Ho said: Perhaps we could enlist the help of some students to perform some of the demonstrations and give talks on various aspects of their course?

Angeline Lee said: 'I think it would be nice if we provided some cookies and soft drinks, free of charge of course.'

The Principal then asked for a volunteer to coordinate all arrangements. Miss Sandra Koh volunteered. It was agreed that she would draft a press release to issue to the local newspapers for insertion for a day before the Open House, encouraging visitors and describing what would happen in the school on that day.

Prepare the press release.

What's wrong with the answer?

PRESS RELEASE

Super Sec Training Centre are pleased to announce their Open Day to be held at their school on 14 September to show off the latest editions to the school.

People will be invited to look around the school's facilities including a demonstration on our new computers and fax machines. A tour will be provided by teachers, showing projects prepared by students and exhibits as well as the well-stocked library. Student's help is being enlisted to give talks on various aspects of the course.

Cookies and drinks will be provided free of charge of course.

Contact: Miss Sandra Koh

ONLINE NEWS RELEASES

If you visit the website of any company you will probably find a heading 'News Releases' or 'Media News'. Companies usually place all their news releases on the Net, with hyperlinks taking readers to connecting stories or sites of interest.

Here is a news release from Singapore Airlines website:

Reprinted courtesy of Singapore Airlines Limited

COMPANY NEWSLETTERS

Many companies publish regular newsletters known as in-house journals or company magazines, which keep staff informed about matters of interest. These regular magazines are very good for improving company/staff relations. They are an effective way of reaching out to members of staff where there are many different branches of a company around the country or even internationally. These newsletters may also be sent to employees who have retired.

Company newsletters contain a variety of information such as:

- new policies/procedures
- updates on products/services
- births/marriages/deaths
- promotions
- sports and social news
- contributions from employees.

Special newsletters may be produced for circulation to customers or members of a special industry. They are a good way of keeping people informed about the latest products, news and developments within the company.

In this example, Pat's School House issues a quarterly magazine to all parents who send children to the school.

Issue 11 Jul-Sep 2004   MITA (P) 037/01/2004

connecting parents & teachers

repeated yet. It's just the Pat's way of doing things, the camaderarie that drives me to want to give my best to the kids. I'm surrounded by such a committed, creative and energetic team – it's hard not to get excited and energised too," she enthuses.

Another set of people that keeps her driven are her young charges. "We can't wait to see their excited faces – that's what keeps us back in school after hours preparing our materials," says Sally. "I may be the teacher but the kids have taught me a lot too, about patience and how each child is an individual and has his or her own learning style," she adds.

Being able to make a difference not just in the kids' lives but their parents' too, gives Sally the job satisfaction to keep going. "I see a lot of myself in the parents. They are like how I was when my kids were young, still learning about parenting yet wanting the best for them. Parents of children with special needs and those who are starting with us at K2 come in apprehensive but when they report to you that their children have opened up since they started at Pat's, it feels really, really good," relates Sally.

Driving Miss Sally

We ask this year's Model Teacher Sally Yap what keeps her passionate about her work.

It was the desire to spend more time with her boys that first got Sally into preschool teaching, back in 1997. For two years, she taught half-day, at Halifax. Today, Sally, is the Assistant Principal of the Katong centre.

"I may have taught for 15 years before that but teaching children needs a different set of skills and methods from adults," recounts Sally who is candid about the demands of teaching preschool kids. "It's hard work. The starting part was the hardest but as my experience and confidence grew, I can now say that I thoroughly enjoy it," she adds.

What kept her motivated, she reveals, was Mrs Patricia Koh's passion and enthusiasm and her colleagues. "I'm not naturally creative so I was really awed by my colleagues. But they are so willing to share their know-how and to let me observe," says a grateful Sally.

"My kids went to Pat's schoolhouse too so I have been to many K2 concerts. Imagine, I have never seen any idea

Listen! Sally's success secret

As far as Sally is concerned, even new teachers deserve recognition as preschool teaching is a challenging job. At the interview, she had no idea yet that she had been named Model Teacher. "I'd be shocked if I am. I relied on observing the experienced teachers so I can hardly claim to have any secret to success," says Sally.

She reveals though, starting with the right attitude really helps and she shares these tips to encourage new teachers:
Listen to the parents They know their children best. What you learn from them about their child's likes, dislikes and habits can help you manage and teach more successfully.

Listen to the child Children take time to warm up and have their own way of explaining and talking. Don't assume or jump to conclusions half way through their stories.

Listen to your colleagues Each may have something you can learn, including the newcomers to the industry. You never know who can help you teach better.

PAT'S eMail Communication Update

You will be pleased to know that parents can now choose to receive the latest communication update via email. If you are currently not on our email mailing list, please email your **full name** and **email address** to **contact@patschoolhouse.com**

Reproduced courtesy of Pat's Schoolhouse, Singapore

WRITING SKILLS

The same basic writing skills are needed to write articles for in-house magazines as are needed for writing press releases. The following guidelines should be noted:

- use reported speech, third person
- write in an interesting, readable style
- use short sentences and a crisp, snappy style
- try to appeal to human interests
- be as factual as possible
- build the article logically.

Here is a good article showing correct writing techniques:

Punchy headline ———— **SAFETY FIRST**

Give the main gist in the opening paragraph ———— A two-day workshop on Health & Safety in Laboratories was held recently at the group and regional laboratory in York.

Short self-contained paragraphs ———— Staff from factories across the country attended the workshop which was organised by Simon Freeman and Ellie Winn of the regional laboratory and Ian Burke of the group occupational health & safety department.

Give full details and information ———— The speakers considered the legal and company requirements for safety matters, including risk assessments, accidents and their prevention, fire safety, dealing with spillages in laboratories, and the correct procedures for arranging for disposal of wastes.

Humour helps ———— In one of the practical exercises, Simon Freeman 'volunteered' to use the emergency shower, to check that it worked properly and to demonstrate that it is quite difficult to remove clothing whilst standing under a torrent of cold water!

It's a good idea to finish with a quotation ———— Says Simon: "The social side of the workshop was enlivened by joining one of the ghost tours of York during the evening, when we heard stories of York's macabre past."

ST/JKL

24 October 200–

Here's another article from *Copper*, the newsletter of Asia Pacific Breweries::

Technical packaging forums
by Victor Cheong

The Canning Forum was held on 1 July at the Tiger Training Room and on 15 July, the Bottling Forum was held in the Tiger Theatrette.

Forty-six members from the three packaging teams (Cnergy, Packaging Bull and Quality Packers) participated in the forums.

Henk de Bruin gave the opening speech where he highlighted the difficulties and importance of communication among three different teams and the forums were one of the ways to achieve better communication for better progress and improvement.

Bernard Wee took charge of the canning forum and Chay Hua Siang, the bottling forum. They briefed the members on past performance of the lines and shared the analysis.

Goh Yong Ang, Packaging Manager, spoke on Autonomous Maintenance, Sustainable Operational Performance relating to:

- Restoring equipment to original condition
- Establishing standard to keep equipment clean
- Changing mindset of staff
- Working together with production and engineering staff
- Increasing sense of ownership
- Single Minute Exchange of Dies (SMED)

Chua Lip Jeong, Engineer, discussed on Root Cause Failure Analysis (RCFA), a method applied to identify real primary cause of failure to avoid re-occurrence during the Canning Forum whilst Andrew Chee, Senior Engineer, presented on the same topic during the Bottling Forum.

Sharing information on regarding packaging materials identification and quality control in canning and bottling was Lee Kwek Kiong, Section Manager (PC).

Shall I write it down?

Brewing Technologist, Leong Sew Kan, gave an insight into biological tracing of the canning and bottling lines.

Senior Technical Officer 1, Jeffrey Tan, spoke on the subject of Planned Maintenance relating to cleaning, lubrication, inspection, shut down maintenance of machines and the Maximo system.

In between the presentations, question and answer sessions were held. Participants, clustered into working groups listed the problems pertaining to their area of responsibilities; some of which were resolved and some taken up as small group projects to resolve the issues.

After the two fruitful forums, the Technical Department will hold a monthly forum from now onwards.

Reproduced courtesy of Asia Pacific Breweries

E-MAIL NEWSLETTERS

E-mail marketing is probably the most measurable and effective direct marketing ever. There are many software programs available that will help you to set up a database, create a message template and then work with you to craft an effective e-mail campaign. All you have to do is consider the content, and the software does the rest, including providing results of how many people read your message, how many people clicked on links, and much more. E-mail campaigns to customers are known to be about 10 to 20 times more effective than standard direct mail, and the results vary according to the strategy, frequency and professional level of the campaign.

Remember

Successful e-marketing is not just about creating a website. It is about using the power of the Internet and the wonders of e-mail to create, build and maintain prosperous and profitable customer relationships online.

Here is an extract from my own monthly e-newsletter. This is a free e-newsletter, so if you want to sign up please visit www.shirleytaylor.com and type your name in the sign-up box. It's easy!

Shirley Says

E-Newletter Issue 22
August 2004

Greetings

I am writing this month's e-newsletter from my home town of Sheffield in England. I have been home here for a couple of weeks nursing a fractured rib and visiting my lovely Mum.

I'm looking forward to returning to Singapore very soon and to getting back to work - so I hope to meet more of you in my workshops later this month and next. As I'm virtually in 'R&R' mode right now, I hope you will forgive this somewhat shorter than usual newsletter - back to normal next month!

See you again soon.

Shirley

In this issue

- Elvis lives ...
  in Sheffield?
- Birthday Princess Shirley
- E-mail your way to the top
- Send or Take or Bring or Fetch?
- Last but not least

**Elvis lives ...
in Sheffield?**

Yes here I am with Elvis! It was good to catch up with my good friends Caroline and

Ron on my UK trip, and especially to be there for Ron's birthday party. Thanks for a memorable night, and another great sing-a-long-a-Ron!

▶

Birthday Princess Shirley

Thank you Thank you Thank you .... to everyone (and there were LOTS) who sent me birthday wishes. I was overwhelmed with all the e-mails and e-cards, and can't thank you all enough. Special thanks also to all my great friends for putting on a fabulous birthday bash at Original Sin in Holland Village - my favourite restaurant in Singapore!

See more photos in my Photo Gallery

E-mail your way to the top

When I was doing some research for my book Guide to Effective E-mail, a friend of mine said:

When I receive a message that has lots of mistakes - spelling errors, punctuation, grammar - I think the reader has no respect for me because he/she couldn't take just one minute to check it through before hitting 'send'.

I completely agree! The Internet has made it possible for us to communicate with people from all over the world. The only way those people can form an opinion of us is by looking at the way

we write! Your credibility could be ruined with one swift click of the 'send' button!

There are 2 articles on my website about the double-edged sword that is e-mail. I hope you will check them out:

E-mail your way to the top

Netiquette

If you want to **energise your e-mail skills**, why not sign up for my one-day workshop organised by Learner's Choice International. For details please e-mail sam@learners-choice.com or call Sam Loo on 6376 2018.

Continue this article on how to e-mail your way to the top

Send or Take or Bring or Fetch?

Many thanks to Mark Richman for e-mailing me to point out that in last month's newsletter I forgot to include the answers to June's quiz where I asked you to complete some sentences with send or take or bring or fetch.

Many apologies for the delay. Here are the answers now:

1. I would like to **take** you out for dinner tonight
2. My flight is at 7 pm today. Will you please **take** me to the airport?
3. When I see you later, will you **bring** that book you borrowed last week.
4. I will meet you at the airport tomorrow night, and **take** you to your hotel.
5. Please **send** your report to my e-mail address before the end of this week.
6. I would like you to **send** me a copy of your new catalogue when it is published.
7. I don't feel well. Will you please **take** me to the doctor's clinic?

SHIRLEY'S 2004 SCHEDULE OF PUBLIC WORKSHOPS AND CONFERENCES

There are still some places available on my public workshops lined up for the rest of 2004.

For further details of any of these workshops please contact hanin@shirleytaylor.com.

Success Skills for Secretaries and Other Support Staff
SINGAPORE 26 October and 26 November

Power Up Your Business Writing Skills
SINGAPORE 18-19 November and 7-8 December

Power Up Your Business Writing Skills
KUALA LUMPUR 29-30 November

Energise your E-mail Skills
SINGAPORE 9 December

Please e-mail hanin@shirleytaylor.com for further details of any of these workshops.

Check out my full Schedule of Public Workshops and Conferences

Quick Links...

Testimonials on Shirley's workshops

Leave a message in my online guest book

Shirley's workshops and seminars

Shirley's articles on learning

An interview with Shirley

Shirley's books

Shirley's photo gallery

Join our mailing list!
[   ] Join

PUBLICITY MATERIAL – KEY POINTS TO REMEMBER

1 Effective publicity material will be factual and newsworthy.
2 Press releases often result in useful publicity for the company issuing the release.
3 Online news releases often include hyperlinks to stories or sites of interest.
4 Company newsletters are a good way of communicating with all staff or customers and keeping them up-to-date.
5 When writing news releases or articles, use reported speech, third person.
6 Write in an interesting, sharp style, using short sentences.
7 Do not write like an advertisement or invitation.
8 Write as though you are the editor of the newspaper or newsletter, talking about your company as an outsider.
9 Include a quotation from a key person if possible.
10 Remember to answer the questions Who? What? Where? When? Why?

A–Z OF BLOOPERS AND BLUNDERS, COMMON ERRORS AND CLICHÉS: O

Off day or day off

As an expatriate in Singapore, you can imagine my surprise when I first heard the term 'off day' mentioned by a fellow-teacher: She said, 'I'm having an off day on Monday.' I thought she must be psychic or something and could see into the future. Where I come from, an off day is when things aren't going smoothly or things are going wrong. When you are taking leave from your work, it is your day off.

Online/ongoing

Both are one word – no hyphen.

Outstation

The word outstation seems to be used a lot in Southeast Asia. It dates back to colonial times when a person was not at his/her station. Unfortunately many people in the rest of the world would not understand this. Why not say: not in the office, out of the office, overseas?

IN THE BIN: O

ordinarily
other things being equal
overall

TEST YOURSELF

1   One of your employees has just won a local sporting competition. Write an article for the staff magazine. Make up appropriate details – name, job, department, branch, nature of the competition, what it involved, the prize he/she won.

2   You have been given the responsibility of organising the company's annual dinner and dance. Write an article announcing details. Include details of how staff can register.

3   You work at Aurora Holdings plc. Write a memo to Tracie Stannard, Communications Manager, enclosing an article you have written. Ask her to consider this for inclusion in the next issue of the staff newsletter (give it a name). In your article tactfully criticise some aspect of the company (a policy or procedure, organisation, salary structure) and make suggestions for how it could be improved.

4   You work for David Fenworth, Manager of Fenworth Fashions, 117 High Street West, Hale, Cheshire WAS 7TJ. (LCCIEB EFB2 style)

You know that a famous film star, Saffron Sinclair, was born in Hale and lived in the town before she left to go to college to study drama. Saffron has won an award as best actress in the new film 'Silver Vision'. She is your favourite film actress and you plan to write a short article about her for the magazine of the Hale Film Society.

Mr Fenworth knows that you are very interested in Saffron and he tells you that he knew Saffron when she was a young girl. You decide to write an article about when she lived in Hale.

Here are our notes on what Mr Fenworth tells you.

Real name – Pauline Sinclair – changed her name to Saffron when she became an actress.
Born in Hale – went to Hale Grammar School – always loved acting – was the star of school plays – played Juliet in school production of 'Romeo and Juliet' – local newspaper said she has 'star quality'.
Also a good dancer – had to give this up when she hurt her back.

Her mother is a nurse at Bowdon General Hospital – her father is retired – used to be a teacher.
Saffron worked at Fenworth Fashions shop on Saturdays when she was at school to earn pocket money.
Loves music – plays piano and guitar – sang in school choir.
Doesn't like smoking – always hated the smell.
Left Fenworth when she was 18 to go to college – still comes home when she can – sister at Hale Technical College.

Write the article.

5   You work for Florence Cheung, Public Relations Manager at the Pagoda Hotel in your town. She asks you to draft a press release about the new service concepts in the hotel which will gain a new perspective with the opening of the new Regency Suites wing of the hotel.

   Mrs Cheung gives you the following notes which should be included:

Regency Suites wing: opens early 2001
New service concept: a wide range to be expected.

Business Centre: vital for businessmen on the move; extension of operations to 24 hours/7 days; complete range of secretarial services – fax, letters, email, internet, reference library, personal computer, private offices, conference room/lounge.

Housekeeping and laundry services: 24-hour service. Late arrivals catered for; requests for stationery, extra pillows, suits pressed.

Hotel's airport reps: greet guests on arrival, meet during departure. Two limousines plus fleet of 14 others – all times – city tours/business trips can be organised.

Professional concierge team: answer queries – provide information; from dinner reservations to theatre shows or show-makers!

Extra services – hotel positioning itself as a top deluxe hotel – perfect choice. 148 Pagoda Hotels and resorts around the world.

Prepare the press release.

6   You work in the Public Affairs Department of Aurora Bank Sdn Bhd. You have been asked to draft a press release for immediate release to announce the move of your bank to new premises. In a discussion with Neeraj Daryani, Public Affairs Manager, you made these notes:

- *Bank now occupies three floors – total built-up area of 950 sq m. Spacious banking hall = customers can conduct business transactions in comfort.*
- *Services include credit facilities, interest-free banking, many personalised services.*
- *Moved from outskirts to centre of town in Wisma Aurora, Jalan Perak.*
- *Branch Manager = Malik Jemadi. Total staff 35.*
- *New premises officially opened yesterday by Group MD. Lim Cheng Poh. He thanked all customers who have supported the bank since it opened in 1984 – even higher standards in 2000+.*
- *New premises should help us reach out and serve customers better.*
- *150 invited customers attended opening ceremony.*

Unit 14

Notices, advertisements and leaflets

LEARNING OUTCOMES

After studying this unit you should be able to:

- State why notices, advertisements and leaflets may be used

- List guidelines for drawing up notices and leaflets

- Understand the difference between small ads and display ads

- Discuss the special techniques used for compiling advertisements

- Identify effective advertisements and leaflets

- Understand the special writing skills for compiling notices, advertisements and leaflets

- Compose notices, advertisements and leaflets according to given instructions

NOTICES

Notices are also around us everywhere we go – in the supermarket, on the underground, at the entrance of shopping centres, at the railway station, the bus station, the cinema.

Most organisations have notice boards posted around the offices which are used to bring special items to the attention of all staff.

Notice boards may be sectioned according to different topics, for example policy matters, health and safety, staff announcements. It is a good idea to nominate one person to be in charge of each notice board. This person should be responsible for:

- removing obsolete notices
- sectioning notices under appropriate headings where possible
- removing 'dead' notices (but retaining them for a short while in case of queries)
- keeping the notice board tidy and clean.

A NOTICE

ABOUT NOTICES

Notices can serve a number of purposes:

✓ Announce social events

✓ Report on matters of interest to staff

✓ Inform staff of new procedures

✓ Advertise posts for internal appointment

✓ Remind staff of company procedures

Checkpoint

Look around your school or college and consider the merits of the notices you see on the corridors.

DESIGNING NOTICES

When designing a notice your aim must be to ensure that your notice is seen and acted upon where necessary. Long, rambling paragraphs will not achieve this aim. When designing notices bear in mind these guidelines:

- give the notice a clear heading
- use different size print for emphasis
- use sub-headings to break up the main information logically
- use asterisks/bullet points to display points on separate lines
- use the paper effectively to display the notice attractively
- include the name of the writer at the bottom as well as a reference and date.

Remember

When designing a notice make sure you split the words appropriately otherwise you could change the meaning completely.

A notice must contain the essential information displayed attractively so that it receives attention and co-operation. Here are three examples of effective notices that meet all these requirements.

Clear heading and
subheading.

These side headings are
very effective.

A signature, name and title
are useful.

AURORA HOLDINGS

SAFETY PROCEDURES IN THE EVENT OF FIRE

FIRE DRILLS
A fire drill will be conducted every 6 months. Staff must be aware of all fire exits, escape routes and procedures for what to do in emergencies.

HOSE REELS
These will be tested once every 6 months at the same time as the fire drill.

FIRE ALARMS
One fire alarm will be tested every week.

SPRINKLERS
These will be tested every week.

EXTINGUISHERS
These will be checked every week. Fire extinguishers must not be moved from specified location.

EXITS
Exit doors must not be locked during working hours and they must be kept clear at all times.

FIRE EXITS
Fire exit doors must never be jammed open.

FIRE DOORS
Fire check doors must never be jammed open. These will be tested every 3 months to ensure correct operation of the closing mechanism.

GANGWAYS
Gangways must be kept clear at all times.

FIRE CERTIFICATE
The fire certificate must be kept in a safe place in the Safety Manager's office ready for inspection by the Fire Brigade.

R. Wallace

ROBERT WALLACE
Safety Manager

RW/ST
24 July 200—

Give a clear heading. ———————————

Centre for special effect. ——————

Short sentences and
paragraphs. ———————

Include a name and
date/reference. ———————

PHOTOCOPYING COSTS

Would all staff please carefully consider the use of
the photocopier.

The cost of photocopying is rising every month and is
becoming very expensive.

The photocopier should only be used when there are no
cheaper methods available. The printing department can
usually make copies that are cheaper than those from the
photocopier.

Also, please make sure that you only make the number of
copies needed so that waste is avoided.

Unless we can cut the cost of photocopying I will have to
consider ways of introducing limits on the number of copies
staff can make. Alternatively perhaps only senior staff will be
allowed to use the machine.

I hope these measures will not be necessary and look
forward to receiving your co-operation in helping to reduce
photocopying costs.

Rashid Hassan
Langland Manufacturing plc

RH/ST
25 May 200–

Clear heading.

Centre important details.

Use sub-headings where possible.

ELECTRICAL REWRITING

26 and 27 May 200–

We regret that due to essential repairs to the hotel's electrical wiring the electricity will be cut off on 26 and 27 May

between 9.30 and 11.30 am
and
between 2.30 and 4.30 pm

During these times nothing operated by electricity will work. This includes lights, kettles, hairdryers and any other electrical equipment.

Unfortunately this also means that our cleaning staff will not be able to use vacuum cleaners in the rooms. Any rooms not fully cleaned by 9.30 am will be cleaned later in the day.

Lifts: Guests are also reminded that during these times the hotel lifts will not be in operation. If anyone needs help they should contact the Reception desk.

Refreshments: Tea and coffee will be provided in the main lounge for any guests remaining in the hotel during these times.

Fire alarms: Please note that guests will not be in any danger as the fire alarms, which operate on a different system, will still work during these times.

We hope that this important electrical work does not cause problems for you and we regret any inconvenience caused.

Ruth Fairless
Manager

RF/ST
20 May 200–

ADVERTISEMENTS

Many companies advertise in newspapers, magazines or trade journals so as to reach out to a wide, and sometimes specific, market.

- to advertise vacant posts
- to promote products or services
- to announce special events or functions
- to publicise changes in the organisation.

The classified sections of newspapers categorise advertisements according to subject so that you can find any section quickly.

TYPES OF ADVERTISEMENT

There are two kinds of advertisement that you may be involved in helping to design: the *small ad* or *line advertisement*, and the *display ad*.

Small ads or line ads

In these ads the information is run on from line to line, often using the same font throughout, with no special layout. Charges are made by the line and there is normally a minimum charge for three or four lines.

Lots of small ads appear in a relatively small space, so you must try to use an opening which will catch the reader's attention. Then give as much summarised information as possible in as few lines as possible. But make sure you choose the right wording when considering the words to fit in a small space.

Capitol Beta/ MRT City Hall

●●●●●●●●●●●●●●●●●●●●●●●●●●●●●●

**PREMIER SECURITY
PRIVATE INVESTIGATION BRANCH
THE ONE NAME FOR ALL
PRIVATE INVESTIGATION NEEDS**
(Owned by the Singapore Police Multi-Purpose Co-Operative Society Ltd and The Singapore Government Servant's Co-Operative Thrift & Loan Society Ltd).
**Call Krishna at tel: 289 0479 (DIR)
Ronnie at tel: 281 4431 (DIR)
Fax: 2852709**

---

61 Other Personal Services

MR FIX-IT: We fix anything and everything (carpentry, electrical etc). Enquiries: 2540021 anytime.

---

72 Packing/ Storage/ Delivery/ Removal

A BUDGET PRICE REMOVAL SVS
Professional household/ office removal & disposal services. Experienced uniformed workers with effective team leaders pro-

---

73 Office Equipment/ Supplies

USED THOMSON PABX Telephone system with capacity of 6 lines + 20 extns, model: P10-A. $800. Used Nitsuko 516 key telephone system with 5 lines + 12 key telephone set $800. Used Switching system 2 lines + 3 extns $300. Pls. call 2742754.

1ST TELEPHONE EMPORIUM in town for major brand of new & used key telephone system. Ranges from 2 lines 3 extensions to 20 lines 50 extensions. Maintenance service is available. Call Sangai Enterprises at tel: 4713988 for details

G'TEED. BRAND NEW. Canon copiers NP150 $1280 up to A3 copy size. 1 yr. g'tee. NP155: zoom/ enlargement, reduction up to A3 size $550. Key phone $680. Fax $750 Speedcoms 7483375.

NEW MINI-PABX telephone system with 2 lines + 6 extns. c/w 1 unit of loudspeaker phone & speed dial memories & 4 unit of standard set. $980. Call 2748450.

RENT OR BUY Ricoh copier with full warranty and backup service. We also sell liquid copier for photocopy centre. Delta O.A. Tel 2721266

WELL KNOWN KEY telephone available. Reasonable price to suit your budget. Call 2722371 for more information. After 5.30pm. Pg. 7012430

BRAND NEW 7 months Rank Xerox model 6002 electronic typewriter & Rank Xerox model 1012 recopier for sale. Page: 8038774.

BRAND NEW PORTABLE typewriters (electronic and manual) for sale. Economical and durable. Enquries, please call: 5332585.

AUTO NEW FAX $890. Canon enlargement/ reduction copier from $500 typewriter $265 3374968.

BRAND NEW FAX with lines sharing feature avail. at attractive price. Call: 4713988.

CANON NP270, 305, 120, PC20/ 30. Xerox 1012, Minolta EP410Z, 350Z, Toshiba 5511. 7450417

FAX $800 ONLY. Typewriter $328. Low Cost Copier, Shredder, Key Phone. Tel: 2704436.

GOOD BUY. BRAND new typewriters, copier, fax, paper shredder, chequewriter, etc. 3388855.

KEY TELEPHONE HYBRID system (8 lines x 32 ext.) for sale. Call: 256 2214 for details.

NEW KEY TELEPHONE system with 2 lines & 3 units of key telephone sets. $780.00. Call 2706383

Display adverts

Display advertisements may incorporate a variety of font styles and sizes. Artwork or colour may be included. Charges will be based on the number of column centimetres, often with a minimum size. Information can be displayed within the advertisement to attract special attention to specific points.

WRITING STYLE

When asked to compile an advertisement you must be able to pick out the main points or features of whatever is being advertised and then put them over in an interesting, attractive way. It is essential to aim for your advertisement to be 'seen' when it stands next to lots of other advertisements. Here is AIDA from the advertising department explaining the technique for meeting this objective:

Attention	you must attract the reader's attention
Interest	get the reader's interest by mentioning something that will appeal to them
Desire	arouse the reader's desire to buy, to attend a function to find out more or to contact the writer
Action	make the audience want to do something as a result of reading the ad.

You will achieve these AIDA objectives if you follow these guidelines:

- use a company logo, prominently displayed
- compose a catchy headline and display it prominently
- use spacing to advantage, giving special items prominence
- categorise the information using sub-headings, bullet points
- clearly state the action you want the reader to take

- make your advertisement eye-catching
- aim for your advertisement to stand out from all the others around it.

Here is an effective advertisement.

Clear heading stating company and position. —————

Use bullets where possible. —————

State benefits clearly. —————

Give clear instructions for applications. —————

Include a closing date. —————

AURORA HOLDINGS

require a

SUPERVISOR
for the Customer Service Department
at its new superstore in Kowloon

A pleasant manner, tact, diplomacy and the ability to cope under pressure are essential attributes, as well as:

- O level English and Maths (or equivalent)
- the ability to motivate and lead
- a clean driving licence

Previous experience is useful but not essential as training will be given. Working hours 40 a week, Monday to Saturday

Benefits: ✓ Attractive salary
           ✓ Staff discount on purchases
           ✓ Subsidised meals
           ✓ 20 days annual leave plus statutory holidays

Applications should be sent to:

Ms Chew Mei Mei
Human Relations Manager
Aurora Holdings plc
25 Nathan Road
Hong Kong

Closing date for applications. 30 June 200–

Checkpoint

Bring in to class a copy of a local newspaper, journal or magazine. Turn to the classified ads section and see if any adverts jump out at you. What makes these adverts so successful?

LEAFLETS

Most organisations produce leaflets or brochures for any number of reasons:

- to publicise goods or services
- to promote special events and promotions
- to give information of any kind.

Such leaflets may take the form of a single page, so they could be designed as a folded document – A4 size could be folded once or twice to make a four-page or six-page leaflet as shown here:

DESIGNING LEAFLETS

Here are some guidelines to consider when designing leaflets:

1 Use a company logo, prominently displayed.
2 Use an appropriate heading that clearly states what the leaflet is about.
3 Consider carefully the information which needs to be included in the main body of the leaflet. Break it up according to different aspects of the main theme.
4 Use sub-headings and bullet points where possible.
5 Use straightforward, simple language and short sentences.
6 Be as persuasive as possible, making everything sound interesting and beneficial.
7 Use everyday language instead of technical jargon.
8 Aim for an effective and attractive display which uses space to advantage.
9 If you want a response give full details – what to do, who to contact, telephone number, etc.
10 If a portion is to be completed, refer to Unit 15 on form design.

Checkpoint

Is there a leaflet or brochure describing the college where you are studying? While you are out and about, pick up some leaflets in shops or offices and bring them in to class. Have a look at the layout of the leaflets and see how they conform to the guidelines in this unit.

Here is a simple but effective leaflet.

SALE OF THE CENTURY
GOOD QUALITY FURNITURE
AT
BARGAIN PRICES!

We are pleased to announce that we are holding a
GRAND SALE
of surplus and slightly damaged furniture.

The date for your diary is
Saturday 27 September at 10 am

We will be selling a wide range of superb furniture at **half price OR LESS**:

- chairs
- tables
- cabinets
- beds
- wardrobes
- chests of drawers

On this occasion we will not be offering our usual delivery service.
All items bought must be taken away by customers on the day.

Come along and see what we have for sale

from 6 pm on Friday 26 September

BMI Manufacturing plc
Freeman Industrial Estate
Pitt Lane
Portsmouth
Hampshire PO13 7JJ

RH/ST
5 August 200–

Here is part of an effective leaflet:

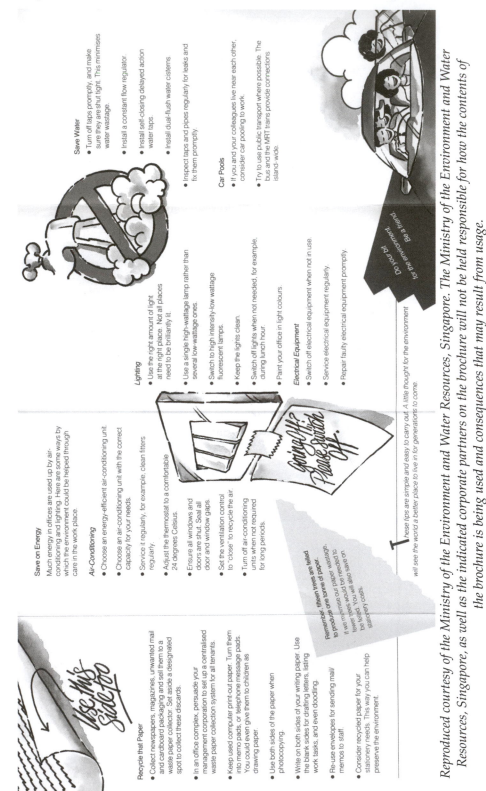

Save on Energy

Much energy in offices are used up by air-conditioning and lighting. Here are some ways by which the environment could be helped through care in the work place.

Air-Conditioning

- Choose an energy-efficient air-conditioning unit.
- Choose an air-conditioning unit with the correct capacity for your needs.
- Service it regularly, for example, clean fitters regularly.
- Adjust the thermostat to a comfortable 24 degrees Celsius.
- Ensure all windows and doors are shut. Seal all door and window gaps.
- Set the ventilation control to "close" to recycle the air.
- Turn off air-conditioning units when not required for long periods.

Recycle that Paper

- Collect newspapers, magazines, unwanted mail and cardboard packaging and sell them to a waste paper collector. Set aside a designated spot to collect these discards.
- In an office complex, persuade your management corporation to set up a centralised waste paper collection system for all tenants.
- Keep used computer print-out paper. Turn them into memo pads, or telephone message pads. You could even give them to children as drawing paper.
- Use both sides of the paper when photocopying.
- Write on both sides of your writing paper. Use the blank sides for drafting letters, listing work tasks, and even doodling.
- Re-use envelopes for sending mail/memos to staff.
- Consider recycled paper for your stationery needs. This way you can help preserve the environment.

Remember, fifteen trees are felled to produce one tonne of paper. If we minimise our paper wastage, fewer trees would be needed to be felled. You will also save on stationery costs.

Lighting

- Use the right amount of light at the right place. Not all places need to be brilliantly lit.
- Use a single high-wattage lamp rather than several low-wattage ones.
- Switch to high intensity-low wattage fluorescent lamps.
- Keep the lights clean.
- Switch off lights when not needed, for example, during lunch hour.
- Paint your office in light colours.

Electrical Equipment

- Switch off electrical equipment when not in use.
- Service electrical equipment regularly.
- Repair faulty electrical equipment promptly.

Save Water

- Turn off taps promptly, and make sure they are shut tight. This minimises water wastage.
- Install a constant flow regulator.
- Install self-closing delayed action water taps.
- Install dual-flush water cisterns.
- Inspect taps and pipes regularly for leaks and fix them promptly.

Car Pools

- If you and your colleagues live near each other, consider car pooling to work.
- Try to use public transport where possible. The bus and the MRT trains provide connections island-wide.

These tips are simple and easy to carry out. A little thought for the environment will see the world a better place to live in for generations to come.

Do Your Bit
Be a friend
for the environment

Reproduced courtesy of the Ministry of the Environment and Water Resources, Singapore. The Ministry of the Environment and Water Resources, Singapore, as well as the indicated corporate partners on the brochure will not be held responsible for how the contents of the brochure is being used and consequences that may result from usage.

Here are some pages from another effective leaflet:

You know that brushing your teeth every day can help you avoid cavities. But that's not enough to keep your teeth healthy. You may be surprised to learn that most tooth loss in adults is not caused by tooth decay—it's caused by gum disease. Gums cover and protect the bone that supports your teeth. This bone is like a foundation that supports a building—if the foundation becomes weakened, the building may fall down, even though there's nothing wrong with the building itself.

Similarly, if the gums are not cared for, the bone underneath can become infected and damaged. You can lose your teeth if the bone is not strong enough to hold your teeth in place—even if you've never had a cavity in your life!

What causes gum disease?

Gum disease is caused by *plaque*—a sticky, colorless film of bacteria that is constantly forming on your teeth. These bacteria produce toxins that can irritate the gums and damage teeth.

The earliest stage of gum disease is called *gingivitis*. This is a swelling of the gums that develops when plaque collects above and below the gumline. With proper oral care every day and regular visits to the dentist, gingivitis can be prevented or reversed because no permanent damage has occurred.

How does gum disease progress?

Left untreated, gingivitis may progress to a more severe form of gum disease called *periodontitis*. Common symptoms of periodontitis are red, swollen gums that have started to pull away from the teeth, creating *pockets*. Periodontitis damages the bone that supports the teeth. Once periodontitis develops, the damage can't be reversed: only a professional treatment program and an improved level of daily oral care at home can keep it from getting worse.

Am I at risk for gum disease?

Yes, gum disease can affect you at any age; however, it most often affects adults. In fact, about three out of four adults over age 35 have gum disease now or have had it in the past.

Your risk of getting gum disease may increase if you smoke or have certain medical conditions. It is therefore vital to keep your dentist informed of your general health.

Can I tell if I have gum disease?

You may have gum disease if you notice that:

- Your gums are tender, swollen, or red.
- Your gums bleed when you brush or floss.
- You can't get rid of bad breath or a bad taste in your mouth.
- There's pus from your gumline or between your teeth.
- Your teeth are loose or separating.
- Your teeth or dentures no longer fit together correctly.

What should I do if I think I have gum disease?

Visit your dentist right away for a cleaning and exam. In most cases, gum disease can be reversed or controlled if caught and treated early enough.

Better yet, by cleaning your teeth properly every day and making regular dental visits you can help prevent gum disease from ever developing.

But remember, cleaning your teeth is a *two-step process* of brushing first followed by cleaning in between your teeth—to get to areas your toothbrush can't reach.

How should I be cleaning in between my teeth?

There are many ways to clean in between your teeth, like flossing. Did you know that if you don't floss, you're leaving up to 40% of your tooth surfaces untouched and uncleaned?

1. Take about 50 cm of floss and loosely wrap most of it around each middle finger (wrapping more around one finger than the other), leaving 5 cm of floss in between.

2. With your thumbs and index fingers holding the floss taut, gently slide it down between your teeth, while being careful not to snap it down on your gums.

3. Curve the floss around each tooth in a "C" shape and gently move it up and down the sides of each tooth, including under the gumline. Unroll a new section of floss as you move from tooth to tooth.

At first, flossing might feel awkward. But stick with it! With just a little patience and practice, it will begin to feel as natural as brushing your teeth.

My gums bleed when I floss; should I stop when this happens?

No. Don't worry about your gums bleeding at first—this is quite common. It may be a sign that you have some form of gum disease. After a few days of flossing, the bleeding should stop as your gums become healthier. If bleeding persists, consult your dentist.

How long does it take for flossing to start paying off?

The fact is, flossing provides unmistakable benefits *that start from day one*. After flossing, your teeth and gums feel cleaner because the floss reaches areas your toothbrush can't. Your breath will be fresher, and the health of your gums will improve.

So, if your dental floss is gathering dust on the bathroom shelf, why not pick it up and try again? Even if it feels awkward at first, keep practicing. Pretty soon, you'll feel the difference and find that it becomes part of your daily routine.

What kind of floss is best?

While there are a number of different kinds of floss (waxed, unwaxed, flavored), they are all designed to reach between the teeth and below the gumline to remove plaque.

So use whatever type of floss you prefer. Some of the newer flosses are easier to use: they are more shred-resistant and slide smoothly between the teeth.

If you have trouble holding or using floss, you may want to try a *dental flossette*. It eliminates the need to wrap and guide the floss between the teeth with the fingers, and can give you better control. Once the flossette is inserted between the teeth, use the same method of flossing as above. Ask your dentist or hygienist to show you if you are unsure.

If you have braces or restorative dental work (such as a bridge) that interferes with normal flossing, you may want to try a *threading floss*. This floss has a stiffened end that allows it to be threaded in between your teeth or under bridgework.

A–Z OF BLOOPERS AND BLUNDERS, COMMON ERRORS AND CLICHÉS: P, Q

Padding

Great grandfather was famous for 'padding', i.e. unnecessary, verbose words or phrases that we should not be using in the twenty-first century business writing. For example: 'You may wish to know that', 'We regret to inform you', 'Please be advised', 'I am writing to inform you', 'in actual fact', 'in this connection', 'at the end of the day', 'in due course', 'in view of the fact that', 'at this moment in time'.

Pass up

When you *pass* something, you move it from one person to another. You do not *pass up* your homework – you *pass in* your homework. *Pass up* is used when talking about chances or offers to do something. When you pass something up you are giving something a miss.

Per cent/percent

British English uses two words, whereas American English uses one.

Per diem

This is a financial term meaning 'by the day'. For example:

We pay speakers a *per diem* of $50.

Practice/practise

British English makes the distinction that *practice* is a noun and *practise* is a verb. All you have to figure out is whether your word is a noun or a verb – sometimes it's not that easy!

Practical or practicable

Practical means useful or sensible. *Practicable* means feasible.

IN THE BIN: P, Q

permit me to say

TEST YOURSELF

1   Design a small line ad announcing a new Business English course starting soon at your college. Mention the duration and how many hours a week. Include a contact number.

2   You work for Aurora School of Physical Therapies in Bedford, telephone 0119 387472. You offer weekend courses in Reflexology, Aromatherapy and Massage – also various post graduate courses. Design a small line ad. Anyone who wants a prospectus can call the school.

3   Design a small line ad regarding an item of office equipment that your company wishes to sell. Make up the details.

4   You work for Mr James Tan, Human Resource Manager at Victory Enterprises Pte Ltd, 201 Nathan Road, Kowloon, Hong Kong. Mr Tan said to you today:

> *'Can you help me to design an ad – we need someone to help Robert in the Sales Department – he needs an assistant because he's away so often. Male or female, a couple of A levels would be good. Not too young though, 25-35-ish. We need someone with lots of common sense, able to work alone. Good telephone manner and diplomacy are essential for this job. You can't be rude to our customers or they'll be off straight away. Good old-fashioned politeness – that's all we ask. Mention that we'll offer a good salary, 4 weeks' holiday, hours 9–5, good career prospects, medical and dental benefits – but in return we expect loyalty and hard work. Try to make it really eye-catching and they'll come flooding in!*

Design a suitable advertisement.

5   You work for Aurora International Ltd, a large travel company based in modern headquarters at Aurora Court, 14–18 Holborn, London EC1N 9JE. The company offers all employees a competitive salary and many benefits including use of worldwide holiday accommodation and discounts on flights. Your fax number is 0208 333 1782. The manager said to you today:

> *Please draft an advert for me. We urgently need bright, intelligent reservation agents to join our team. We provide thorough training so previous experience in the travel industry isn't essential. Applicants do need basic keyboard skills though, and a reasonable geographical knowledge. Oh, and a good telephone manner goes without saying. The next training session will start on the 30th of next month so applicants must be available for that.*
> *Applicants need to be interested in quality customer service, a real people person.*
> *Faxes only I think so don't give our address.*

Design a suitable advertisement.

6 You work for Mr David Fenworth, Manager of Fenworth Fashions, 117 High Street, Hale, Cheshire WA5 7TJ. (LCCIEB EFB2 style)

Mr Fenworth has just been told that some urgent repair work is being made to the staff car park next week and the car park will be closed for three days from 8 to 10 August. During this time staff who use their cars to come to work can use the customers' car park but there isn't a lot of room in this. It would be helpful if staff didn't use their cars for these three days and would use the bus or make alternative transport arrangements to get to the shop. It would also help if staff could give each other lifts to work so there won't be so many cars using the car park. Mr Fenworth has asked you to write a notice about the car park to be placed on the staff notice boards.

Write the notice.

7 There have been some problems recently with the fire alarm system in the offices of *Link Services*. The fire bell has sounded when no-one has touched any part of the alarm system and when there has not been a fire. This has caused confusion in the offices as well as a lot of disruption.

The system is going to be repaired next Thursday. At 1400, staff from *Southern Security* will be carrying out this work and have said that they will need to test the bell on several occasions. The work will take about 2 hours. You have been asked to **produce a notice** to be placed in each office announcing this. Your manager, Mr Claude Bernard, says this to you:

'Of course, staff should ignore the fire bell while the security staff are repairing the system. But if there is a real fire during this time, our staff will quickly go through each office and tell people to leave the building.

'Once the system is repaired, any time that staff hear the fire bell they must follow the usual procedure and get out of the building immediately. It could be a real fire.

'Please make all of this very clear and thank everyone for cooperating.'

Task

Write the notice. (LCCIEB EFB2 style)

8 You work at a local health centre where the aim is to provide a high standard of service for all patients. To help to meet this aim there is a team of fully qualified and trained practice nurses and health visitors. You have been asked to design a leaflet to highlight the work of the nursing team. Here are your notes of what must be included:

Practice Nurses and Health Visitors = role developed to bridge the gap between medical and nursing care. They see anyone with minor illnesses (sore throats, earache, coughs/hayfever/asthma, diarrhoea and vomiting, minor traumas, sticky eyes, infant colic, feeding problems)
Doctors = more time for more serious consultations.
Nursing Team always works closely with Doctors to ensure best possible care for all.

Practice Nurses are available Mon–Fri 8.30–12.15, Mon/Wed/Fri 2.00–6.00, Tue/Thurs 4.00–6.00.

Design a leaflet (either A4 size, or fold A4 into three to make a six-sided leaflet) to issue to patients at the health centre.

9   You work for Mrs Ruth Fairless, Office Manager of the Bateman Hotel, Norland Road, Tenwick, Cumbria C49 8JY. (LCCIEB EFB2 style)

The hotel is well known for its Christmas lunches and often guests enjoy staying over the Christmas period. For the first time this year the hotel is planning to offer something similar on New Year's Eve and New Year's Day. Many people enjoy celebrating the New Year and Mrs Fairless has asked you to draft a leaflet to send to all the guests who have ever stayed at the hotel informing them about these New Year celebrations.

You made some notes when speaking to Mrs Fairless, as follows.

Guests staying for one night on 31 December and will be able to go to the hotel's grand dinner and dance that evening. A special five course dinner will be served and guests will be able to celebrate until 2 am.
On the following day there will be a special boat trip on the lake next to the hotel and lunch will be served on the boat. Afternoon tea will be served back at the hotel before guests leave.
Entertainment will be provided for children on 31 December and there will be a disco for older children.
All included in special price.
Children who stay in their parents' room will be free.
If guests stay on longer, regular rates will apply.

Draft the leaflet.

10   You work for *Eastern Jewels*, a company that buys and sells second hand jewellery, from its shop in Central Arcade in the city of Metroville. You assist the shop manager, Mr Alexander Pletnev.

There have been a lot of new housing developments in Metroville recently and Mr Pletnev feels that it would be a good idea if a leaflet was produced, for delivery to all these new houses. Mr Pletnev says this to you.

'Please draft a leaflet for us. If you design it I can get a friend of mine who is a printer to publish it. So if you want to include any picture, maps etc., just say what you want.

'Basically, I'd like the leaflet to tell everyone that we will give a good price to anyone who wants to sell any jewellery. You'd better remind everyone that we are a very reputable company (we've been in Metroville for over 30 years now) and we'll always give a fair price.

'I'm sure you can do a good job to make the leaflet interesting. You can tell people that they should not keep old jewellery when they can get good money for it.

'You'll need to give our address, but you say that anyone can call in to see us with their jewellery, but we'll also visit anyone in their own home if they wish.'

Eastern Jewels' telephone number is 01457 666224 and its e-mail address is easternjewels@freemail.net

Task

Write the leaflet. You do not have to draw any pictures but you can indicate where you want any of these to appear. (LCCIEB EFB2 style)

Visual and oral communication

Unit 15

Forms and questionnaires

LEARNING OUTCOMES

After studying this unit you should be able to:

- State reasons why forms and questionnaires are used

- Explain the techniques used to design effective forms and questionnaires

- Identify poor design of forms and suggest improvements

- Design forms for use internally and externally

- Illustrate the types of questions used on questionnaires

- Design effective questionnaires

THE REASON FOR FORMS

Form-filling is almost an everyday occurrence. In almost every aspect of our personal lives forms cannot be avoided. This is also true in the business world. Even with the impact of information technology, pre-printed forms are being used more and more for a variety of reasons:

- They are extremely valuable for collecting data in procedures that are standardised.
- They ensure that every piece of information required is completed by the form filler.
- The sequence of information is included in a priority order.
- They act as computer data input sources.
- They provide useful sources of reference.
- New forms can be designed easily to meet new policies or revised procedures.

Here are a variety of well-designed forms in everyday use in business:

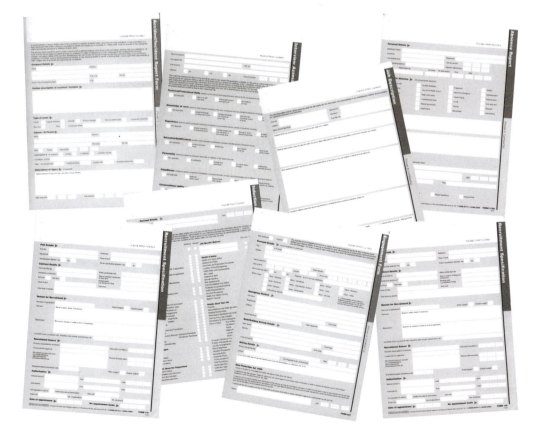

Reproduced for educational purposes only courtesy of Waterlow Business Supplies Limited

DESIGNING FORMS

One reason why some people hate forms is because some designers do not allow sufficient space for the person completing the form to insert all the information.

If you have ever had a similar experience in completing a form, this should help you to ensure that your created forms are a pleasure to use. Effective form design can save many people valuable time, so study these guidelines for some useful techniques.

1   Consider these questions:
    (a) Who will be completing the form?
    (b) Who needs the information?
    (c) Why is this information needed?
    (d) How would the information be most effectively presented?

2   Make a checklist of all the information needed, for example: name, address, telephone number, fax number, age, date of birth, sex, nationality.

3   Divide your checklist into appropriate sub-sections and choose titles for each section.

4   Decide on a logical structure for the form according to priority.

5   Design your form in draft, making sure that you
    (a) word your questions carefully so that they will obtain the required response
    (b) use options boxes where a variety of responses could be given
    (c) leave sufficient spaces and lines where the required information will fit
    (d) allow sufficient space when asking open questions
    (e) ensure questions and instructions are simple, clear and unambiguous.

6   Try your form out on a colleague and ask for constructive criticism. Make any amendments based on the useful information obtained from this trial.

7   Print the form properly but monitor the first few forms completed. Check that users understand requirements completely and that sufficient space for answers is provided.

8   Monitor forms regularly and ask yourself, is the form
    (a) essential?
    (b) straightforward and simple to complete?
    (c) logical in the sequence of questions?
    (d) printed on appropriate paper (colour/size/quality)?
    (e) relevant?
    (f) suitable for the purpose for which it is intended?

REPLY FORMS

On many occasions in business replies are required from recipients of letters. In Unit 12 we discussed tear-off slips which are often used when sending out circular letters. Sometimes when a tear-off slip is not big enough for the information required a separate reply form may be necessary.

A reply form enables the sender to specify the information required from everyone to whom the form is sent. This guarantees that the correct information will be obtained and is a much better way of obtaining information than by requesting a written reply.

Sometimes reply coupons are included in advertisements so that interested parties can reply easily.

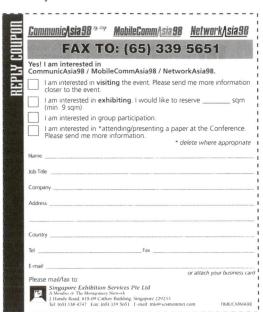

Reproduced courtesy of Singapore Exhibition Services Pte Ltd

When you design a reply form, remember that if you omit important details or word a question badly, it could result in your receiving many phone calls asking for clarification. Alternatively you could have to make hundreds of phone calls requesting extra information which you forgot to ask for on the form. Bear this in mind when you are designing forms.

Headers and footers

Two important features of reply forms are the details shown at the head and foot. These details will differ on forms used within an organisation and forms used externally. Here are examples of header and footer details for forms used both internally and externally:

Internal forms

Date, name and title only ———

Internal forms don't need
company name/address, etc ———

REPLY FORM

Please return by 25 May 200– to Mrs Mavis Tan, Training Manager

Signature .... Date ....

Name (in capitals) ....

Designation/Department ....

Extension Number ....

External forms

Forms used externally
need full name/title/
company name/address ———

Always remember
signature and date ———

Remember to allow sufficient
space for appropriate details ———

REPLY FORM

Please return by 20 August 200– to   Mrs Rosehannah Wethern
                                        Marketing Manager
                                        Timeless Traders Ltd
                                        219 Rue de Chanson
                                        Bridel L-85-96
                                        Luxembourg

Signature .... Date ....

Name (in capitals) ....

Designation/Department ....

Company ....

Address ....

....

.... Post code ....

Telephone Number .... Fax Number ....

Remember

When thinking of the opening and closing details for forms, just ask yourself who will be completing the form and what details you need to know!

SPECIMEN FORM

Here is an example of a reply form sent out with a letter to clients of a training organisation. Clients were asked to specify whether or not they would like to attend a one-day management conference, when accommodation will be required, and enclose a cheque to cover the cost.

Always give a return by date and address ——————

Use same heading as on covering document ——————

Use numbered points where appropriate ——————

Use options/tick boxes where relevant ——————

Use I/my as if the person completing the form is speaking ——————

Always include signature and date ——————

Choose appropriate details here dependent upon the person completing. Use double spacing ——————

Don't forget the footnote if applicable ——————

REPLY FORM

Please return by 15 February 200– to   Mr Sim Fook Chin
Training Manager
Professional Training Sdn Bhd
126 Buona Vista Boulevard
13006 Kuala Lumpur
Malaysia

**ONE-DAY MANAGEMENT CONFERENCE
SATURDAY 3 APRIL 2000–**

I wish/do not wish* to attend this conference.

I require accommodation on

❏ Friday 2 April

❏ Saturday 3 April   (please tick)

My cheque for M$500 is attached (made payable to Professional Training Sdn Bhd)

Signature ....   Date ....

Name (in capitals) ....

Designation/Department ....

Company ....

Address ....

....

....   Post code ....

Telephone Number ....   Fax Number ....

* Please delete as necessary

What's wrong?

After reading this assignment carefully, study the answer given. Discuss what is wrong with the reply form and then rewrite it correctly.

The Human Relations Manager has written to all employees informing them about the company's 25th anniversary dinner and dance to be held in three months' time. You have been asked to design a reply form for employees to return to you. Staff must let you know if they will be attending and also if they will be bringing a partner. You need a full list of names of those attending. Design a suitable form.

REPLY FORM

To be returned by 31 April to

Human Relations Manager
Aurora Holdings plc
Aurora House
Temple Street
London
SE1 4LL

I, ... (name) from ....

(department) do/do not* wish to attend the dinner and dance on 12 May.

I will/will not* be bringing my partner.

Signed ....

* Please delete

QUESTIONNAIRES

Questionnaires are a special type of form designed to record opinions or suggestions from different groups of people. They are widely used in business, for example:

- for researching the preferences of consumers
- for investigating public attitudes to major issues
- for requesting the opinions of staff on issues like canteen facilities and flexihours.

A questionnaire may well form part of the research undertaken in the preparation of a formal report, as discussed in Unit 9.

All the guidelines mentioned about the design of forms apply also to the presentation of questionnaires. People who complete a questionnaire are often under no pressure to do so; therefore their design is even more important because they are dependent on the public's desire to help. To avoid putting people off, the questionnaire must be as straightforward as possible. Humour also helps, as in this extract from a feedback form used at Changi Airport, Singapore.

Please tick on the appropriate faces

	Excellent	Good	Average	Poor
Check-in Facilities & Services	☺	☺	😐	☹
Arrival Facilities & Services	☺	☺	😐	☹
Transit/Transfer Facilities & Services	☺	☺	😐	☹
Airport Cleanliness	☺	☺	😐	☹
Friendliness of Airport Staff	☺	☺	😐	☹
Shopping Facilities	☺	☺	😐	☹
Other Facilities (Please specify)	☺	☺	😐	☹

Reproduced courtesy of Civil Aviation Authority of Singapore

To achieve the objective of ensuring that people fill in your questionnaire, follow these guidelines:

- Ensure your questionnaire is clear and attractive.
- Use language that is simple and direct; it should not offend anyone.
- Use wording that will create a good relationship with the reader.
- Include only essential questions so the form is not made unduly long.
- Begin with a polite request to the reader to complete the form and briefly mention why the information is needed.
- Include an assurance that all information will be treated in confidence.
- Thank the reader for completing the form.
- Include clear instructions about where to send the form after completion.

Here is a well-designed questionnaire used by the National Health Service to obtain feedback from patients about the quality of the food provided.

CATERING SATISFACTION SURVEY

NHS

We aim to provide you with excellent food and catering services during your hospital stay. We know that if we listen carefully to your opinions, we can make our services even better. You do not need to give us your name - we'd still be very interested in your views.

Please take a moment to answer the questions below, and feel free to use the box at the end if you have any other comments about our catering services.

Ward number or name: _____ Month: _____
Name of patient: (optional) _____
Are you MALE ❑ or FEMALE ❑
Year of Birth: _____
Approximately how many days have you been in hospital? _____ days

(please tick √)

1. Was the menu easy to understand?	❑ Yes	❑ No
2. Were you offered the kinds of meals you like to eat?	❑ Yes	❑ No
3. Was there enough choice for:		
a) Breakfast?	❑ Yes	❑ No
b) Midday meal?	❑ Yes	❑ No
c) Evening meal?	❑ Yes	❑ No
4. Were there enough menu choices to suit your religious beliefs?	❑ Yes	❑ No ❑ Not Applicable
5. Was there enough choice of vegetarian or vegan food?	❑ Yes	❑ No ❑ Not Applicable

(please tick √)

6. Were you made comfortable before the meal service?	❑ Yes	❑ No
7. Were you given the chance to freshen up before the meal service?	❑ Yes	❑ No
8. Were the meal times suitable?	❑ Yes	❑ No
9. Was the ward atmosphere pleasant during meal times?	❑ Yes	❑ No
10. Were the staff serving the meals friendly and helpful	❑ Yes	❑ No
11. If you needed help with eating, was it available?	❑ Yes	❑ No ❑ Not Applicable
12. Did you always get the meal you wanted from the trolley or ordered from the menu?	❑ Yes	❑ No
13. Could you get a drink or snack when you wanted?	❑ Yes	❑ No
14. If you missed a meal was a replacement offered?	❑ Yes	❑ No
15. Were you given enough to eat?	❑ Yes	❑ No

	Excellent	Good	Acceptable	Poor	Very Poor
16. How would you rate:					
a) the taste of meals?	❑	❑	❑	❑	❑
b) the temperature of food?	❑	❑	❑	❑	❑
c) the appearance of meals?	❑	❑	❑	❑	❑
17. How would you rate your overall satisfaction with the catering service?	❑	❑	❑	❑	❑

Comments

Thank You

PTO

For office use only

Reproduced courtesy of the Department of Health

TYPES OF QUESTION

Different techniques can be used for asking questions on a questionnaire.

Alternative questions are used to establish facts and circumstances before asking further opinions. Care must be taken to ensure that the alternative answers are specific.

How often do you buy cold drinks?

✗ Often/sometimes/rarely/never

✓ Several times a day/every day/twice a week/once a week/less often/never

Closed questions require specific answers. The most basic closed questions are those requiring yes/no answers:

Have you bought any drinks from the college
vending machines during the past month?   Yes/No

Do you feel a vending machine for snacks should
be provided?   Yes/No

Multiple choice questions are those giving a list of responses to be ticked. This type of question needs planning carefully to ensure complete coverage of possible answers:

Which of the following drinks have you bought recently?

Coffee	Sprite
Tea	Cola
Chocolate	Diet Cola
Milo	Orange juice

(please tick)

Rating or preference questions ask for an opinion. Gradings are provided for ticking:

What is your opinion on the quality of the drinks from the vending machine?

	Good	*Average*	*Fair*
Coffee			
Tea			
Chocolate			
Milo			
Sprite			
Cola			
Diet Cola			
Orange			

Open questions invite comment:

> Name any additional items you would like to be available from the college vending machines.

> Drinks ....

> Snacks ....

Here is a questionnaire inserted in boxes of The Sunshine Supplement Kira (St John's Wort) by manufacturers Lichtwer Pharma UK Ltd. They use various different questioning techniques in this leaflet to obtain feedback to assist them in developing the product suitably.

About Kira

Is this the first time you have tried Kira?

Yes ☐   No ☐

How did you first hear about Kira?

Newspaper Advertisement ☐	Radio ☐
Newspaper Article ☐	TV ☐
Magazine Advertisement ☐	Friend's Recommendation ☐
Magazine Feature ☐	Chemist's Recommendation ☐
Saw in-store ☐	Doctor's Recommendation ☐

In which type of shop did you purchase Kira?

Healthfood ☐   Chemist ☐

Please tell us your reasons for buying Kira _____

_____

Have you ever bought Hypericum products for health reasons before?

Yes ☐   No ☐

If yes, please specify which product and why? _____

_____

How satisfied are you with Kira?

Too soon to say ☐   Very Satisfied ☐   Satisfied ☐   Dissatisfied ☐

Do you intend to buy Kira again?

Definitely Yes ☐   Probably Yes ☐   Probably Not ☐

Definitely Not ☐   Why? _____

How much do you spend on supplements per month? _____

If there are any further comments which you would like to make to us we would be delighted to receive them on a separate piece of paper enclosed with your questionnaire.

Please Tell Us About Yourself   Male ☐   Female ☐

Title _____ Name _____

Address _____

_____

Age   Up to 25 ☐   25–35 ☐   36–50 ☐   51–65 ☐   Over 65 ☐

Occupation

Administration/Clerical ☐	Housewife ☐
Manual ☐	Professional/management ☐
Retired ☐	Student ☐
Unemployed ☐	Other ☐

May we contact you again?   Yes ☐   No ☐

Data Protection: the information you supply will be treated in the strictest confidence and will not be linked with your name. Relevant data will be recorded on our database. It is our policy never to rent out or release our lists to other companies for their use.

Thank you for completing this questionnaire.

Please send to (no stamp required):

Lichtwer Pharma UK Limited FREEPOST SL 1171 Marlow Bucks SL7 1BT

Reproduced courtesy of Lichtwer Pharma AG

SUMMARY

If they are designed and used correctly, questionnaires can make life much easier for all concerned. They can ensure that an organisation obtains the information it needs, thus leading to an improved public image and increased customer rapport. Here is part of a feedback form used at the Marché Restaurant in Singapore which would certainly achieve these objectives:

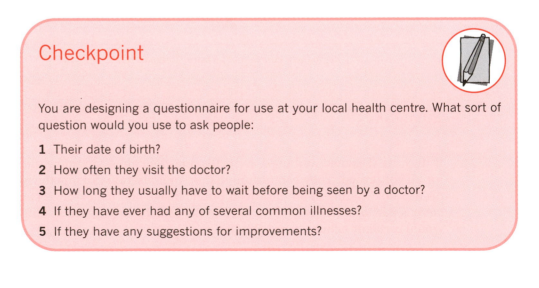

Marché
MÖVENPICK
RESTAURANT

Day/Date of Visit: _____   Sex: Male ☐   Female ☐

Time: ☐ 11:30am – 2:00pm   ☐ 2:00pm – 5:30pm   Local ☐   Tourist ☐
            ☐ 5:30pm – 8:00pm   ☐ 8:00pm – 11:00pm   Age:

No. of people in your party: _____   Occupation:

Area that you sat in: _____   Student ☐   Executive/Professional ☐   Homemaker ☐
                                                      Others (please specify) : _____

| 1 = Unacceptable | 2 = Needs improvement | 3 = Acceptable | 4 = Good | 5 = Excellent |

A.   Food & Beverage:

Choice/Variety: 1......2......3......4......5

Freshness/Quality   1......2......3......4......5

Presentation   1......2......3......4......5

Pricing:
Pasta/Pizza   inexpensive......fair......expensive

Seafood   inexpensive......fair......expensive

Grilled Meats   inexpensive......fair......expensive

Salad   inexpensive......fair......expensive

Dessert   inexpensive......fair......expensive

Beverages   inexpensive......fair......expensive

Comments:

_____
_____
_____

B.   Staff

Presentation: 1......2......3......4......5

Friendliness   1......2......3......4......5

Efficiency   1......2......3......4......5

Attentiveness   1......2......3......4......5

Comments:

_____
_____
_____

C.   Restaurant

Cleanliness   1......2......3......4......5

Ambience   1......2......3......4......5

Decor   1......2......3......4......5

Background Music   1......2......3......4......5

Comments:

_____
_____
_____

Reproduced courtesy of Marché Restaurant Singapore

Checkpoint

You are designing a questionnaire for use at your local health centre. What sort of question would you use to ask people:

1 Their date of birth?

2 How often they visit the doctor?

3 How long they usually have to wait before being seen by a doctor?

4 If they have ever had any of several common illnesses?

5 If they have any suggestions for improvements?

What's wrong?

Your colleague has been asked to find out the opinions of staff on the food and service provided in the staff restaurant in your company. The results of this research will be analysed carefully to form the basis of a report. Discuss what is wrong with this questionnaire so that you can tactfully suggest to your colleague how it could be improved. When you have done this, redesign the questionnaire more appropriately.

CIRCULAR

Please complete this form and return it to Susan Gingell as soon as possible.

1   Which lunch sitting do you attend?   _____

2   How many times a week do you use
     the staff restaurant?   _____

3   What else do you sometimes do at lunch time?   _____

4   Do you ever have to queue for meals?   _____

5   Are you satisfied with the selection of food available?   Yes/No

6   Are you satisfied with the service provided?   Yes/No

7   Are you satisfied with the food?   Yes/No

Any other comments?

....

....

....

....

Signature ....   Date ....

A–Z OF BLOOPERS AND BLUNDERS, COMMON ERRORS AND CLICHÉS: R

Refer

Great grandfather used to say things like 'We refer to your letter dated' … or 'With reference to' … or expressions like 'Your letter of … refers'. Remember, great grandfather is dead, and we need to kill off his old-fashioned expressions. 'Please refer' is also no good, as it tells the reader to do something. There are ways we can say the same thing without using these archaic expressions, for example:

Instead of	*Say*
We refer to our meeting on ….	It was good to meet you on …
I refer to your letter dated …	Thank you for your letter dated …

Reiterate or repeat

Reiterate is a more formal way of saying *repeat*. To repeat is to do something again, so neither of these words should be followed by the word *again*.

Request

You do not *request for* something. *Request* means to ask for. So if you say, for example, 'I want to request for new stationery' you are really saying 'I want to ask for for new stationery'. Cut out the extra word. (See also discuss, emphasise, investigate, mention.)

Return

Many people use the phrase *return back*. This is not correct. We *return* faulty goods. We *return* to our favourite island resort. We do not need the word back.

Revert

Many people are using sentences like 'Please revert to me on this matter soon'. The word *revert* means to regress or go back to a former condition. We can refer to Clark Kent changing into Superman and then reverting to being Clark Kent. *Revert* should not be used when you mean reply or let me know. Why not say 'I hope to hear from you soon'.

IN THE BIN: R

rather
really
regarding
respectively

TEST YOURSELF

1   Your manager has written a circular letter to all customers announcing a cocktail evening to celebrate your company's 10th year of trading. Prepare a reply form to be returned stating whether or not customers will attend.

2   Your manager has written an open letter to all employees announcing the retirement of the chairman and inviting them to attend a special presentation. This will be held at a local hotel in 2 months' time. Design a form to be sent with the letter for employees to return to you with the necessary information.

3   You are responsible for organising the company's annual dinner and dance. When you write to employees they will need to let you know whether or not they are attending. You also need to know if they are bringing a partner. Full payment must be sent with replies. Design an effective form.

4   You have written to departmental heads in all branches of your company asking them to nominate staff in their departments to attend a training workshop on effective communication. This will be a half-day course held in 2 months' time. Design a form to send with the memo for departmental heads to complete and return to you.

5   You work at a large hotel in your country. Design a small feedback form to be completed by visitors to any of your many coffee houses/restaurants. Use your initiative to decide which categories and statements should appear on the questionnaire so that it will be valuable to management in gauging customers' opinions.

6   You work at Rapid Repair car repair workshop with many branches in the region. You specialise in tyres, exhausts, batteries, shock absorbers and many other items. The General Manager has asked you to design a simple questionnaire to be completed by customers so that standards can be maintained and improved. Use the following notes to help you to design the questionnaire:

This visit – what did they buy?

Why us? (TV, radio, newspaper, yellow pages = think of others here)

Questions – seat covers used? frank and honest appraisal given? informed of cost before work started? finished work examined in customer's presence? any parts removed offered to customer? depot clean/tidy?

Overall rating?

Include any other details you think are appropriate and design a questionnaire.

Unit 16

Visual presentation

LEARNING OUTCOMES

After studying this unit you should be able to:

- State the reasons for choosing visual presentation of information

- List the main forms of visual presentation and describe each one

- Choose the best method for presenting different types of information

THE APPEAL OF VISUAL PRESENTATION

Visual presentation of information is having an increasing impact on our lives. You only need turn on the television set or open any newspaper to appreciate the widespread use and effectiveness of such presentation. Visual presentation is beneficial for many reasons:

- Complex facts and figures can be much more easily absorbed.
- Visual presentation adds impact to the information.
- It enables quicker understanding due to its simplified format.
- It enables comparisons to be made and recognised easily.
- Audiences are more likely to be interested in a chart or diagram than a long explanation or lots of words.
- Charts or diagrams can easily be transferred onto overhead transparencies for presentation to large groups.

This illustration shows the percentage of information remembered when it is seen as compared to other means of communication. Compare too the illustration with the table shown alongside it. The pictorial presentation of the information is much more vivid, simpler and more effective compared to the words and figures.

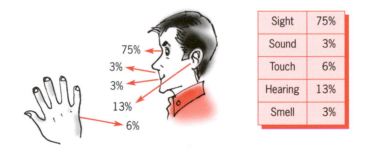

Sight	75%
Sound	3%
Touch	6%
Hearing	13%
Smell	3%

METHODS OF PRESENTATION

To ensure the effectiveness of the presentation, it is important to select the most appropriate method. There are many ways in which information can be presented:

- tabulated data
- line graphs
- bar charts
- Gantt charts
- pie charts
- pictograms

- maps and diagrams
- cartograms
- flowcharts
- visual planning boards
- computer graphics.

TABULATED DATA

Information is very often provided in the form of tables. Tables present data in an immediate and carefully ordered way, but they rely on the reader to interpret the data shown on them. This often means that the full significance of the data is not always immediately obvious until it has been carefully studied.

Turnover by region (%)

	1995	1996	1997	1998	1999	2000
Europe	52	50	49	46	45	40
Australasia	21	20	18	20	19	20
Africa and Middle East	11	10	14	10	14	12
USA/Canada	16	20	17	24	22	28

Checkpoint

How could this information be presented in a different format so that the breakdowns for each year are easy to see at a glance?

Some tabular displays can be highly inventive and unusual with symbols and graphics to attract the reader to the page, making all the information very easy to interpret at a glance, as shown in these extracts from a leaflet produced by Boots the Chemists.

Your Quick Guide to Hayfever Symptoms and Treatments

Symptoms		Minor	Moderate	Severe
Eyes		✔	✔	✔
Nose		✔	✔	✔
Throat			✔	✔
Chest				✔
Suitable Treatments	**P8**	Antihistamine tablets	Antihistamine tablets	Antihistamine tablets
	P10	Decongestant nasal spray/drops for occasional use	Preventative nasal spray/drops for season long use	Preventative nasal spray/drops for season long use
	P11	Eye drops for occasional use	Preventative eye drops for season long use	Preventative eye drops for season long use
			Throat lozenges for immediate relief	Throat lozenges for immediate relief

Reproduced courtesy of Boots Group plc

Hayfever Calendar

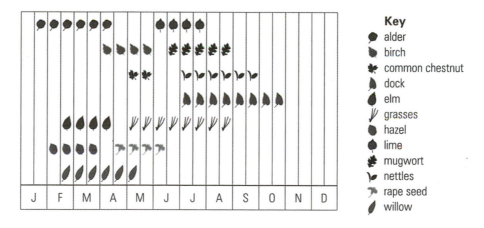

Key
- alder
- birch
- common chestnut
- dock
- elm
- grasses
- hazel
- lime
- mugwort
- nettles
- rape seed
- willow

J	F	M	A	M	J	J	A	S	O	N	D

Reproduced courtesy of Dr Jean Emberlin, National Pollen and Aerobiology Research Unit, University College Worcester

LINE GRAPHS

Line graphs are useful to show comparisons or indicate trends. Two sets of figures are used – the horizontal scale (or *x* axis) from left to right, and the vertical scale (or *y* axis) from top to bottom. Two or more items may be shown on the same graph by using contrasting lines or different colours.

A single line graph

A multi-line graph

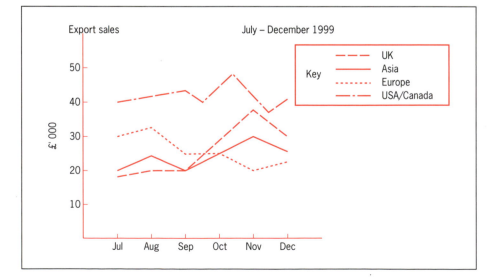

BAR CHARTS

Bar charts may be displayed vertically or horizontally and can be made up of single or multiple bars. They are useful for showing comparisons:

A vertical bar chart

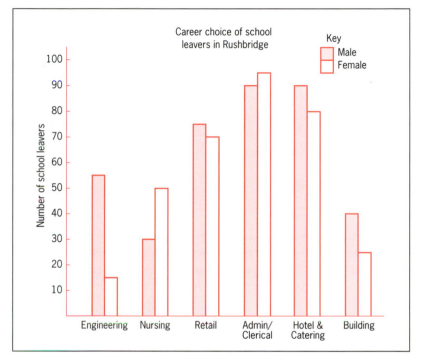

A horizontal bar chart

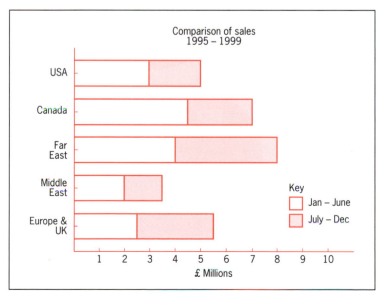

GANTT CHARTS

A Gantt chart is used to show the comparison between work that has been scheduled and work that has actually been accomplished in relation to time. In this example, scheduled work is represented by a pale line and completed work by a dark line. In practice, colour could be used to good effect in such a chart.

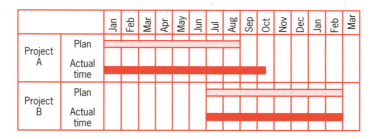

PIE CHARTS

Pie charts are often used when it is necessary to show the relationship of parts to a whole. It is preferable not to use too many segments in the pie, otherwise the impact could be lost. Shading may be used to focus special attention on a single element, or the segment may be separated from the remainder of the pie.

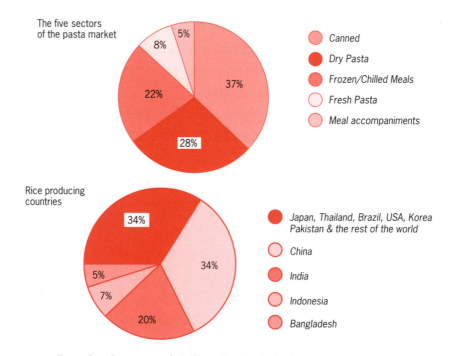

Reproduced courtesy of Unilever UK Foods. Unilever is not responsible for the accuracy of this information

PICTOGRAMS

A pictogram shows information represented in the form of figures or symbols. The value of each figure is indicated by either the size or the number of figures shown. Pictograms are visually interesting and easily understood.

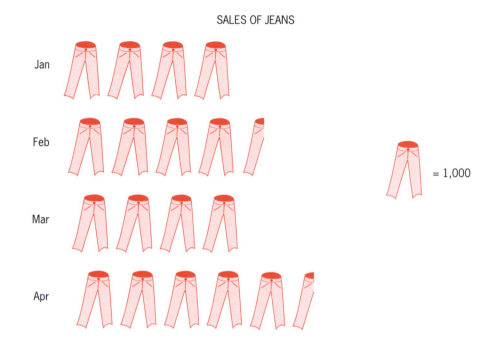

SALES OF JEANS

= 1,000

MAPS AND DIAGRAMS

Maps can be an effective visual aid (consider the weather forecast maps shown on television). Maps or diagrams may also be sent out to delegates of a conference or to customers showing a new company's location. Such maps have obvious advantages over the written word.

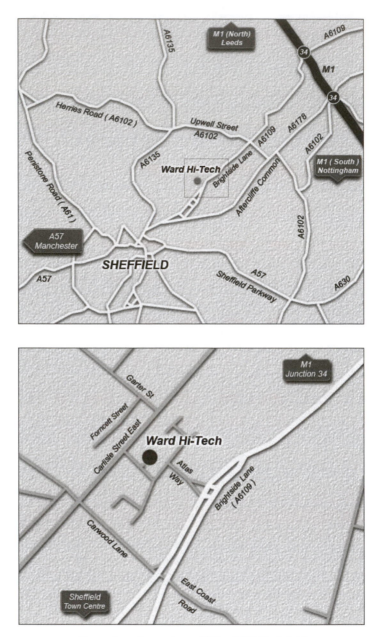

Reproduced courtesy of Ward Hi-Tech Ltd

CARTOGRAMS

A cartogram is a special kind of map used to give information about the distribution of people or things within a country or region. Things that may be depicted clearly in a cartogram are, for example, the density of population in China, the number of dog owners in Britain. Here is a cartogram showing the number of Aurora Hotels in Europe, and another showing the location of Corus Hotels in the UK.

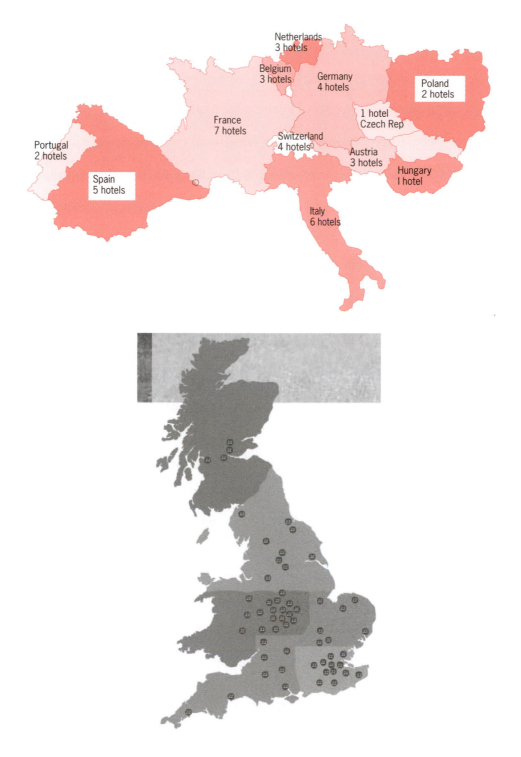

Reproduced courtesy of Corus Hotels

FLOWCHARTS

A flowchart is a diagram showing a sequence of decisions or instructions involved in a process. Flowcharts are often used in business to work out the stages of writing a computer program. However, they can also be very valuable in highlighting the separate steps or procedures involved in a sequence of events. It is often useful to construct a flowchart when faced with the task of achieving a new objective or simplifying a procedure. This process is useful in encouraging logical thought.

Here are two very effective flowcharts included in the publicity material of Cadbury Ltd.

The first flowchart shows the sequence of events involved in the production of chocolate, from the cocoa bean to the end product.

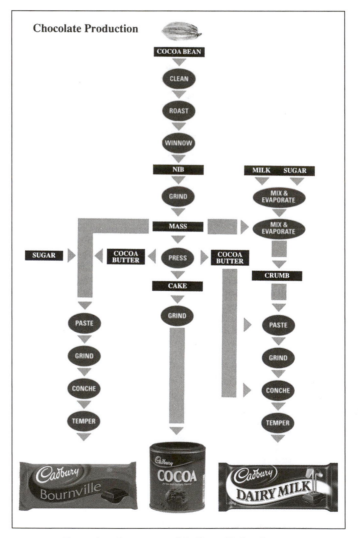

Reproduced courtesy of Cadbury Trebor Bassett

This flowchart highlights the steps involved in market research and new product development, from the initial idea through to the final launch and continuous research.

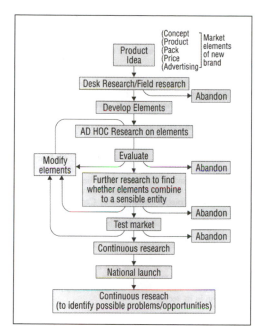

Reproduced courtesy of Cadbury Ltd

VISUAL PLANNING BOARDS

Visual planning boards can be built up to show virtually any information – from a simple plan showing staff holidays to a complex plan showing activities of a company over a 12-month period, featuring a number of variables. Visual planning boards offer flexibility and ease of updating. They enable future trends to be plotted, changes to be foreseen and realistic forward planning to be made. Many visual planning boards are available, from simple paper charts to sophisticated magnetic wall boards using shapes, strips and symbols.

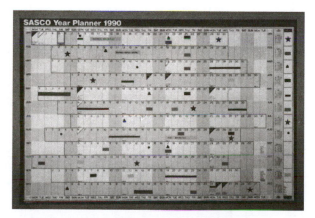

Reproduced courtesy of Acco UK Limited

COMPUTER GRAPHICS

Most managers are very busy and they welcome information being presented to them in the form of high quality graphics – as charts, graphs, maps, coloured tables, and so on. These are visually attractive and easily interpreted.

The use of graphics application software packages has increased rapidly over recent years, enabling users to present data easily and quickly in any graphics format.

It will be advantageous for anyone working in the business world today to become familiar with the range of graphics software. This will become part of your own 'package' to offer future employers.

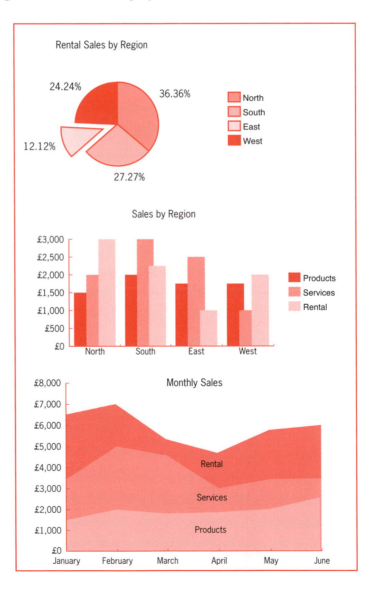

A–Z OF BLOOPERS AND BLUNDERS, COMMON ERRORS AND CLICHÉS: S

Said

'Said' was used by great-grandfather instead of 'above-mentioned'. The 'above mentioned conference…,' 'the said invoice…'. Just like 'above-mentioned', we should not use 'said' in this context today.

Send/take

If you 'send' your children to school in the morning, you do not go with them. If you mean that you drive them or walk them to school, then you should use the word 'take'. Use *take* when you are going to hand something to someone, or when you are asking someone to do the delivery. For example:

Please send your report by e-mail before Friday.
Will you please take me to the airport on Monday?
I must take these flowers to Mandy in hospital.
Please take this form to John in Accounts.

NB: See also Bring/fetch

Should

Phrases beginning with 'Should' are old-fashioned. Use 'If' instead. For example:

If you have any questions, please give me a call on xxxxx.

Sometimes, sometime, some time

Sometimes means occasionally. *Sometime* means at an indefinite time.
Some time means a period of time. For example:

Do you have some time tomorrow to discuss this report?
Sometimes it's easy to decide which word to use. Other times it's hard.
I hope we can meet sometime soon to discuss this.
Let me know when you have some time free for a meeting.

Stay

We use 'stay' for short periods only. for example, 'I am staying at the Oberoi Hotel when I visit Singapore'. If you live somewhere, that's the word you should use for example, 'I live in Holland Village, Singapore'.

IN THE BIN: S

seemingly
seems to indicate
somewhat
sort of
such

TEST YOURSELF

1   You work for Collectibles plc, a company that deals with anything people collect –
    autographs, model cars, dolls, stamps, etc. Study these pages from your collectibles
    catalogue and then answer the following questions. (LCCIEB EFB1 style)

STAMPS AND COVERS

Item	Ref	Very good	Good	Poor
Penny Black	SPB	£1000	£700	£200
Penny Black Cover	SPBC	£2000	£1000	£500
Twopenny Blue	STB	£600	£400	£100
Victoria Jubilee	SVJ	£100	£60	£25
Seahorses Set	SSHS	£450	£300	£125
Seahorses Cover	SSHC	£600	£400	N/A
George V Jubilee	SGVJ	£200	£100	£50
Edward VIII Set	SEE	£40	£20	N/A
George VI Coronation	SGC	£50	£30	£10
George VI Silver Wedding	SGSW	£300	£200	£60

AUTOGRAPHS

	Ref	Personalised	Photograph	Plain
Frank Sinatra	AFS	£500	£300	£100
Elvis Presley	AEP	£2000	£1000	£300
The Beatles	ATB	£4000	£2000	£600
Marilyn Monroe	AMM	£2000	£1800	£400
Martin Luther King	AXK	£500	£100	£50
Nelson Mandela	ANM	£750	£400	£100
Laurence Olivier	ALO	£1000	£600	£200
Laurel & Hardy	ALH	£650	£300	£100
Mike Tyson	AMT	£175	£125	£60
Harry Houdini	AHH	£2000	£1000	£250

POSTCARDS

Type	Ref	Posted	Unposted	Poor
Seaside Views	PSV	£1	£2	–
Train Crashes	PTC	£5	£2	£1
Teddy Bears	PTB	£10	£20	£2
Father Christmas	PFC	£5	£10	£3
Trams	PT	£1	£2	-
Comic	PC	£2	£3	£1
Military	PM	£3	£5	£2
Birthday Cards	PBC	£10	£5	£1
Royalty	PR	£9	£3	£1
Film Stars	PFS	£3	£5	£1

1   What is the price of item SSHC in good condition?   ....

2   What is the reference for Mike Tyson's autograph?   ....

3   How much would you pay for a Teddy Bear postcard
    in poor condition?   ....

4   How much is a photograph/autograph of Marilyn Monroe?   ....

5   What is the cheapest price for a George VI Silver Wedding
    set of stamps and coins?   ....

6   To what does ATB refer?   ....

7   How much is an unposted Royalty card?   ....

8   Does the shop list more autographs than postcards?   ....

9   To what does SEE refer?   ....

10 How much is a plain autograph of Nelson Mandela?   ....

11 How much is a good set of the Victoria jubilee stamps?   ....

12 How much would you pay for a Teddy Bear card that
    had been posted?   ....

13 Is a plain Laurence Olivier autograph more expensive
    than a personalised Mike Tyson autograph?   ....

14 Which stamp would you pay £2000 for?   ....

15 Which postcard is the most expensive?   ....

16 How much is the cheapest item under ref SGVP?   ....

17 How much would you pay for a photograph/autograph
    of Frank Sinatra?   ....

18 To what does PC refer?   ....

19 Which postcard would cost you £9?   ....

20 How much would you pay for a personalised
    Beatles autograph?   ....

2   You work for Sporting Ventures plc. Your company owns five golf clubs in the South of England. Each of the golf clubs is named after a famous golfing professional – Faldo, Woods, Player, Nicklaus and Else. This table shows the features of each of these golf clubs. Use the information in the table to answer the following questions. (LCCIEB EFB1 style)

Club features	FALDO	WOODS	PLAYER	NICKLAUS	ELSE
Holes	18	18 + 9	18 + 18	18	18
Driving range/s	2	No	4	1	No
Tuition	£25 ph	£20 ph	£40 half day	£18 ph	None
Joining fees	£100	£150	£250	£125	£180
Car park spaces	100	200	345	80	50
Opening dates	March–October	All year	All year	February–September	April–September
Practice greens	Yes	No	Yes	No	No
Age limits	None	21+	18+	None	None
Floodlight putting	Yes	No	No	No	No
Licensed bar	Yes	Yes	Yes	No	No
Restaurant facilities	No	Yes	Yes	Yes	Small cafeteria
Changing rooms	Male	Male & female	Male & female	No	No
Buggy hire	£10 ph	£20 ph	£40 (3 hrs)	No	No
Visitor fees	£30 half day	£35 half day	£50 per day	£20 half day	No
Visitors	Weekdays only	Weekends only	Thursdays	Any time	No visitors
Insurance	£25 pa	Own scheme	Included in fee	£50 pa	£50 pa
Annual fee	£500	£500	£750	£350	£200
Professionals employed	1	1	3	2	1
Languages spoken	French Japanese	French Italian Japanese	German Japanese	German Italian	None
Shop hours	9–5.00	10–4.00	8–8.00	10–4.00	None

QUESTION   ANSWER

  1 Which club has most holes?

  2 How many clubs have more than one driving range?   ....

  3 Which club offers the cheapest tuition for one hour?   ....

  4 Which club does not offer any tuition?   ....

  5 Which club is the most expensive to join?   ....

  6 Which club is the cheapest to join?   ....

  7 How many clubs provide more than 60 parking spaces?   ....

  8 Which club has fewest parking spaces?   ....

  9 How many clubs are closed on 25 February   ....

10 How many clubs have practice greens?   ....

11 How many clubs do not accept 20-year-olds?   ....

12 Where could you practise putting at night?   ....

13 How many clubs do not have a licensed bar?   ....

14 How many clubs do not have a restaurant?   ....

15 How many clubs have no changing rooms for ladies?   ....

16 Which club charges the most for a buggy for three hours?   ....

17 How many shops are open at 9.30 a.m.?   ....

18 How many clubs do not have an age limit?   ....

19 How many clubs accept visitors on a Friday?   ....

20 Which club offers a visitor the cheapest rate for a full day?   ....

21 How many clubs charge a specific sum for insurance?   ....

22 How many clubs charge more than £400 for their annual fee?   ....

23 How many clubs employ fewer than three professionals?   ....

24 Which foreign language is most readily available?   ....

25 Which club(s) would be most suitable for a 17-year-old German speaker?   ....

3 These three pie charts show the breakdown of season ticket holders for a particular football club over three years. The charts indicate the proportions of men, women, under-16s and over-65s. Study the charts and answer the questions that follow:

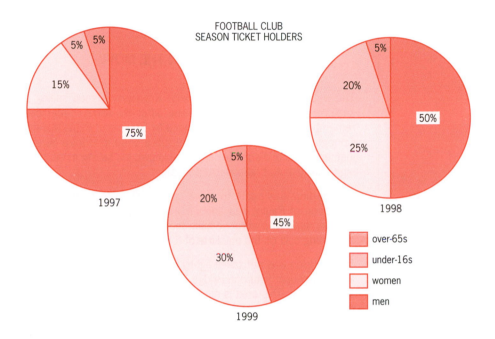

FOOTBALL CLUB
SEASON TICKET HOLDERS

1997 — 5%, 5%, 15%, 75%

1998 — 5%, 20%, 25%, 50%

1999 — 5%, 20%, 30%, 45%

over-65s
under-16s
women
men

1 Less than _____ the total season ticket holders in 1999 were males.

2 In 1998 the relationship of male to female supporters was _____

3 In 1998 and 1999 there were _____ numbers of under 16s and over 65 season ticket holders _____.

4 From 1997 to 1999 the percentage of women season ticket holders _____.

5 The number of male season ticket holders has _____ every year.

6 The number of women season ticket holders has _____ every year.

7 The number of over 65 season ticket holders has _____ every year.

8 The number of under 16 season ticket holders has _____ since 1997.

9 If this trend continues, in the year 2000 there may be almost an _____ number of male and female supporters.

10 Draw a graph to show the changing patterns in season ticket holders.

11 Prepare a series of bar charts to show the same information.

12 Which form of presentation, if any, do you consider is more effective in this case?

4 Read carefully the announcement *On the Move* below, then say whether the statements following are *True* or *False*. Then *quote* the words or phrases from the passage that support you answer. Do not write more than 6 supporting words for each answer. You will lose marks if you write more than this. (LCCIEB EFB1 style)

ON THE MOVE

The well known company, *Marinello Brothers*, a shop selling good quality boots, shoes and other footwear, is moving, after 60 years. Older people in the area will remember that the shop was founded by Bruno and Paulo Marinello, who come from Conegliano in North Italy. They set up a shop in Bridge Street to sell shoes and leather goods and soon became well known for selling items that were stylish and of high quality, but at reasonable prices.

But the time has come to move on. The shop manager, Michael Marinello, great-grandson of Paulo, has announced that *Marinello Brothers* will move in three months' time to a purpose-built shop in the Falcon Centre, the shopping precinct now being built on the outskirts of town.

The decision was not taken lightly by Mr Marinello. 'We know that our shop is seen as a permanent fixture in Bridge Street. We have done well for 60 years, but things are changing. This area is now better known for bars and restaurants. People come to Bridge Street for night-life and entertainment. Most of the major stores will be in the Falcon Centre, so that is where we must be now. The Falcon Centre will be the major bus and train terminus for the town and there will be 10,000 free car-parking spaces. Car parking is a major problem in Bridge Street, where it is difficult to find and expensive.'

Today most shoppers in town were sorry to hear the news. 'Bridge Street without *Marinello Brothers* will not be the same', was a typical comment. But other people welcomed the move, and we should remember that the Falcon Centre will be an attractive indoor precinct with a great range of shops. Indeed, the news that Marinello Brothers are to relocate will surely help to attract other stores.

We know that *Marinello Brothers* will continue to be the store that makes sure that local people – men, women and children – can wear top quality, stylish shoes.

ON THE MOVE

Write your answers on the line marked A

1   *Marinello Brothers* is famous in the area.
A   _____

2   The original Marinello Brothers were Italian.
A   _____

3   *Marinello Brothers* have moved.
A   _____

4   It was an easy decision to take to move.
A   _____

5   People think of Bridge Street mainly as a shopping area.
A   _____

6   People will be able to travel easily by public transport.
A   _____

7   Car parking is plentiful and free in Bridge Street.
A   _____

8   Most shoppers welcomed the announcement to move.
A   _____

9   The Falcon Centre will be a covered shopping area.
A   _____

10 *Marinello Brothers* only sells ladies' shoes.
A   _____

Example:

Statement: *Marinello Brothers'* shoes are expensive.
Answer: *False* – reasonable prices

5   You work for a large company. You have been asked to check how many people who work for the company are *First Aiders* (that is, they have a First Aid Certificate) and how many of these have been trained how to use the Fire Equipment.

Task

Look at the information in the table below and then answer the questions that follow.

Write your answers in the answer column, as a single word, a name, or a figure. (LCCIEB EFB1 style)

FIRST AIDERS – STAFF WHO HAVE A FIRST AID CERTIFICATE

Name of member of staff (First Aider)	Department	Number of staff in department	Age	How long First Aid Certificate held	Trained how to use fire equipment?
Mr John Lane	Finance	24	61	5 years	Yes
Ms Yvonne Kramer	Marketing	9	28	1 year	No
Ms Anne Brunner	Administration	28	53	4 years	No
Mr Tomasz Pilenski	Administration	28	48	3 years	Yes
Mr Deming Cheng	Finance	24	29	4 years	No
Miss Julie Kay	Human Resources	8	31	2 years	Yes
Ms Gerald Larek	Sales	14	35	1 year	No
Ms Ingrid Paulson	Finance	24	40	3 years	Yes
Mr Inderjit Singh	Marketing	9	35	3 years	Yes
Mr Joshua Masenda	Customer Service	6	53	4 years	Yes

Answers

1 Who is the oldest person with a First Aid Certificate?   ....

2 How many people in the Administration Department are First Aiders?   ....

3 Who has been a First Aider for 2 years?   ....

4 Which department has the most First Aiders?   ....

5 Who is the youngest man with a First Aid Certificate?   ....

6 Has the First Aider from Human Resources been trained to use Fire Equipment?   ....

7 Which male First Aider is 35-years-old and works in the Marketing Department?   ....

8 How many people gained the First Aid Certificate *more than* 3 years ago?   ....

9 Is Ms Ingrid Paulson younger than Miss Julie Kay?   ....

10 In which Department has no one trained how to use the Fire Equipment?   ....

11 Which First Aider works in Administration and is 48-years-old?   ....

12 How many First Aiders are women?   ....

13 Which female First Aider is in the Administration Department?   ....

14 Which department has the most members of staff?   ....

15 Are Mr John Lane and Ms Ingrid Paulson from the same department?   ....

16 How many years has the youngest female First Aider held a certificate?   ....

17 Who has held a First Aid Certificate for 4 years and is also trained in how to use Fire Equipment?   ....

18 In which department is the male First Aider who has held a First Aid Ceriticate for the **shortest** time?   ....

19 How many First Aiders have **NOT** been trained in the use of Fire Equipment?   ....

20 Does the department with the *fewest* staff have a First Aider who is over 50 years of age?   ....

6   Next month the company you work for is holding a conference at the *Gourmet Hotel*. The hotel has given you some information about the 6 conference rooms to help you decide which one to use. The table below shows this information, including which member of the hotel's staff supervises each room.

Task

Look at the information in the table, then answer the questions that appear after the table. Write your answer in the answer column as a single word, a name or a figure. (LCCIEB EFB1 style)

Conference Rooms in the Gourmet Hotel

Room name	Size of room (number of guests it can accommodate)	Name of supervisor of room	Equipment in room	Tea/coffee Machine
Pisces	40	James	Audio-visual equipment, whiteboard	Yes
Capricorn	100	Tracey	Audio-visual equipment, computer, whiteboard	Yes
Libra	20	Irena	Whiteboard	No
Gemini	30	James	Computer, whiteboard	No
Aries	40	Irena	Computer, whiteboard	Yes
Taurus	60	Claude	Audio-visual equipment, computer, whiteboard	Yes

Answers

1 Which room can accommodate the largest number of guests? ....

2 Does the smallest room have a computer? ....

3 How many rooms have a tea/coffee machine? ....

4 Which room can take 40 guests and has audio-visual equipment? ....

5 Which member of staff supervises the smallest room? ....

6 How many rooms can accommodate more than 50 guests? ....

7 Which member of staff supervises 2 rooms with a total of 70 guests? ....

8 Are there any rooms without a whiteboard? ....

9 Which is the smallest room with audio-visual equipment, a computer and a whiteboard? ....

10 Which other room is supervised by the member of staff who supervises the Aries room? ....

11 How many guests can Claude's room accommodate? ....

12 Which room with *only* a computer and a whiteboard is the largest? ....

13 How many guests can be accommodated in *all* the rooms with computers? ....

14 Who supervises the largest room *without* a tea and coffee machine? ....

15 What equipment is in *both* the largest and the smallest room? ....

16 How many of the rooms supervised by Irena have a tea and coffee machine? ....

17 Which room takes 30 guests and is supervised by James? ....

18 Which is the largest room that Irena supervises that has a tea and coffee machine? ....

19 How many staff supervise only 1 room? ....

20 'The Gemini Room is the largest room supervised by James.' Is this statement true or false? ....

Unit 17

Reformulating and summarising

LEARNING OUTCOMES

After studying this unit you should be able to:

- complete 'look and write' production tasks involving labelling a diagram, form or flow chart

- complete 'reformulation' tasks involving expanding, reducing or selectively rewriting a passage of English for a specific purpose

- use summarising skills effectively

- produce a business summary from a given passage of English

- produce a summary in the form of a list

WHAT IS A SUMMARY?

To make a summary means to convey all or most of a section of text using a reduced number of words. We use summarising skills all the time in response to questions like 'What did you do last night?' or 'So how was your holiday?' This is usually done orally instead of in writing.

The written summary will not be new to you. It is something most of us have done throughout our school days. However, it is very rare in business to be asked to do a straightforward continuous prose summary. Summaries in business may be written in the form of an advertisement or notice, an article for the staff newsletter, a handout for issue to trainees. These are all exercises in summarising, picking out relevant and important information and then presenting it in an appropriate manner.

It is to this type of more realistic exercise which many examiners are now turning in order to provide realistic tasks which an employee may very well be asked to perform in the business world. This type of 'business summary' will be discussed in more detail later.

USING SYNONYMS

When summarising or reformulating you may be expected to use your own words as far as possible, instead of quoting huge chunks of the original passage. This exercise is designed to give you practice in choosing synonyms for words.

Provide synonyms for each of the following words (remember that very often more than one word could be used):

1	huge	_____	
2	afraid	_____	
3	regularly	_____	
4	retain	_____	
5	impression	_____	
6	accurate	_____	
7	honesty	_____	
8	specimen	_____	
9	common	_____	
10	immune	_____	

11	certain	_____
12	vital	_____
13	price	_____
14	desire	_____
15	apparent	_____
16	inquisition	_____
17	objective	_____
18	reluctant	_____
19	inadequate	_____
20	terminate	_____

REDUCING PHRASES

There are many expressions in the English language that are long-winded and could be expressed in a simpler or shorter way. This exercise will help you be aware of such expressions and spot them, and others like them, when summarising.

Reduce the expressions shown without changing the meanings. Use the number of words shown in brackets:

1 in the near future (1)   _____
2 it appears that (1)   _____
3 put up with (1)   _____
4 the same amount of (1)   _____
5 in modern times (1)   _____
6 as a result   _____
7 because of this (1)   _____
8 always bear in mind (1)   _____
9 a lot of   _____
10 at all times (1)   _____
11 at the beginning of each day (2)   _____
12 owned by private individuals (2)   _____
13 equipment should be checked (2)   _____
14 make a record of all appointments (3) _____
15 on the day of the interview (3)   _____

ONE WORD FOR MANY

Summarising means saying the same thing but in not so many words. In these sentences replace the section in italics by providing just one word.

1 When the meeting is over, you must produce the *accurate transcript of the main discussions which took place and the decisions made.*   _____

2 She's not interested in work – only in *tennis, swimming, hockey, golf – anything requiring physical activity.*   _____

3 The next meeting of the Board is coming up soon. I must prepare the *list of items to be discussed at the meeting.*   _____

4 The *person who greets visitors to an organisation* must portray a good impression.   _____

5 When goods have been purchased, it is usual to send out an *itemised statement informing the buyer of the quantity, description and price of the goods which were bought.*   _____

6 We must send out a *document to all the customers on our mailing list.*   _____

7   This is a *list of all the duties which the employee may be required to perform.* (2 words)

    _____

8   Some job advertisements require applicants to send a *separate schedule showing their education, qualifications, employment history and other personal details* when applying for jobs. (2 words)

    _____

RETAIN OR REMOVE?

Summarising anything requires the ability to find and remove unimportant details or, more to the point, choose which details should be retained. A lot of information that can be removed from summarising exercises can be categorised, e.g. examples, definitions, additions and rephrasing. 'Clues' are often given in such cases, as shown below.

Categories	*Clues*
1 Examples	'For example…'
	'…, e.g.…'
2 Definitions	'This is…'
	'This means…'
3 Rephrasing	'In other words…'
	'That is…'
	'…, i.e.…'
4 Additions	'…, especially…'
	'…, particularly…'

Example: (the information to be removed has been italicised)
It has been argued, (1) *especially in recent years*, that an examination summary is not a realistic exercise, (2) i.e. *not the type of summary one is required to do in the business world*.

Number 1:   Why should it be removed? (addition)
               What was the clue given? (especially)

Number 2:   Why should it be removed? (rephrasing)
               What was the clue given? (i.e.)

The sentences below all contain some information which should be removed from a summary – examples, definitions, rephrasing or additions. Highlight the details which should be *retained*, and state the reason why the rest should be *removed*, together with the *clue* given.

1 An essential part of any documentary evidence, for example letters, invoices, orders, is that it should have the names and the addresses of both parties to the correspondence.

Reason?   _____

Clue?   _____

2 References often include departments and file numbers, especially in correspondence with government departments.

Reason?   _____

Clue?   _____

3 All business documents should be grammatically correct, i.e. they should contain no errors in grammar, spelling or punctuation.

Reason?   _____

Clue?   _____

4 It is becoming popular for larger organisations to use a 'house style' for their correspondence. This means all typists and secretaries present correspondence in the same, standardised formats.

Reason?   _____

Clue?   _____

5 Business letters should be free of slang and other colloquialisms, i.e. expressions used only in conversation.

Reason?   _____

Clue?   _____

6 Some circular letters are unsolicited. This means the recipients have no particular interest in the message.

Reason?   _____

Clue?   _____

7 It is important to retain grammatical precision when writing business documents. In other words, all sentences in a series should consistently follow the same grammatical pattern.

Reason?   _____

Clue?   _____

8 Many companies, particularly the larger ones, are turning more and more to computerisation of their clerical procedures.

Reason?   _____

Clue?   _____

9 A quorum must usually be present at formal meetings, e.g. Annual General Meetings, meetings of shareholders.

Reason?   _____

Clue?   _____

10 Certain items appear on the agenda of many regular meetings, e.g. any other business and date of next meeting.

Reason?   _____

Clue?   _____

REMOVING REASONS

Read the following passage and use it to complete the table below:

In the name of safety, gangways between desks should not be blocked with boxes, files or wastebins as employees may trip over them causing injury. Filing cabinet drawers should be closed immediately after use, or the cabinet may become unbalanced and topple over. Torn or frayed floorcovering could cause a person to fall, so it should be repaired or replaced. Office doors should be locked and windows secured at the end of the day. This will prevent burglars from breaking in. To avoid a fire hazard electrical appliances should be unplugged and switched off at the end of each day.

SAFETY PRECAUTION	REASON
1 Do not block gangways between desks with boxes, files or wastebins.	_____
2 _____	_____
3 _____	_____
4 _____	_____
5 _____	_____

NB: Retain consistency of expression by using verbs at the start of each item in column one.

COUNTING THE WORDS

Summary assignments normally state the number of words to be used. This will usually be expressed in one of two ways:

1 *Use no more than 160 words*
In this case, do not exceed 160 words. 150–160 will normally be accepted, but anything less than 155 will be penalised.

2 *Use approximately 160 words*
Here, 155–165 will not be penalised.

What to count

When counting the number of words used, do not count the words in the heading or any numbers used in your display. Sub-headings, however, should be included in your word count.

Will the examiner check?

An examiner with many scripts to mark will know approximately how much space your summary should take up on your answer sheet. He/she will be able to see if yours looks too long or too short.

If you indicate that you have used the precise number of words instructed (perhaps a white lie?) then the examiner may just spot that it looks too long or too short, and will double-check.

If you do not indicate the number of words used, you will also be penalised.

The best option is to try to stick within the word limit and always include it at the end in brackets.

GUIDELINES FOR WRITING SUMMARIES

1   Read the instructions carefully and determine what is required in your summary. Maybe only a certain theme from the passage needs to be picked out, or perhaps it should all be summarised. Whatever, many students produce very good summaries, but lose marks because they have not done what the instructions requested.

2   Read the passage through carefully twice – the importance of this reading period cannot be over-emphasised. You really need to 'think yourself into the theme' of the passage and ensure a complete grasp of the topic before continuing.

3   After checking the instructions again, go through the passage highlighting the information which should be included in your summary.

4   Re-check what you have highlighted in case you have missed something or highlighted something incorrectly.

5   Make a rough draft from your highlighting, using your own words and avoiding the language of the original passage wherever possible.

6   Check your draft carefully against the original, making sure that you have not left out anything of importance, or added anything which is not relevant.

7   Write out the summary in its final form. Take every possible opportunity to rephrase in an attempt to cut down on the number of words used.

8   Count the words used, and if necessary make some more amendments to keep within the limit prescribed.

9   Read your summary through carefully to check for grammatical, punctuation or spelling errors.

BUSINESS SUMMARIES

The summaries we have looked at so far have been 'continuous prose', i.e. a straightforward paragraph or two. However, the recent trend is towards realistic summaries, summaries to suit a specific purpose. Virtually any type of presentation could, therefore, be required. It is important that the instructions are studied carefully so that you pick out only the information required in your summary, and that you display it appropriately.

These follow some examples of different types of business summaries which you could be asked to produce.

Advertisement/notice

Obviously an advertisement or notice should be presented suitably. Items should be centred to attract attention. Perhaps points can be listed, with subheadings. Use capitals and underscoring to add to effect.

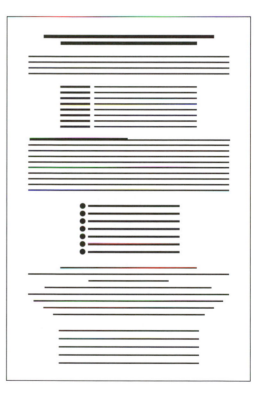

Checklist

Enumeration is required in any checklist. Perhaps an introduction is necessary also. Take care with consistency of expression, so that all points on the checklist follow the rule of grammatical parallelism. (A useful word-saving ploy here is to use verbs at the start of each point.)

Handout/information sheet

Sub-headings may be appropriate, as well as numbered points. Again, take care with consistency of expression

Notes for a speech

For reference when making a speech, again enumeration would probably be easier to follow, perhaps also with subheadings for different aspects of the main theme.

NB: There can be no hard and fast rule to say 'Oh it's a handout – I must do it like this', or whatever. The instructions will tell you for what purpose your summary is to be used. After reading the passage carefully, and double-checking the instructions, careful thought should be given to using the most suitable format.

Covering memo

When instructed to compose a business summary of the type discussed, it may be relevant for a covering memo to be written to the person who requested it. Your memo should be short and state the source of the material which has been used. For example:

```
SAFETY IN THE OFFICE

As requested, I have made a summary of the article that appeared
in the May edition of 'Business Digest' for its inclusion in the
next issue of the staff newsletter.

I hope you find this satisfactory.

Enc
```

A worked example of a business summary

As with any assignment, it must be remembered that no two people will produce identical summaries, yet many could be suitable for the purpose intended. However, this worked example of a business summary is given to illustrate the principles and procedures involved in effective summarising.

Step 1

Read the instructions carefully, marking the important points.

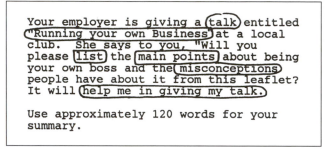

```
Your employer is giving a talk entitled
"Running your own Business" at a local
club.  She says to you, "Will you
please list the main points about being
your own boss and the misconceptions
people have about it from this leaflet?
It will help me in giving my talk."

Use approximately 120 words for your
summary.
```

Step 2

Consider a suitable format. Your summary is to be used by your employer as reference when giving a talk about 'Running Your Own Business'. Your employer stresses she wants a list of the 'main points' as well as 'misconceptions'. These two terms give you a clue as to sub-headings which could be used. Also important here is the word 'list' – obviously your employer does not want to read from a script, so continuous prose will not be suitable. A list will be easy to refer to, and your employer will be able to expand on each point, thus making her talk sound very natural.

Step 3

Read the passage carefully several times, highlighting the important points.

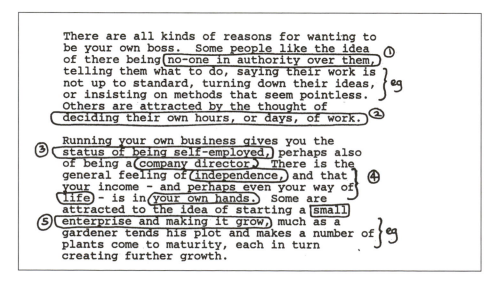

```
There are all kinds of reasons for wanting to
be your own boss.  Some people like the idea      ①
of there being no-one in authority over them,
telling them what to do, saying their work is
not up to standard, turning down their ideas,     eg
or insisting on methods that seem pointless.
Others are attracted by the thought of
deciding their own hours, or days, of work.       ②

    Running your own business gives you the
③  status of being self-employed, perhaps also
    of being a company director.  There is the
    general feeling of independence, and that      ④
    your income - and perhaps even your way of
    life - is in your own hands.  Some are
    attracted to the idea of starting a small
⑤  enterprise and making it grow, much as a
    gardener tends his plot and makes a number of  eg
    plants come to maturity, each in turn
    creating further growth.
```

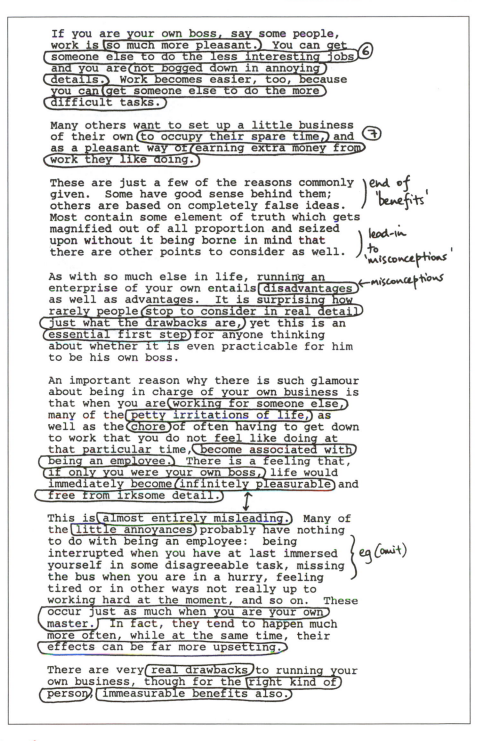

If you are your own boss, say some people, work is so much more pleasant. You can get someone else to do the less interesting jobs and you are not bogged down in annoying details. Work becomes easier, too, because you can get someone else to do the more difficult tasks. ⑥

Many others want to set up a little business of their own to occupy their spare time, and as a pleasant way of earning extra money from work they like doing. ⑦

These are just a few of the reasons commonly given. Some have good sense behind them; others are based on completely false ideas. Most contain some element of truth which gets magnified out of all proportion and seized upon without it being borne in mind that there are other points to consider as well. 〉 end of 'benefits' 〉 lead-in to 'misconceptions'

As with so much else in life, running an enterprise of your own entails disadvantages ← misconceptions as well as advantages. It is surprising how rarely people stop to consider in real detail just what the drawbacks are, yet this is an essential first step for anyone thinking about whether it is even practicable for him to be his own boss.

An important reason why there is such glamour about being in charge of your own business is that when you are working for someone else, many of the petty irritations of life, as well as the chore of often having to get down to work that you do not feel like doing at that particular time, become associated with being an employee. There is a feeling that, if only you were your own boss, life would immediately become infinitely pleasurable and free from irksome detail.

This is almost entirely misleading. Many of the little annoyances probably have nothing to do with being an employee: being interrupted when you have at last immersed yourself in some disagreeable task, missing the bus when you are in a hurry, feeling tired or in other ways not really up to working hard at the moment, and so on. These occur just as much when you are your own master. In fact, they tend to happen much more often, while at the same time, their effects can be far more upsetting. 〉 eg (omit)

There are very real drawbacks to running your own business, though for the right kind of person, immeasurable benefits also.

Step 4

Produce a rough draft or notes from the original, referring to the instructions again to ensure you are picking out what is required.

Step 5

Go through your draft/notes and make marginal notes regarding amendments/
synonyms/rephrasing. Remember that your summary should be expressed in your
own words wherever possible.

MAIN POINTS *(Benefits)*

- No-one to give you instructions *(answer to no one)*

- Choose own hours/working arrangements } *link?*

- Self-employed status - director? *accountable?*

- Independent, responsible for own
  income/life *self-reliant?*   *company/business*

- Satisfaction from seeing enterprise
  grow   *pleasure*   *simple?*

- Less interesting work - other people
  also more difficult work *laborious?* } *Delegation!*

- Business occupies spare time - earn *create income*
  money too.

MISCONCEPTIONS

vital

Few consider all details - essential first
step.

Being the boss seems glamourous - thinking
that life would be better if no mundane
chores, no annoyances, like employees -
wrong!   *annoyances*

Irritations also when you are boss - more
often? Effects more upsetting!   *far-reaching?*

CONCLUSION *consequences*   *disagreeable?*

Consider drawbacks carefully. *(disadvantages)*
If right for you - immeasurable benefits.
   limitless/
   countless?   *rewards?*

Step 6

Produce your final summary by linking up the notes into full sentences. Count the
words. If necessary, make further amendments. Make sure your summary reads
smoothly and is correct in spelling and punctuation. Finally, ask yourself if your
summary is a satisfactory condensed version of the original, and also if your
summary could be used for the purpose mentioned in the instructions.

Step 7

Don't forget to produce a brief covering memo for summaries of this nature.

```
M E M O R A N D U M

To      Mrs Eileen Starr, Managing Director

From    Sharon Tan

Ref     GS/ST

Date    12 July 200-


RUNNING YOUR OWN BUSINESS

I have summarised the leaflet you gave to me,
listing the main points about being your own
boss, together with misconceptions.  This is
attached.

I hope this helps you in giving your talk next
week.

Sharon

Enc
```

```
RUNNING YOUR OWN BUSINESS


BENEFITS

1   You have no-one to answer to, and have
    self-employed, maybe director, standing.

2   You make your own choices, including
    working hours.

3   You are self-reliant, accountable for
    your own income.

4   You obtain pleasure from seeing your
    company grow.

5   Delegation is possible - of the simple
    and the laborious jobs.

6   It can fill your spare time and create
    income from work you enjoy.
```

▶

```
MISCONCEPTIONS

1   Some do not consider the drawbacks - a
    vital preliminary step.

2   Some feel life would improve without
    the aggravations often encountered as an
    employee.

    However, most of such aggravations occur
    to employers as well as employees, but
    with more disagreeable consequences.

CONCLUSION

Consider the disadvantages carefully.
If it is for you, the rewards are
limitless.

(115 words)
```

A–Z OF BLOOPERS AND BLUNDERS, COMMON ERRORS AND CLICHÉS: T

That/which

'That' is a defining, or restrictive, pronoun. For example:

> The books that have blue covers are new.

This sentence implies that only the books with blue covers are new. The word 'that' restricts the sentence – it limits the books we are talking about.

'Which' is non-defining, or non-restrictive (and commas are needed). For example:

> The books, which have red covers, are new.

This sentence implies that all the books are new. The words 'which have red covers' are adding information about the books. They tell you more about the books than you would otherwise know.

In other words: Use 'which' (surrounded by commas) if a group of words adds information. Use 'that' if it restricts. For example:

> This is the house that Jack built.
> This house, which Jack built, is falling down.

Thank you in advance

A phrase like this, or 'Thanking you in anticipation', is unnecessary. They are from great-grandfather's era. Don't thank readers before they have done something. Wait until they have done it, then say thank you.

The fact that

We commonly hear or see 'Due to the fact that', 'Despite the fact that', 'In spite of the fact that', etc. These words are totally unnecessary and should not be used.

Time

It is never *12am* or *12pm*. It is either *noon* or *midnight*. It's either *3am* or it's *3 o'clock in the morning*. It is never *3am in the morning*.

Trust

Another great grandfather word that should not be used today. Use 'Please' instead. For example, instead of 'I trust that you will send me a copy of your new catalogue', say 'Please send me a copy of your new catalogue' or 'I hope to receive a copy of your new catalogue'.

IN THE BIN: T

take the liberty of
take this opportunity to
the above
the fact of the matter is
the month(s) of
the said
this is to inform you
to all intents and purposes
to tell you the truth
type of

TEST YOURSELF

1   As part of a college project, you have just interviewed Harold Weston, Course Director of Aurora Management Consultancy Group. The following is a verbatim record of the information he gave you in answer to your questions.

Use the information to complete the diagram.

I have overall responsibility for all the courses offered by the Aurora Management Consultancy Group. My three assistants are very valuable though – James Lee runs the part-time courses. Keith Chan is responsible for intensive courses and Rita Wong deals with in-company training.

The secretarial work is dealt with by Wendy Roberts – she reports to the Administration Manager, Yong Wai Kee. Wai Kee also supervises the Security Chief, Graham Voon.

The Chief Executive of the Group is Dr Dean Franks – he's quite a tough cookie, but I guess he has to be. His PA is Prema Viswanath and she seems to be able to handle him OK.

I suggest you should talk to Ganesh Karuppiah about marketing matters. He's in charge of that area. Individual areas are taken care of by Frank Dupont (Western Europe), Jim Smith (UK and Southern Europe) and there's also our new man Donnie McLellan in charge of Scotland and Northern Ireland.

Legal matters – you should talk to Sham Hassan – she's the Company Secretary as she's expert in all things legal.

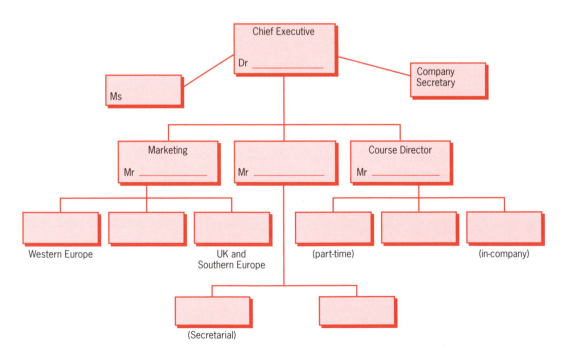

2 You work in the Travel Section at Minton Engineering Group, 46 Tower Avenue, Hong Kong, telephone 45223456. The Marketing Director, Ong Hee Huat, is going to Singapore on Wednesday 22 June. Study this note from him and complete the hotel booking form.

> *Thanks for booking my flight to Singapore. Please book me in at the Sheraton Towers – I'll check in as soon as I arrive (early) rather than go straight to our regional office.*
>
> *I'll stay in the hotel until Sunday morning – my friends will collect me and I'll stay at their home until I fly back here the following week.*
>
> *In the hotel I'll need space to work and entertain so please book an executive suite with sitting room.*

(LCCIEB EFB1 style)

HOTEL BOOKING FORM

Please complete in block capitals

City	
Hotel	
Guest	
Mr/Mrs/Miss/Other	
Company	
Address	
Telephone	
Arrival	
AM/PM	
No of nights	
Room	
Rate	
Date	

3   You work for Aurora Golf Clubs, a company that owns 5 golf clubs in England. On 29 May you answer a telephone call from Mr James Milton. Below are your notes of the telephone call. Use these notes to complete the standard complaint form.

> *Visited Player Golf Club yesterday at 9.00 am with 4 business colleagues.*
>
> *Difficult to find entrance as no sign on the main road.*
>
> *Many staff rude and unhelpful.*
>
> *Whole place untidy, even the greens. Two trees had fallen on the fairways – no attempt was made to remove them.*
>
> *Hired a set of clubs – 2 had damaged handles.*
>
> *Helped by very civil girl in Reception but would like to shoot the waiter!*
>
> *Restaurant cold and food unappetising.*
>
> *Unlikely to visit again.*
>
> *Colleagues found the club expensive and poor quality.*
>
> *Mr Milton's tel no: 0208 330 2349*

(LCCIEB EFB1 style)

AURORA GOLF CLUBS
COMPLAINT FORM

Name ....   Tel No ....

Date of visit ....   Time ....

Club visited ....

1 General comments

    Reception area ....

    Reception staff ....

2 Equipment

    Equipment hired ....

    Condition ....

3 Course

    Comments on Fairways ....

    Comments on Greens ....

4 Restaurants

    Food ....

    Staff ....

Any other comments ....

....

....

Name of person recording complaint ....

Date ....

4   You are secretary to the Principal of a secretarial college and the Principal feels the following article contains useful points for students who will be leaving shortly, in preparing them for job interviews. Rewrite as a checklist for the Principal to issue to teachers for use in class discussion. Use no more than 70 words.

Interviews – experiences which some people love, and some hate. Whichever category you belong to, a few tips should be borne in mind to ensure interview success.

In nearly all meetings, the first impression is that which makes the strongest impact on new acquaintances, be they colleagues, friends or other associates. If that goes wrong, it may be impossible to correct. Secretaries are often seen as status symbols, so an employer would prefer a smart and presentable person to fulfil this role. Not many employers would be impressed by a provocative evening-type dress and hair tossed seductively, and it certainly would not be everyday office attire, so plan your wardrobe carefully. Personal freshness is also important, particularly when under stress. You must consider the effect you may have on the people around you. If you have ever stood next to someone on a bus whose personal 'aura' makes you rush to get off before your stop, then you know what I mean. Give your teeth a good going-over too, to make sure they sparkle and that your breath smells fresh. Long tapering nails also wouldn't be able to whizz across a keyboard if you are asked to do a typing test, so give yourself a good manicure and ensure your nails are attractive.

The evening before the interview, get all your clothes ready so as to avoid a panic and not being able to decide what to wear. Make sure your hair is clean and shining too. A rumbling tummy is a sure sign of nerves, so avoid embarrassment by having a hearty breakfast. Nerves can often make your nose run too, for no apparent reason, so be sure to carry tissues. If you are wearing tights, make sure you carry a spare pair in case you damage them on the way to the interview.

Before you walk into the interview room, take a few deep breaths to calm your nerves – always a useful calming technique. And when you walk in, smile! Don't get carried away so that your smile looks forced, but be as natural as you can. Be friendly in the interview itself, and it will make it easy for the interviewer to conduct the interview. However nervous you feel, sit in as relaxed a manner as you can, and don't keep twitching nervously, with your fingers, with the strap of your handbag, with your skirt hem, or whatever. Look at the interviewer directly and don't avoid eye contact or it will not give a good impression. When answering questions, avoid using 'yes' or 'no' – they tell an interviewer absolutely nothing and result in a very dull interview. Try to answer as fully as possible, without going off the mark.

Remember that the aim of an interview is to allow the interviewer(s) and the interviewee to get to know each other in a short space of time in order to decide quickly if it would be possible to work together. It is not intended to be like entering the torture chamber. Relax – and try to enjoy it!

5   All the secretaries in your organisation use audio transcription, as the employers prefer not to use shorthand dictation. In informal talks with many secretaries personally, you know there is a considerable amount of frustration because of poor audio dictation technique by their employers. You recently came across the following article in a secretarial magazine, and feel it includes helpful advice for employers on effective audio dictation techniques. You decide to summarise it as a checklist for employers to follow when dictating, and to send it to the editor of the staff magazine asking him to consider it for inclusion in the next issue. Use approximately 100 words.

Using dictation machines saves considerable time, as the secretary does not need to be present, thus it leaves the secretary free to deal with her other responsibilities while the boss dictates his correspondence. But how many secretaries out there continually bang your head against the office wall in frustration because the boss has coughed loudly in your ear? Does your boss mumble, talk too loudly occasionally and then almost whisper? How many times have you rewound and listened to an unfamiliar word 20 times and just wished the boss had the sense to spell it out?

Well maybe your boss is an admirable Accountant or a marvellous MD, but good dictation technique requires considerable practice. I hope this advice will be helpful – perhaps you can casually put it on your boss's desk with his coffee in the morning, but don't admit where it came from of course!

Before starting dictation, it is essential to be organised. All the necessary papers should be to hand. Otherwise you'll get frustrated and start scrambling about in the midst of dictation and it will be especially infuriating for your secretary if you forget to switch off the mike during this process!

Interruptions will affect your train of thought during the dictation so try to time your recording when you know you have some time free and do it in a room which is free from noise.

Once these preparations have been made, you're off. Before starting dictation on each piece of correspondence, do state the exact nature of the document, e.g. 'short letter', 'long report', etc. Also give an indication of the number of copies which will be required. This type of information is invaluable to your secretary as to the correspondence to be transcribed.

As for the dictation – the microphone is not a lollipop, so don't try to eat it! Hold it two or three inches away from your mouth. If you hold it too close, your speech will be blurred; too far away and you won't be heard at all. Don't mumble into the mike, but try to ensure your speech is clear. And please don't go like a bull at a gate – a secretary will not thank you if you dictate at 50 miles an hour!

When you have dictated the first sentence or so, listen to it again by playing back the recording, so that you can make any necessary adjustments – the sound may be too high or too low, so it's much better to correct it at this point than deafen your secretary later!

If the volume's OK, then go ahead. We all need to pause for thought now and again, so when you find it necessary to do so, or when the phone rings, remember to switch off the mike. Your secretary doesn't want to listen to a few minutes of nothing, or to a conversation with your wife about what's for dinner!

Wherever you can, try to include a mention of new paragraphs, and give clear instructions to your secretary regarding headings and any items which need to be numbered.

Your secretary will also need to clarify things with you every few minutes if you don't spell out personal names, place names, foreign names – anything which she may be unfamiliar with. Numbers too – prices, sums of money, percentages, etc.

When you've successfully reached the end of a document, mark the length of the document on the index slip – this will be a valuable reference tool for your secretary on the size of paper to use for the correspondence.

Finally, make sure you keep any letters, memos, reports, files and other relevant documents connected with the dictation in a special pile, and pass all this to your secretary with the recording. In this way all the information she needs will be just where she can find it, and she won't need to bother you with queries.

If you follow the above advice, it should save your secretary much frustration – and a happier secretary makes your life easier too, doesn't it?

Happy dictating!

6   You have been asked to give a talk at a secretarial seminar on the secretary's duties in connection with meetings, and the text of your speech is printed below. You have also been asked for a one-page summary of your speech for inclusion in the seminar booklet which delegates will keep for future reference. Using an appropriate format make your summary in not more than 150 words.

Meetings form an essential part of business life and, as secretaries, our role is to ensure that they are organised and administered efficiently, and that all the paperwork is dealt with correctly. I would like to talk to you today on the various things we have to think about when preparing for meetings, and the documentation involved.

Once it has been agreed that the meeting will take place on a particular day there are many practical tasks you should attend to. First of all make sure you enter the date of the meeting in your boss's diary and your own. This will, of course, avoid the risk of a clash of appointments at a later date. Then check the venue for the meeting, and if there is a regular room make sure it is available. This may be the company's own board room, or in the case of a departmental meeting perhaps you will use the manager's office. You then need to prepare and circulate the notice of meeting and agenda. If you will turn to page 41 of your seminar booklet you will see examples of the wording and layout of the notice and agenda.

(NB: Discuss from examples printed in seminar booklet page 41.)

Any additional documents for distribution, such as reports, statistics, etc., should be circulated with the notice and agenda, so that members may become thoroughly familiar with their contents prior to the meeting. Remember also to make additional sets of such documents – isn't it always the case that someone forgets to bring their copies on the day of the meeting, and we end up having to get extra copies for them at the last minute! If you take extra copies to start with, you will avoid this last-minute rush.

In consultation with your Chairman you should then produce a draft of the Chairman's agenda which he may amend as necessary. The Chairman's agenda is a little more detailed than the ordinary members' agenda. It is for use only by the Chairman, containing extra notes for his own reference in helping him to conduct the business of the meeting efficiently.

(NB: Discuss Chairman's agenda from page 42.)

So much for the preliminary documentation, what about other matters? If you have a regular caterer, a provisional order should be made for refreshments at this stage, which will be confirmed when the number of participants is known nearer the date.

Any equipment which may be required at the meeting should be arranged, including making sure any visual aids required will be available if necessary. (Does anyone require the overhead projector, spirit pens, video recorder, etc.?)

Place names should be prepared if these are needed to identify the participants at the meeting. Obviously these will not be necessary at a departmental meeting where everyone knows everyone else, but at more formal meetings they may be useful.

Once these provisional arrangements have been attended to, you can more or less relax until the day of the meeting itself. Then you will need to make sure everything is organised as efficiently as possible, using a bit of the foresight we are supposed to develop as secretaries. First of all arrange the meeting room, attending to such things as seating arrangements, water and glasses, writing paper and pencils, and ashtrays. Any documents to be used during the meeting should be laid out on the table. Spare copies of the agenda and minutes of the last meeting should be at hand, as well as the official minute book and any other reports which I mentioned earlier. You should also check that any equipment and accessories required are in the right place and in working order. You don't want your boss to switch on the OHP during the meeting only to find the bulb has blown, or for him to write on a transparency only to find the spirit pen has run out!

Next reconfirm that refreshments will be served at the appropriate time, and give any last-minute instructions regarding the number of members attending the meeting.

The switchboard and receptionist should also be given a list of participants at the meeting, together with instructions for diverting their calls as necessary. Perhaps a colleague will be called upon to take all calls, or the switchboard operator herself may be required to take messages. Whatever the arrangements, make sure the relevant people know what is required of them.

If you are attending the meeting as secretary, gather your own paperwork together with suitable materials to take down the minutes. Ensure that you have your own and your boss's diaries available to check details of appointments when future dates have to be arranged during the meeting. Finally place a 'meeting in progress' notice on the door. This will ensure no one walks in and disturbs the progress of the meeting. I will not mention anything about Minutes here because my colleague will be discussing that with you in detail later in the programme.

Arranging meetings can be a bit of a headache – collating all the reports and material for the meeting, making sure all the documentation is issued at the appropriate time, and all the various other matters which we have to attend to. But if you think them through logically, step-by-step, and use the summarised checklist which I have included in the seminar booklet, you can ensure that nothing is overlooked.

So whether you are organising your first meeting or your fiftieth, I wish you success.

Unit 18

Oral presentation skills

LEARNING OUTCOMES

After studying this unit you should be able to:

- Describe the steps involved in making a presentation

- Attract and keep an audience's attention

- Put forward ideas that flow naturally and develop as the presentation unfolds

- Vary the pace, pitch, stress, volume and tone of your voice

- Speak clearly

- Communicate in a non-verbal way

- Overcome anxiety and increase confidence in public speaking

- Create and take advantage of effective visual aids

- Deal with questions from the audience

- Manage the presentation

In the work environment, we make presentations all the time. It is another form of communication. To all of us in the workplace, almost every day presents opportunities for us to give a presentation, whether it is formal or informal, individual or group, impromptu or prepared.

This unit has been written by Ricky Lien, to whom I am very grateful. Ricky is a professional speaker and trainer on leadership, communication skills and motivation. Check out his website at www.mindsetmedia.com.sg and sign up for his free monthly newsletter. Ricky is a good friend and an excellent presenter – and that's why I asked him to write this unit for me. Thanks Ricky!

WHAT IS A PRESENTATION?

A presentation is any opportunity to communicate your point of view or ideas to an audience. This can be informal or formal, impromptu or prepared, individual or group.

Although we may not address the media or large groups of people, in business we may make presentations to our:

- bosses
- new employees
- customers
- colleagues
- suppliers.

Also, let's not forget that in a social setting, almost everyone may be required to make a speech at a party, a social gathering, a wedding, or at a party.

Did you know?

The truth is, nobody is born a good speaker – good speaking is learned and takes a great deal of hard work.

This unit will introduce you to the art of making presentations or public speaking where you will be more powerful, more persuasive and more impressive as a public speaker. And also more confident as you will face the opportunity of making a speech with less fear.

We will cover the following important topics:

- *Planning*
    1 Get to know your listeners
    2 Analyse the circumstances around your talk
    3 The location and the size of the audience

- *Writing*
    4 Brainstorm the topic
    5 Get the hard information
    6 Write a draft and read it aloud
    7 Use visual aids
    8 Beyond the rough draft

- *Completing*
    9 Practice, practice, practice
    10 It's natural to feel nervous

- *Deliver the presentation*
    11 Delivery of your speech
    12 Handling questions

1 GET TO KNOW YOUR LISTENERS

One of the most common communication barriers in presentations is the speaker's assumption that they know and understand the audience. If you want to achieve your purpose, if you want your listeners to see the world from your perspective, then you need to construct messages that start with their way of seeing the world.

Good speakers, in their preparation, clarify the interests and needs of their listeners and determine what values, hopes, advantages, fears and concerns their listeners have before they determine what it is they could say to those listeners.

Here are some you need to ask of two or three of the people who will be attending your presentation:

- What do you want to know about the topic? Be careful and tactful here as most people don't like to be exposed as ignorant or unknowledgeable.
- Do you know the knowledge level of the audience on this topic?
- Do you know why I'm giving this talk and why you're here?
- What sort of work have you done in this area?
- Why are you attending this presentation?
- Do you think that my topic will have an impact on your work?
- How interested are you in this topic?
- How long do you want me to present for?

Naturally, if you already have a certain amount of time allotted to you for your presentation, the last question may already be answered. If you question people carefully you may find they want you to talk briefly and then open up the meeting to questions and answers.

Remember

Questions are a better, more realistic form of communication. It is easy to switch off when someone is just talking to you. When specific questions are being answered there is a real need to listen and participate.

For example, asking, 'Are you interested in a 20-minute talk about Apple and IBM type computers?' will elicit a very different response from 'Have you ever used an Apple Computer? What did you like about it?' The first question can be answered by a simple 'Yes', or 'No'. The' second question demands a detailed answer.

So the more you know about your audience, the more you will be able to talk to them in language they understand. It's a good idea to start with the person who invited you to present. Quiz them as they will be able to make some suggestions as to how you can get a better feel of your audience.

Learn to answer questions strategically

'What's in it for me?' Your listeners always listen with this question in mind. This should guide both your topic and your sentence construction.

'What do I want to say?' You will have particular points that you want to make. Your goal must be to align your listener's needs and attitudes with your needs and attitudes.

'What is the most effective way of constructing and presenting the particular things I want to say to achieve my purpose?' Get to know about both your topic and your listeners. The two are always related.

Learn your audience's demographics

To establish your listener's values, priorities, and concerns you will need to have an idea of their demographic characteristics. You may be able to learn their age, gender, cultural identity, ethnic background, race, religious affiliations, and group memberships.

Remember

Good speakers can become that way only by becoming good listeners first. Disciplining ourselves to take the time to listen first can be hard work. Our more automatic and probably more egocentric response is to think first about what we want to say. However, if we think of our listeners first, and seriously consider their interests and concerns as our interests and concerns, it will pay dividends. Being disciplined in this way, we will be rewarded with endless resources to achieve their goals because it starts in the place where our listeners are.

A checklist on listening

- To be a good speaker, be a good listener.
- Audience analysis makes successful presentation planning. It is the starting point for the planning of any presentation.
- Make it a habit to gather information on demographic features of your audience – age, gender, occupation, cultural background, group memberships.
- Understand the role of the audience's attitude towards you as the speaker.
- Good presentations start where the audience is and then move them towards the speaker's point of view.
- What does the audience expect of you?
- Why are they here?
- What is their knowledge level?
- Do you expect friendliness, indifference or hostility?
- Will they be able to use what you are going to tell them?

2 ANALYSE THE CIRCUMSTANCES AROUND YOUR TALK

Your presentation will be affected by location and the audience. In adjusting your presentation to the audience, you have to decide:

- What level of language and style to use?
- What is the circumstance and occasion of your speech or talk?
- Is it a sales presentation, a speech at a wedding, or an informational speech?
- Is it a light-hearted, persuasive, political, joyful, passionate speech?
- What is the time length and situation of the presentation?

Remember

Learn about and understand your audience, and don't make any assumptions.

A checklist of questions about the audience

*   How many people will there be in the audience?
*   What is the age group of the audience?
*   What are the language, literacy and numeracy levels of the audience?
*   What is the gender make-up of the audience?
*   What sort of work do the people do?
*   Is the audience enthusiastic or depressed about the topic you have chosen?
*   What has brought your audience together?

Remember

If you are to make a memorable presentation, it is your job to address all these important issues.

3 THE LOCATION AND THE SIZE OF THE AUDIENCE

The location of a meeting and the facilities provided will have a major bearing upon your ability to give an interesting presentation. If you have video, slide, audio, and overhead projector facilities, you will be able to illustrate your report.

A checklist for the venue

- The room size, seating arrangements, layout, set-up and acoustics
- The technical arrangements, e.g. microphones (either hand held or lapel mikes), power points, computer use, audio-visuals, lighting, music, and whether assistance is available (and have you notified your requirements in advance?)
- What controls are there for air-conditioning (too cold, too hot), lighting, moving people in/out?
- What are the seats like?
- Are there coffee facilities?

4 BRAINSTORM THE TOPIC

To get further ideas on what you want to say, you should brainstorm the topic. This consists of writing down everything about the topic that comes into your head. Jot down anything you feel may be useful – quotes, ideas, anecdotes, facts, figures, examples, anything. Don't worry about organising it yet, you can do that later. Just get your brain working and write down all you can think about the topic you are going to speak about.

Imagine that you are going to talk about a holiday trip to the snow mountains, and the enjoyment that can be had from such an adventure. So your brainstorming page might look something like this:

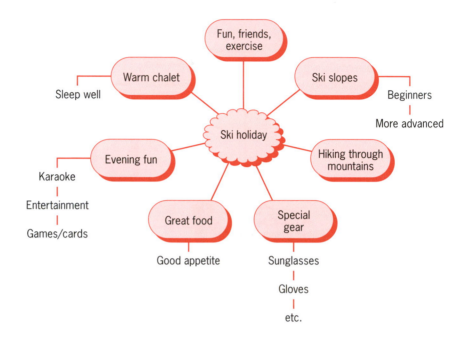

If you then have a close look at the notes you have written, you can probably find a theme that you can develop and that can become the central idea of the talk. Keep the early points in mind. Remember who the audience is going to be, try to include stories of your own, or stories that your audience don't already know. If you have some personal anecdote that will illuminate the story, jot it down.

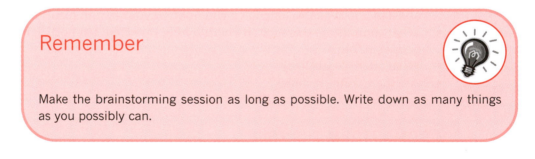

Remember

Make the brainstorming session as long as possible. Write down as many things as you possibly can.

At the end of the brainstorming you will have worked out a theme for your talk. You could argue that having a holiday in the snow mountains is a really refreshing and different holiday!

A checklist for brainstorming

- Do you already have some good stories, analogies or examples?
- Do you have the facts and statistics necessary to support your argument?
- Have you got the must-know, should-know and the nice-to-know points?
- Do you have more material than you need in case you need to stretch the presentation out?

5 GET THE HARD INFORMATION

Now that you have your ideas in some kind of order, you have to gather sufficient evidence to back up your ideas. The quality of a good speech is often determined by the quality of the information it provides. Start now to read up and research as much information as possible on holidaying in the snow mountains. Can you find any interesting statistics? Some unusual facts? Something that will keep your audience interested?

For example, you could gather information from tourist associations about the frequency of visits to particular snowy areas of the world. You could research holiday packages from the backpacking variety right up to the five-star quality range! You could find out which country offers the best variety of snow ski holidays. Why not also get facts about how the holiday resorts started, and a bit of their history?

The facts, statistics, quotes and opinions that your research produces will add to the persuasiveness of your presentation. Remember to present statistics in an interesting and dramatic way. The value of facts and figures is two-fold. They lend authority to your presentation and increase your confidence.

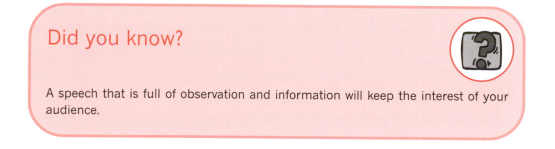

Did you know?

A speech that is full of observation and information will keep the interest of your audience.

Checklist for your key facts

- Have you collected sufficient facts and figures to support your argument?
- Do you have good quotes that are entertaining and memorable for your audience?
- Have you checked to ensure that your information is relevant and up-to-date?
- Have you double-checked your information to make sure that it will withstand criticism and is accurate?

6 WRITE A DRAFT AND READ IT ALOUD

Once you have come up with a good idea and theme, done your research and have good quotes and a good solid body of interesting information, the best way to develop your speech is to let it stew for a while. The more time you let the ideas float around in your head, the clearer they'll become and the easier you will be able to write them down.

When you write the first draft of your speech, it should contain the three basic elements:

- The introduction
- The discussion
- The conclusion

You will want to change the speech as you read over it and as you practise it. During this process, you will be able to polish your draft, add some things to it, and take some things away. Some things you will want to expand on and you will be able to improve your expression and provide better examples as you keep on drafting.

Let us look at these three basic elements in detail.

The introduction

If the speech is a formal one, it is customary to thank the people who invited you there. You might also have to address and thank important people who are there at the presentation. Spend about 10% of your allotted time on your introduction.

It has become an accepted procedure to grab the attention of your audience immediately. Much like a newspaper headline, hit the audience between the eyes with a catchy headline that grabs their attention immediately. To help you, study the headlines in newspapers, or have a look at the headlines in the monthly magazines, and get an idea of how to write attention grabbing headlines.

Remember

We are living in a world where every form of mass media – from radio and television to newspapers and magazines – uses the opening to excite and capture the attention of the audience. A speech is no different. It should have an exciting and interesting opening that captures the audience's attention.

After you have delivered the headline, follow it by a clear and concise statement of what you intend to talk about, 'Today, I'm going to show you how to …' Express your point clearly and concisely so that your audience knows where you stand on this issue.

Checklist of questions to ask yourself about your introduction

- Do you have a headline that will 'grab' your audience's attention?
- Have you included a statement that clearly states your topic and expands your headline?
- Have you clearly stated your point-of-view and where you stand on the issues?
- Have you tested and practiced your introduction so that it is clear and easy to understand?

The discussion

In the discussion or body of your presentation, you develop your arguments and convince your audience of your conviction. Your research now comes into use and you quote facts, provide information from authorities, use logical argument and support your argument with examples. This is the major portion of your speech and should take up about 80% of the allotted time.

Checklist of points to remember

- Keep your examples on a personal level. People want to listen to your story, not a heap of dry facts.
- Verbal communication is the least successful way of communicating so keep to a fairly low number of points.
- Make your points clear.
- Use appropriate audio-visual aids to keep your audience interest up.
- Use the appropriate body gestures to help get your points across.
- Make sure you signposts along the way, i.e. keep your audience informed of where you are in your speech, 'There are five points, and the third point is…' so the audience knows how you are progressing and when you are going to finish.
- Do you have sufficient evidence to 'sway' or to persuade your audience to take action or to agree with your point of view?
- Have you picked several 'must-know' points that are powerful?
- Do you have a logical flow to your argument?
- Are your facts presented in an easy fashion so that the audience understands the information?

The conclusion

Audiences tend to remember the beginning and end of a speech. These are the parts of speech that your audience finds easiest to remember, so they can become the parts in which the most important information can be conveyed. So remember to signpost your audience when you are finishing your talk by pausing and announcing clearly 'in conclusion' or 'to sum up'. Once your audience knows that you will be winding up your presentation soon, they will pay more attention again and this is an opportunity for you to explain your main argument, or the points that you want to make, again.

Checklist to remember about your conclusion

- Repeat the important points.
- Use different words and different illustrations to get your point across.
- Keep your conclusion short and to the point (around 10% of the total speaking time).
- Try and end with a big bang. If you can think of a one-liner or a memorable expression, now is the time to use it.
- Use a key transition statement to show you are coming to the end of your presentation.
- Decide how you are going to summarise your argument.
- Have a clear call to action so that your audience will take action after you have finished your talk.

7 USE VISUAL AIDS

It is important to consider which visual aids may be used to enhance the presentation of mere facts. Visual aids help to create interest and to illustrate points that may be hard to explain using words alone. They also help the speaker to remember details of the presentation and, if used tastefully, they can help to improve the speaker's professional image.

Here are some visual aids that you might consider for your presentation:

- Overhead projector and transparencies.
- Whiteboard.
- Flip charts to prepare.
- Video clips.
- Models and/or samples.
- A computer-based program such as Microsoft PowerPoint.

Did you know?

Up to 50% of information is taken in through the eyes, you should consider adding visual aids to enhance your presentation.

Let's look at these visual aids in more detail:

Overhead projector and transparencies – Pieces of clear plastic that contain your text and/or graphics. Place this onto the overhead projector for projection onto a screen. You can either create the drawings by hand or use a computer and a printer to prepare them.

White board – A flat writing surface in which you can either draw or write your illustrations as you make your presentation.

Flip chart – Using felt tip colour markers, you record ideas generated during the presentation. You can also pre-prepare them and use them as illustrations during your talk.

Video clips – Recordings can be used to show clips of specific instances that you want to be discussed. The modern use of DVD and VCD players is beginning to overshadow the older technology of video tapes.

Photographs and prepared diagrams – These are pre-printed and can be used at the precise moment to illustrate your points.

Models, actual samples of the things being talked about – The physical samples of the objects being talked about can be introduced at the appropriate time so that your audience is able to see, feel and touch the salient points of the article being discussed.

PowerPoint slides – Coupled to an LCD projector, most speakers draw upon this technology to assist them with their presentations. The PowerPoint computer software is powerful and designed specially to be used for presentations.

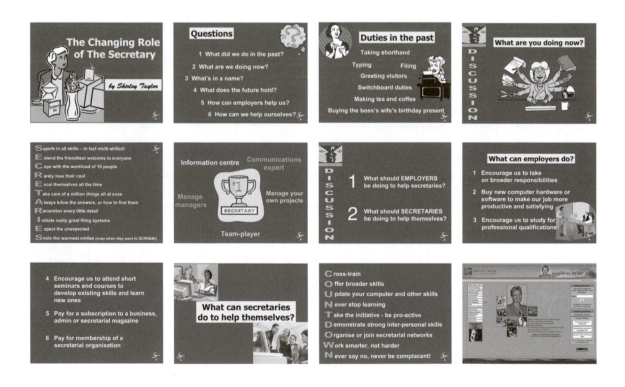

8 BEYOND THE ROUGH DRAFT

Once you have written out your notes, break them up into a number of simple, easy-to-remember points. In these points, you might want to write down a single word, a memorable phrase, and a symbol of something to remind you of what to say.

After you have practised your speech a few times, you will find that you will remember the important bits, and all you need are some notes to prompt your memory.

Eventually, when you have done enough and you are really confident, you will find yourself making mental notes and just remembering the sequence of ideas and topics.

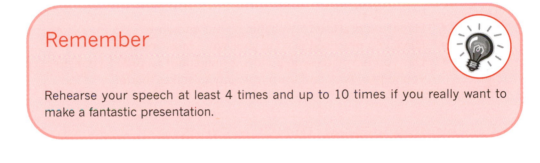

Remember

Rehearse your speech at least 4 times and up to 10 times if you really want to make a fantastic presentation.

9 PRACTISE, PRACTISE, PRACTISE

It is rare for anyone to remember a speech perfectly. If you want to deliver a really interesting, confident and memorable speech, you will need to practise. Speaking in public is a little like acting, you must rehearse, and you have to know your lines. The more rehearsals and the more practice you do, the better you will become.

During these practices, you will become less dependent on your notes, so that finally you are simply glancing down at them to ensure that you are presenting the points in the correct order and that you include the vital bits of information.

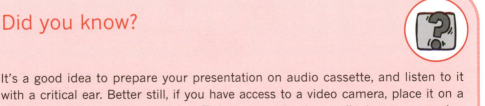

Did you know?

It's a good idea to prepare your presentation on audio cassette, and listen to it with a critical ear. Better still, if you have access to a video camera, place it on a tripod and film yourself practising. Tighten your structure, adjust your expression or change your order if you need to. Leave it for 48 hours before you listen to it again. You may have new thoughts, as you are now quite a distance from your initial attempt.

As you rehearse, consider how you look and sound. Remember to:

- Try not to stand behind a lectern.
- Express your power to your audience by speaking confidently.
- Stand tall.
- Make good use of facial expression and gesture to add feeling and greater meaning to your presentation.
- Use your voice well.

Checklist on practising

- Have you practised reading out your speech at least four times?
- Are you so familiar with your presentation that you hardly need to look at your notes?
- Have you practised 'eye-balling' your audience?
- Have you practised making your voice more interesting?
- Did you have access to a video camera and recorded your practice sessions for you to play back and learn from any mistakes made?

10 IT'S NATURAL TO FEEL NERVOUS

Even after you have practised constantly, you will still probably feel nervous when you finally get out there in front of your audience.

If you follow some of the pointers below, they will certainly help you to ease your nervousness and will make the experience much more pleasant.

1 When you feel nervous, take a deep breath, hold it. Then let it out with a confident smile. You will be amazed at how this helps to calm your nerves.
2 Pause to take deep breaths.

3 Look at your audience.
4 Use gestures appropriately, move your arms around to demonstrate your points.
5 Respond to the looks and body language of your audience.
6 Say to yourself, 'I have something of value to say, and these people love to listen to me'.
7 Just because you are nervous doesn't mean that you must freeze and do a bad job.
8 Keep on practising until your material becomes second nature. It will be there in your head.
9 Remind yourself that you are there to help the audience take something of value away.
10 Just imagine that you are the idol and your audience is there to soak away your message.
11 Dress one level better than your audience is dressed – this gives you further confidence and makes you look professional.
12 Leave yourself with plenty of time – don't rush about.
13 Be early.
14 Eat and drink only lightly.
15 Have a glass of warm water with a slice of lemon by your table.
16 Speak slowly, clearly and with impact.
17 Project your voice to reach the back row of the audience.

It's also very important to be willing to work on your self-esteem. Here are three exercises to help you build your self-esteem and confidence.

Exercise 1

- Make a list of all your accomplishments.
- List all the skills you've developed on the way – include everything from swimming badges to helping somebody to learn to ride a bicycle, from great meals you've cooked to getting your present job. Make it a long list.
- Recognise that you are a unique individual and worthy of success.

Exercise 2

- Make a list of all your essential qualities and values as a human being.
- Ask: What's distinctive about me?
- Ask 3 or 4 good friends to say what they think makes you who you are.

Exercise 3

- Imagine future presentations as if you are watching them on TV or a large film screen. 'See' yourself being a brilliant presenter and exactly as you wish. Play this positive picture story regularly in your mind, and as many times as you can throughout the day.
- Do this also last thing at night before you go to sleep.

11 DELIVERY OF YOUR SPEECH

We're now on our feet at last, facing our audience. The following seven factors will contribute towards our success during the presentation. Your critical success factors are:

- Your start.
- Audience mood.
- Your voice.
- Body language.
- Your visual aids.
- Timing.
- Conclusion.

The start

The greatest battle is won when you make a great start. Bear the following points in mind:

- Do not apologise.
- Be confident.
- Know the topic well.
- Be confident.

Audience mood

- Be empathic with your audience mood.
- Watch your audience's body language.
- Watch their facial expressions, glances exchanged, shuffling of feet.
- Be professional.
- Project the right degree of formality.
- Use good pace and drive.
- Don't be arrogant – this will turn your audience against you.
- Controll your enthusiasm.

Your voice

- Use it with skill.
- Be clearly audible.
- Use a microphone if necessary.
- Keep your head up.
- Open your mouth wider than during normal speech.
- Speak more slowly so the audience can digest what you are saying.

- Stress on the consonants.
- Accent on the last syllable of each word for clarity.
- Use the right pace, i.e. the speed of speaking.
- Use a good pitch – the musical tone of your voice. Vary it. High notes convey urgency, the low notes convey emphasis.
- Use the right volume, i.e. the loudness should be sufficient for all to hear comfortably.

Body language

The body can help or hinder a good presentation. Pay attention to the following:

- Positioning of our body – stand in a good posture, do not pace around too much.
- Use your hands in proper gestures to support your points.
- Good use of eye contact – gains and holds attention and establishes rapport.
- Avoid mannerisms that irritate, e.g. swaying side to side, fiddling with marker pens, pointers or spectacles.
- Placing hands in pockets.
- Pacing to and fro.

Your visual aids

- When using flip charts or white boards, write from the side.
- Write legibly.
- Stand so that you do not block the view of the screen or flip chart.
- Do not speak to the board or screen.

Timing

Make sure you end on time. Nothing is worse than going overtime unless you have checked with the audience first. Keep to your allotted time.

Conclusion

Finish with a bang. Go out on a high note. Ask the audience for action. Whatever else, leave no doubt in your audience's mind that you have come to an end of your presentation.

12 HANDLING QUESTIONS

You must also be prepared to answer any questions from the audience. If there is a question that you are afraid of, prepare your answer and consider it carefully before giving it.

The question and answer section is an important part of a presentation. Questions from the audience clarify their thinking on what you have just said. Maintain your professionalism, self-control and control of the situation.

   You may want to leave questions until the end or inform your audience that you will take questions as you go along.

*   Probably leaving questions until the end is a better timing as your train of thought can easily be broken by the interruption.
*   Look directly at the questioner as you speak, repeat the question for all to hear.
*   Answer the question by also looking at the audience and not just at the person who asked you the question.
*   Regard question time as an opportunity, not as a threat.

Remember

If you do not know the answer to a question, ask whether somebody in the audience knows, if not tell the questioners that you will get back to them as soon as possible with the answer.

Questionnaire to test presentation skills

The skill	1 Poor	2	3	4	5	6	7 Excellent
1 Did the speaker speak clearly so that the audience understood easily?							
2 Did the speaker use language and vocabulary that the audience could understand?							
3 Was the tone of the presentation correct? Was it enthusiastic, serious or light-hearted to fit the occasion?							
4 Did the speaker choose relevant information?							
5 Was clear structure used and a sense of clear organisation used?							
6 Did the speaker present the topic in a logical, flowing manner?							
7 Were the ideas at the heart of the presentation presented clearly?							
8 How successfully did the speaker hold and keep the audience's attention and interest?							
9 Did the speaker keep to the appropriate time and finish off what was supposed to be said?							
10 Did the speaker use appropriate body language, gestures?							
11 Did the speaker vary his/her voice, pace, stress words, correct pitch and was the volume comfortable for all to hear?							
12 Did the speaker use appropriate visual aids to enhance the presentation?							
13 Did the speaker handle questions well from the audience?							
Other comments:							

A–Z OF BLOOPERS AND BLUNDERS, COMMON ERRORS AND CLICHÉS: U, V, W, X, Y, Z

Undersigned

Great-grandfather used to refer to himself as a third person, i.e. 'Please do not hesitate to contact the undersigned if you require any further information.' Unfortunately, I still see people using this in their messages. What we should be writing is 'Please call me at xxxx if you need any further information'.

Use/utilise

Use is much better than utilise. For example, 'I used the dishwasher', 'John used the scissors to open the box', 'You should use a tissue to blow your nose'.

While/whilst

'Whilst' is an old-fashioned word. Use 'while'.

Who/whoever/whom/whomever

'Who' and 'whoever' are subjects, for example, 'Who put sugar in my coffee?' 'Whoever loves me must also love my dog.' 'Please take these receipts to whoever is responsible for petty cash.'

 'Who' and its related forms refer only to people, not to animals, things or ideas.

 'Whom' and 'whomever' are objects, for example: 'Teenagers often fall out with friends whom they have fought with', 'You always find fault with whomever I bring home.' Unless you understand 'who', 'whoever', 'whom' and 'whomever' well, it is best to rephrase your sentences so that you don't use these words. (NB: That's what I do!)

Whose/who's

Many people confuse these words because the way to form the possessive of most words is to add an apostrophe and an 's'. For example, Mary's desk, John's advice.

 However, pronouns like 'whose' do not follow this rule. 'Whose' is possessive but it does not need an apostrophe. For example, 'The person whose suggestion is chosen will receive a special award.' *Who's* is a contraction meaning *Who is*. For example, 'Who's the right person to ask about petty cash claims?', 'Martha is the person who's co-ordinating this project.'

Your/you're

After a few SMS's (text messages) with a friend, I received one that read 'Your funny'. I wondered what she meant – 'Your funny face?', 'Your funny smile?' 'Your funny feet?'

Of course, what she meant to say was 'You are funny'. To use the contraction correctly, it should be 'You're'.

Remember, *your* is possessive. It describes the word or words immediately following it. For example: 'Your experience', 'your confidence', 'your hair', 'your nose'.

'*You're*' is a contraction that means 'you are'. For example, 'You're the right person for this job', 'Please give me a call when you're next in Singapore'.

IN THE BIN: U, V, W, X, Y, Z

we are writing to inform you
well and good
when all is said and done
wish to advise
wish to state
with all due respect

Appendix

FREQUENTLY CONFUSED WORDS

These pairs of words sound similar, so you must be careful not to use the wrong one. Be sure you know their meanings.

NB: It's also a good idea to make sure you can pronounce them all correctly.

accede	to agree or comply with
exceed	to go beyond
accept	to receive or take
except	to exclude
access	entrance
excess	extra or surplus
advice	suggestion
advise	to suggest
adverse	unfavourable, unpleasant
averse	hesitant, unwilling
affect	to influence
effect	the result
all ready	completely prepared
already	previously, before now
allusion	reference, mention
illusion	false impression
alternate	to rotate or interchange
alternative	options, choices
cite	to quote
sight	a view
site	a location or place
complement	go well together, make up for, allowance
compliment	to flatter or praise
defer	to put off until later
differ	to be different
dependant	charge or responsibility
dependent	reliant
device	a piece of equipment, gadget
devise	to plan or concoct
die	to stop living, to break down
dye	colour, to colour
discreet	diplomatic, tactful
discrete	separate, detached

elicit	to draw out, to extract
illicit	illegal, dishonest
eminent	well-known, famous
imminent	coming up, impending, about to happen
ensure	to make sure
insure	to cover, indemnify
envelop	to surround
envelope	wrapper for a letter
farther	beyond, at a distance
further	additional, extra
forth	forward
fourth	number four
hangar	shed, shelter
hanger	coat-hanger, hook
human	person
humane	compassionate, caring
incidence	frequency
incidents	events, occurrences
instance	example
instants	split seconds, moments
later	afterwards, subsequently
latter	the second or concluding
loath	unwilling, reluctant
loathe	to hate or detest
loose	unrestricting, slack
lose	to misplace
moral	ethical, decent, a message
morale	sense of well-being
overdo	to exceed, do too much
overdue	behind time, late
peace	harmony, end of war
piece	part or portion
pedal	a foot lever
peddle	to sell
persecute	to hound or torment
prosecute	to put on trial, to sue
personal	private
personnel	employees, staff
precedence	priority
precedents	instances, examples, standards

principal	sum of money, main, chief
principle	general rule
rain	water, downpour
reign	period in office, sovereignty
rein	bridle, harness
rap	to knock or tap
wrap	to cover or enfold
residence	home
residents	inhabitants, occupants
right	correct
rite	ceremony
write	to put pen to paper, to inscribe or mark
role	part to play, position or job
roll	to rotate or tumble, a tube or reel
shear	to cut or trim
sheer	total, complete, steep, fine
stationary	motionless, still
stationery	paper, envelopes
their	belonging to them
there	in that place
they're	contraction of 'they are'
waive	to put aside, ignore
wave	a gesture, a swell of water
weather	climate or conditions
whether	if
who's	contraction of 'who is' or 'who has'
whose	possessive form of who

Weblink

http://dictionary.reference.com

Dictionary.com
Links to websites on grammar, style and usage.

http://www.thesaurus.com

Thesaurus.com
Guide to antonyms and synonyms.

COMMONLY MISSPELLED WORDS

Even the best spellers have to look up the spelling of some words occasionally in a dictionary. Here are some of the most commonly misspelled words – try to memorise them. (Note that UK spellings have been used here.)

NB: Do you know all their meanings?

absence	chargeable	exceed
accessible	clientele	exhaust
accessory	collateral	existence
accommodate	committee	exorbitant
accumulate	comparatively	expatriate
achieve	competitor	extraordinary
advantageous	concede	extravagant
affiliated	concerted	extreme
aggressive	congratulations	
alignment	connoisseur	familiar
allege	consensus	fascinate
amend	controversial	flexible
analyse	controversy	fluctuation
apologies	convenient	forty
apologise	converse	friend
apparent	convertible	fulfil
appropriate	corroborate	
argument	criticism	gauge
assistance		gesture
assistant	definite	grammar
asterisk	definitely	grateful
auditor	description	grievous
average	desirable	guarantee
	desperate	
bankrupt	dilemma	haphazard
bankruptcy	disappear	harass
beautiful	disappoint	harassment
behaviour	disappoint	hierarchy
believable	discrepancy	humorous
brilliant	dissatisfied	humour
bulletin	dissipate	
business	distraught	illegible
		immediate
calendar	eligible	immigrant
campaign	embarrassing	impending
category	embedded	incidentally
ceiling	endorsement	indelible
changeable	exaggerate	independent

indispensable
insinuate
insinuation
insistent
instalment
intermediate
irresistible
itinerary

jewellery
judgement
judicial

legitimate
leisure
liaise
license

maintenance
manoeuvre
mathematics
mediocre
miniature
minimum
misconstrue
misspell

necessary
negligence
negligible
negotiable
negotiate
niece
noticeable

occasion
occur
occurrence
omission

opponent
original

parallel
pastime
pedestal
perceive
peripheral
permanent
perseverance
persistent
personnel
persuade
possess
possesses
potato
precede
predictable
predominantly
preferred
privilege
procedure
proceed
pronounce
pronunciation
proverbial
psychology
pursue

questionnaire

receive
recommend
repetition
restaurant
rhythm
ridiculous

saleable

secretary
seize
separate
skilful
similar
sincerely
succeed
success
succession
suddenness
supposedly
sufficient
superintendent
supersede
surprise

tangible
tariff
technique
technology
tenant
tomorrow
transferred

unanimous
unfortunately
until
useful

vacillate
vacuum
vegetarian
vehicle
vice versa
vicious

weird
wilful
withhold

Weblink

http://www.yourdictionary.com/
Dictionaries in over 200 languages.

http://english2american.com/
Translations for Americans on English words.

http://www.encyberpedia.com/
Website contains links to numerous dictionary, glossary and encyclopedia resources.

THE A TO Z OF ALTERNATIVE WORDS

This list was produced by the Plain English Campaign (www.plainenglish.co.uk) and was reproduced with their permission.

This guide gives hundreds of plain English alternatives to the pompous words and phrases that litter official writing. On its own the guide won't teach you how to write in plain English. There's more to it than just replacing 'hard' words with 'easy' words, and many of these alternatives won't work in every situation. But it will help if you want to get rid of words like 'notwithstanding', 'expeditiously' and phrases like 'in the majority of instances' and ' at this moment in time'. And using everyday words is an important first step clearer writing.

Using the A to Z

If you find yourself about to write, type or dictate a word you wouldn't use in everyday conversation, look it up in the A to Z. You should find a similar alternative. Often there will be a choice of several words. You need to pick the one that best fits what you are trying to say.

New words

We have put more than 20 years' experience of writing, editing and training into this guide. But please let us know if you don't find the word you are looking for.

Original word	Possible alternatives

A

(an) absence of	no, none
abundance	enough, plenty, a lot (or say how many)
accede to	allow, agree to
accelerate	speed up
accentuate	stress
accommodation	where you live, home
accompanying	with
accomplish	do, finish
according to our records	our records show
accordingly	in line with this, so
acknowledge	thank you for
acquaint yourself with	find out about, read
acquiesce	agree
acquire	buy, get
additional	extra, more
adjacent	next to
adjustment	change, alteration
admissible	allowed, acceptable
advantageous	useful, helpful
advise	tell, say (unless you **are** giving advice)
affix	add, write, fasten, stick on, fix to
afford an opportunity	let, allow
afforded	given
aforesaid	this, earlier in this document
aggregate	total
aligned	lined up, in line
alleviate	ease, reduce
allocate	divide, share, add, give
along the lines of	like, as in
alternative	choice, other
alternatively	or, on the other hand
ameliorate	improve, help
amendment	change
anticipate	expect
apparent	clear, plain, obvious, seeming
applicant (the)	you
application	use
appreciable	large, great
apprise	inform, tell
appropriate	proper, right, suitable
appropriate to	suitable for
approximately	about, roughly

as a consequence of	because
as of the date of	from
as regards	about, on the subject of
ascertain	find out
assemble	build, gather, put together
assistance	help
at an early date	soon (or say when)
at its discretion	can, may (or edit out)
at the moment	now (or edit out)
at the present time	now (or edit out)
attempt	try
attend	come to, go to, be at
attributable to	due to, because of
authorise	allow, let
authority	right, power, may (as in 'have the authority to')
axiomatic	obvious, goes without saying

B

belated	late
beneficial	helpful, useful
bestow	give, award
breach	break
by means of	by

C

calculate	work out, decide
cease	finish, stop, end
circumvent	get round, avoid, skirt, circle
clarification	explanation, help
combine	mix
combined	together
commence	start, begin
communicate	talk, write, telephone (be specific)
competent	able, can
compile	make, collect
complete	fill in, finish
completion	end
comply with	keep to, meet
component	part
comprise	be made up of, include
(it is) compulsory	(you) must
conceal	hide

concerning	about, on
conclusion	end
concur	agree
condition	rule
consequently	so
considerable	great, important
constitute	make up, form, be
construe	interpret
consult	talk to, meet, ask
consumption	amount used
contemplate	think about
contrary to	against, despite
correct	put right
correspond	write
costs the sum of	costs
counter	against
courteous	polite
cumulative	added up, added together
currently	now (or edit out)
customary	usual, normal

D

deduct	take off, take away
deem to be	treat as
defer	put off, delay
deficiency	lack of
delete	cross out
demonstrate	show, prove
denote	show
depict	show
designate	point out, show, name
desire	wish, want
despatch or dispatch	send, post
despite the fact that	though, although
determine	decide, work out, set, end
detrimental	harmful, damaging
difficulties	problems
diminish	lessen, reduce
disburse	pay, pay out
discharge	carry out
disclose	tell, show
disconnect	cut off, unplug
discontinue	stop, end
discrete	separate
discuss	talk about

disseminate	spread
documentation	papers, documents
domiciled in	living in
dominant	main
due to the fact of	because, as
duration	time, life
during which time	while
dwelling	home

E

economical	cheap, good value
eligible	allowed, qualified
elucidate	explain, make clear
emphasise	stress
empower	allow, let
enable	allow
enclosed	inside, with
(please find) enclosed	I enclose
encounter	meet
endeavour	try
enquire	ask
enquiry	question
ensure	make sure
entitlement	right
envisage	expect, imagine
equivalent	equal, the same
erroneous	wrong
establish	show, find out, set up
evaluate	test, check
evince	show, prove
ex officio	because of his or her position
exceptionally	only when, in this case
excessive	too many, too much
exclude	leave out
excluding	apart from, except
exclusively	only
exempt from	free from
expedite	hurry, speed up
expeditiously	as soon as possible, quickly
expenditure	spending
expire	run out
extant	current, in force
extremity	limit

F

fabricate	make, make up
facilitate	help, make possible
factor	reason
failure to	if you do not
finalise	end, finish
following	after
for the duration of	during, while
for the purpose of	to, for
for the reason that	because
formulate	plan, devise
forthwith	now, at once
forward	send
frequently	often
furnish	give
further to	after, following
furthermore	then, also, and

G

generate	produce, give, make
give consideration to	consider, think about
grant	give

H

henceforth	from now on, from today
hereby	now, by this (or edit out)
herein	here (or edit out)
hereinafter	after this (or edit out)
hereof	of this
hereto	to this
heretofore	until now, previously
hereunder	below
herewith	with this (or edit out)
hitherto	until now
hold in abeyance	wait, postpone
hope and trust	hope, trust (but not both)

I

if and when	if, when (but not both)
illustrate	show, explain
immediately	at once, now

implement	carry out, do
imply	suggest, hint at
in a number of cases	some (or say how many)
in accordance with	as under, in line with, because of
in addition (to)	and, as well as, also
in advance	before
in case of	if
in conjunction with	and, with
in connection with	for, about
in consequence	because, as a result
in excess of	more than
in lieu of	instead of
in order that	so that
in receipt of	get, have, receive
in relation to	about
in respect of	about, for
in the absence of	without
in the course of	while, during
in the event of/that	if
in the majority of instances	most, mostly
in the near future	soon
in the neighbourhood of	about, around
in view of the fact that	as, because
inappropriate	wrong, unsuitable
inception	start, beginning
incorporating	which includes
incurred	have to pay, owe
indicate	show, suggest
inform	tell
initially	at first
initiate	begin, start
insert	put in
instances	cases
intend to	will
intimate	say, hint
irrespective of	despite, even if
is in accordance with	agrees with, follows
is of the opinion	thinks
issue	give, send
it is known that	I/we know that

J

jeopardise	risk, threaten

L

(a) large number of	many, most (or say how many)
(to) liaise with	to meet with, to discuss with, to work with (whichever is more descriptive)
locality	place, area
locate	find, put

M

magnitude	size
(it is) mandatory	(you) must
manner	way
manufacture	make
marginal	small, slight
material	relevant
materialise	happen, occur
may in the future	may, might, could
merchandise	goods
mislay	lose
modification	change
moreover	and, also, as well

N

negligible	very small
nevertheless	but, however, even so
notify	tell, let us/you know
notwithstanding	even if, despite, still, yet
numerous	many (or say how many)

O

objective	aim, goal
(it is) obligatory	(you) must
obtain	get, receive
occasioned by	caused by, because of
on behalf of	for
on numerous occasions	often
on receipt of	when we/you get
on request	if you ask
on the grounds that	because
on the occasion that	when, if
operate	work, run
optimum	best, ideal

option	choice
ordinarily	normally, usually
otherwise	or
outstanding	unpaid
owing to	because of

P

(a) percentage of	some (or say what percentage)
partially	partly
participate	join in, take part
particulars	details, facts
per annum	a year
perform	do
permissible	allowed
permit	let, allow
personnel	people, staff
persons	people, anyone
peruse	read, read carefully, look at
place	put
possess	have, own
possessions	belongings
practically	almost, nearly
predominant	main
prescribe	set, fix
preserve	keep, protect
previous	earlier, before, last
principal	main
prior to	before
proceed	go ahead
procure	get, obtain, arrange
profusion of	plenty, too many (or say how many)
prohibit	ban, stop
(to) progress something	(replace with a more precise phrase saying what you are doing)
projected	estimated
prolonged	long
promptly	quickly, at once
promulgate	advertise, announce
proportion	part
provide	give
provided that	if, as long as
provisions	rules, terms
proximity	closeness, nearness
purchase	buy
pursuant to	under, because of, in line with

Q

qualify for	can get, be able to get

R

reconsider	think again about, look again at
reduce	cut
reduction	cut
referred to as	called
refer to	talks about, mentions
(have) regard to	take into account
regarding	about, on
regulation	rule
reimburse	repay, pay back
reiterate	repeat, restate
relating to	about
remain	stay
remainder	the rest, what is left
remittance	payment
remuneration	pay, wages, salary
render	make, give, send
report	tell
represent	show, stand for, be
request	ask, question
require	need, want, force
requirements	needs, rules
reside	live
residence	home, where you live
restriction	limit
retain	keep
review	look at (again)
revised	new, changed

S

said/such/same	the, this, that
scrutinise	read (look at) carefully
select	choose
settle	pay
similarly	also, in the same way
solely	only
specified	given, written, set
state	say, tell us, write down
statutory	legal, by law
subject to	depending on, under, keeping to

submit	send, give
subsequent to/upon	after
subsequently	later
substantial	large, great, a lot of
substantially	more or less
sufficient	enough
supplement	go with, add to
supplementary	extra, more
supply	give, sell, delivery

T

(the) tenant	you
terminate	stop, end
that being the case	if so
the question as to whether	whether
thereafter	then, afterwards
thereby	by that, because of that
therein	in that, there
thereof	of that
thereto	to that
thus	so, therefore
to date	so far, up to now
to the extent that	if, when
transfer	change, move
transmit	send

U

ultimately	in the end, finally
unavailability	lack of
undernoted	the following
undersigned	I, we
undertake	agree, promise, do
uniform	same, similar
unilateral	one-sided, one-way
unoccupied	empty
until such time	until
utilisation	use
utilise	use

V

variation	change
virtually	almost (or edit out)
visualise	see, predict

W

ways and means	ways
we have pleasure in	we are glad to
whatsoever	whatever, what, any
whensoever	when
whereas	but
whether or not	whether
with a view to	to, so that
with effect from	from
with reference to	about
with regard to	about, for
with respect to	about, for
with the minimum of delay	quickly (or say when)

Y

you are requested	please
your attention is drawn	please see, please note

Z

zone	area, region

EXAMINATION PAPERS WRITTEN IN THE STYLE OF LCCI EXAMINATIONS BOARD ENGLISH FOR BUSINESS

This paper has been written in the style of LCCI Examinations Board English for Business Level 1.

Question 1

Situation

You work in a large bookshop called *Brilliant Books* as an assistant to the manager, Ms Martha Olsen. The shop has rules about what the staff should wear, and a copy of the rules is given to everyone when they start work at the shop. All staff must follow these rules, even those who work in the office and who do not meet customers. The contract rules say that all staff should wear black or dark blue trousers or skirts with a white shirt or blouse.

Ms Olsen says to you:

'I'd like you to send a memo to the office supervisor, Mrs Nicola Hester. I've noticed that some office staff have not been following the clothing rules recently. Please remind her that we expect all staff to follow the rules, and suggest that she should have a quiet word with any of her staff who are not following the rules. For example, I've seen some of the office with long hair that is not pinned up or tied back. This can look very untidy. I've even seen one or two of the office staff wearing trainers and not the correct shoes, which should be plain blue or black. Mrs Hester needs to remind staff to look back over the rules they received. I want you to mention in particular that a small amount of jewellery can be worn, such as a ring, but nothing too much. You'd better use my name in the memo.'

Task

Write the memo to Mrs Hester about the company's clothing rules and ask her to make sure her staff follow the rules. (LCCIEB EFB1 style)

(30 marks)

Question 2

Situation

Your company is holding a conference at *Hyfields Hotel*. Your manager wants you to find out about the hotel and its services as many members of staff will stay at the hotel for 3 days.

Task

Read the **Hotel Information** below then say whether the following statements are **TRUE** or **FALSE**. Then write down **only the word or phrase** from the passage that supports your answer. Do not write **more than 6 words** for each answer. You will lose marks if you write more than 6 supporting words. (LCCIEB EFB1 style)

HOTEL INFORMATION

All of us at the Hyfields Hotel hope you will have a most enjoyable stay with us. We have listed below the most important services we offer, but if there is anything else you need please contact reception (by dialling 0) and someone will try to help you.

Bedrooms
All our bedrooms have fitted toilets and bathrooms (some with showers only). All rooms have tea/coffee making facilities. Other services (for example irons, hairdriers) are available from reception.

Restaurant
Our award-winning restaurant is open for breakfast between 0700 and 0900, lunch between 1200 and 1400 and dinner between 1900 and 2200. Full meals or lighter snacks are available for each meal, and a vegetarian option is always available. There is also a limited room service menu.

Car parking
Cars can be parked at the rear of the hotel. Whilst the car park is camera controlled, parking is at the owner's risk.

Television
Each bedroom is fitted with a television which provides a range of channels. A movie channel is available for an additional cost.

Heating
You can change the room temperature by adjusting the control near the door. Please note that all bedroom windows can be opened apart from ground floor windows.

Conference rooms
We have 10 rooms of varying sizes available for conferences or meetings. All conference rooms have Internet access.

Fire precautions
For your own safety you should study the notice on the back of each room door. This will direct you to the nearest fire exists. Our fire alarms are tested at 1000 each Monday.

Room cards
Each door is opened by a room card. The lock operates when the door is closed. Please show your card when you need any meals or other hotel services.

Checking out
You should leave your room by no later than 1000 on departure day.

Write your answer on the lines marked A.

1. All rooms have hairdryers.
   A. _____

2. At lunchtime the restaurant is open for 2 hours.
   A. _____

3. People who do not eat meat can use the restaurant.
   A. _____

4. The hotel takes responsibility for cars parked in the car park.
   A. _____

5. A free movie channel is available on each television.
   A. _____

6. You can make your bedroom hotter or colder.
   A. _____

7. Most conference rooms have Internet access.
   A. _____

8. Fire alarms are tested late in the week in the afternoon.
   A. _____

9. Your door is opened with a key.
   A. _____

10. On the day you depart, you must leave your room by 1000.
    A. _____

(30 marks)

Question 3

Situation

You are thinking about taking a course to improve your computer skills. A local training organisation has published its new programme of evening courses. The programme appears in the chart below.

Task

Use the information in the chart to **answer the questions below**. Write your answer as a **name, a course, a single word, a figure or a length of time**. You will lose marks if you write more than this. (LCCIEB EFB1 style)

Course	Level*	Tutor	Room	Evening	Length of course
Starting out	B	Mr Schulz	18	Tuesday	4 weeks
Introduction to the Internet	B	Mrs Patel	21	Wednesday	6 weeks
Spreadsheets	B	Mr Schulz	16	Friday	6 weeks
Web pages	I	Ms Chitonga	21	Monday	6 weeks
Networking	I	Ms Rosetti	18	Monday	8 weeks
Databases – sorts/searches	I	Ms Rosetti	16	Wednesday	8 weeks
Advanced applications	A	Mr Khan	14	Tuesday	10 weeks
Developing Internet	A	Mrs Patel	21	Friday	12 weeks
Telematics	A	Ms Rosetti	17	Thursday	14 weeks

* Courses are at 3 levels – *Beginners* for those with no experience, *Intermediate* for those with some experience, *Advanced* for those with a lot of experience.

Answers

1. Which is the longest course?

2. How many Beginners courses are there?

3. Which tutor has only one Advanced course?

4. Which room is used the most?

5. Which is the shortest course on Tuesday evening?

6. On which evening is the Spreadsheets course?

7. Which Advanced course has the shortest length?

8. Which Monday course lasts 6 weeks?

9. How many tutors are women?

10. Which evening has the fewest courses?

11. What level is the Networking course?

12. What is the highest level course on a Wednesday evening?

13. How many male tutors have courses on a Tuesday evening?

14. Which rooms are used on Wednesday and a Friday evening?

15. Which is the shortest Beginners course with a male tutor?

16. Apart from Starting Out, which other course takes place on a Tuesday evening?

17. Who is the tutor on the highest level 6 week course?

18. Which is the shortest Advanced course where the tutor is a woman?

19. Which tutor has the most Beginners' courses?

20. How much longer is the Developing Internet course than the Introduction to Internet course?

(20 marks)

Question 4

You work for a large company that uses many computers and information technology systems in its offices. The company employs a computer technician to maintain the computers and help the staff. Up to now this technician has been sent to a department when a problem arises, but this has not worked very well. It has been decided that the technician will now be based in each department for two hour sessions starting at 0830 each morning and finishing at 1730.

The manager of the company has asked you to organise the technician's timetable for the week. The manager says this to you.

'I've started the timetable for you by putting him in Administration for the first session on a Monday as this department has the most computers. He should go there at first on Wednesday also. It would be helpful if he could keep Wednesday afternoons free so that he can then be a standby for problems anywhere. He should spend two sessions in Finance, one at the beginning of Friday and one last session on Monday. For the other first sessions, one should be in Marketing and one in Sales. Leave Sales as late in the week as you can. I'd like him to finish the week in Security.

'Straight after lunch on Monday, Tuesday and Friday he should go to Human Resources and if there is still a session after lunch, he should go to Marketing. He should also go to Marketing on Monday morning.

'I suppose he should spend more time in Administration. Give him one session (anything that's left) on Friday and, if possible, one session at the end of any other day.

'We should have 3 sessions before lunch left. He should go to the warehouse then. I think that covers the whole week.'

Task

Complete the technician's timetable printed below.

	08.30 – 10.30	10.30 – 12.30	12.30 – 13.30	13.30 – 15.30	15.30 – 17.30
Monday			Lunch		
Tuesday			Lunch		
Wednesday			Lunch		
Thursday			Lunch		
Friday			Lunch		

(20 marks)

(LCCIEB EFB1 style)

This paper has been written in the style of LCCI Examinations Board English for Business Level 2.

Choose 1 (one) from these 3 options:

Question 1(a)

Situation

The *Hotel Splendide* in the town of Farchester has been very successful in attracting guests and visitors in recent years. The hotel is now building a new block with lecture rooms and it hopes to expand its business by running conferences and other events for organisations and the public.

You work as an assistant to the Hotel Manager, Ms Miriam Lee. The directors of the hotel have just told Ms Lee that they would like to give the new block an interesting name but they were having difficulties in thinking of one. They have decided to hold a competition amongst the hotel staff. All staff will be asked to suggest a name and the directors will then decide which is the most suitable. The person who suggests the best name will be given a cash prize of $500 and will also be asked to take part in the naming ceremony.

Ms Lee has asked you to prepare a notice to be placed in all staffrooms in the hotel and said this to you:

'We hope everyone enters this competition, whatever their job. It will be good fun trying to think of a name and there's a good prize as well.

'We don't mind what type of name is suggested. The new block is going to be used mainly by businesses so maybe the name could have something to do with business but it doesn't have to be. It could be named after someone from Farchester or another famous person, possibly someone from history. But it could be given any type of name, as long as it is interesting. Anything will be better than the "Conference Block"!

'The deadline for entries is three weeks today. Staff can enter more than once if they can think of more than one name, but we need to know their name and department.'

Task

Write the notice.
(LCCIEB EFB2 style)

Question 1(b)

Situation

You work in the office of *Fancy Footwear*, a shop selling all kinds of shoes, boots and other footwear. One of the shop assistants, Mrs Colette Muldoon, has worked at the shop for nearly 50 years and the Manager feels that this remarkably long period of service should be publicised.

The local newspaper has agreed to publish a **short article** if someone from the company writes this. You have interviewed Mrs Muldoon and made notes of what she said.

You:	Well, Mrs Muldoon. You have worked for Fancy Footwear for 50 years. How did you start?
Mrs Muldoon:	I started working in the shop the day after I left school. I didn't serve customers at first though. I did odd jobs like cleaning and moving stock about.
You:	But you then started selling ladies shoes?
Mrs Muldoon:	Oh, no. I first sold shoes in the Children's Department. That was hard work. Young children hate trying on new shoes. After about 5 years I moved to the Ladies' Department.
You:	And you have been there since then?
Mrs Muldoon:	Yes, I became a supervisor and then manager of the Department about 20 years ago.
You:	I bet you have seen some changes over the years.
Mrs Muldoon:	Oh yes. We all had to wear a uniform when I started. There were stiff collars that were very uncomfortable. Now we can wear what we like, as long as we are comfortable.
You:	Have the shoes we sell changed?
Mrs Muldoon:	Well, they have, I suppose. But our top quality shoes are very similar to those we sold 50 years ago.
You:	What about the prices?
Mrs Muldoon:	Oh, yes. The price of one pair of shoes today is about the same as my monthly wages 50 years ago. And it was all cash in those days. Now we have credit cards, debit cards and cheques. Very few people pay cash.
You:	What about yourself? Do you plan to retire?
Mrs Muldoon:	Well, I love my work, but I am getting older. I think I will retire within the next couple of years.
You:	What will you do then?
Mrs Muldoon:	I have 6 grandchildren now, so I will enjoy spending more time with them. And as you might know, I love cooking. I hope to do much more of this.
You:	Well, Ms Muldoon, we are very grateful for all your hard work at the shop. We shall miss you when retire, but we wish you well.

You have been asked to write a brief but interesting article about Mrs Muldoon. You should give the article an interesting heading.

Task

Write the article.
(LCCIEB EFB2 style)

Question 1(c)

Situation

You work at one of the many branches of *NUCF International*, a large multinational manufacturing company. Managers and staff at the company are very excited because in two weeks time the President of the Company, Mr Kyu Kowaguchi, will be visiting your branch from the company headquarters in Japan. The date of the visit (date), has just been confirmed and the Branch Manager, Mr William Carson, has asked you to send a memo to all heads of department to confirm the date.

Mr Carson says this to you.

'I've had the pleasure of meeting Mr Kowaguchi and he is a very charming and pleasant man. He wants the visit to be informal so we haven't arranged a detailed timetable for the visit. But he will want to look round the branch so he might come in to any department. Tell everyone not to worry if he does, but it might be wise to make sure that everything is as tidy as possible on the day. Mr Kowaguchi speaks good English so staff need not worry if he asks any questions.

'Please give a big hint that we should try to make to make a good impression on Mr Kawaguchi. He is Company President so he will make the final decisions about which branches expand in future, and possibly which ones might close!'

Task

Write the memo.

(40 marks)

(LCCIEB EFB2 style)

Question 2

Situation

You work for Apex Building Company. The manager of the company, Mr Parajit Singh, has shown you this letter he has received today:

Flat 43
Victoria Mansions
Station Road
Uptown

The Manager
Apex Building Company
116 Dock Road
Millfield

Dear Sir

I live opposite Woodbridge School where your company is building an extension. When I returned home today I was shocked to see that your workmen had cut down the fine row of mature trees next to the entrance to the building.

These were beautiful trees and must have been 100 years old. The entrance to the school looks terrible now. Even if you planted new trees they would take years to be as good as the trees you cut down.

I do not know if what you have done is legal but it was a great mistake. There are not many mature trees in this area and we cannot afford to lose any.

Yours sincerely

Carlo Cragnetti

Mr Singh explains to why the trees had to be cut down and asks you to write a letter to Mr Cragnetti. These are the notes of your conversation.

Trees – were very old and very nice – but had to go – some had diseases – would have died anyway – disease would have spread further if trees not removed. Also the roots were damaging school's foundations – and could even be unsafe – some trees block views of entrance for car drivers in street – children could run from behind them into road – Apex Building Company intends to plant quick growing trees – site will be fully landscaped when buildings finished.

Task

Write the letter to Mr Cragnetti.

(30 marks)

Question 3

Situation

The Manager of *Econoserve*, a company offering a range of services to business in the area, is very proud of her company's use of computers and Information and Communication Technology (ICT). Most communication with customers is now by means of e-mail.

However, the Manager, Ms Suzanne Stolte, is less happy that staff seem to receive many e-mails that they neither want nor need. These e-mails which are unsolicited are called *Spam*.

Ms Stolte has asked you to investigate how and why Spam is sent and received and what can be done about it, and **write a report** for her.

You speak to various experts in ICT and the notes of your conversation are as follows.

Spam – unsolicited or 'junk' emails – usually advertising material sent by other companies – most of it is useless – but occasionally there might be a good offer.

It is sent because it is cheap – once something is written it can be sent to thousands of email addresses without costing anything.

Sometimes (rarely) Spam can be dangerous as it can contain a virus that will damage the information held in the computer – anti-virus software is available.

You should be careful about your email address – it could go on spam mailing lists. It can waste a lot of ink and paper if you print these 'junk' emails out – better to delete them straight away – maybe glance at them to make sure that they are rubbish.

Don't ever contact people who send spam – this just confirms that your email address is genuine and you'll get even more spam.

Task

Write the report.

(30 marks)

(LCCIEB EFB2 style)

Index

Shirley Taylor's training programmes

Power Up your Business Writing Skills (one or two days)

One of the biggest challenges in business has always been to communicate effectively, especially in writing. This has become even more crucial in today's fast-paced e-world. In this popular workshop, you will learn proven, practical tools and techniques that will make you a better business writer. You will learn how easy it is to make your writing crisper, clearer, more proactive and more interesting to read. You will acquire the basics of organising your words and thoughts on paper, structuring your messages logically, presenting your documents attractively, and improving the format, style, language and tone of all your written communications. **Using these guidelines, you will learn a set of practical skills that will be useful to you every day for the rest of your life.**

Remember: You are what you write – so you should learn to write well!

"Shirley captivated my attention from the very beginning. She managed to keep the session alive with her witty jokes and experienced delivery of the topics."

"I have gained a lot from Shirley's class. She is a very interesting and dynamic trainer. She uses words that everybody understands. She is very lively and encouraged class participation."

Energise your E-mail Skills (one day)

E-mail has become an essential and fundamental part of the way businesses work. When e-mail is used effectively it can be very powerful indeed. But when it is used ineffectively it can be costly, annoying and it can quickly damage a company's reputation. The Internet has made it possible for us to communicate with people from all over the world. The only way those people can form an opinion of us is by looking at the way we write – so it pays to learn to write well! **In this practical workshop you will learn how to make technology work for you, not against you, and become a better business writer in the process.**

"Shirley's teaching was very precise and detailed. Her workshop really taught me a lot. Not boring at the least."

"It has helped me to realise some of the outdated phrases that we always use."

Other books by Shirley Taylor

Model Business Letters, E-mails and Other Business Documents, 6th edition, is an international best-seller, popular all over the world. A practical, comprehensive guide to helping you put the key rules of good business writing into action. It not only tells you how to do it, but also gives you easy to use examples that you can lift straight off the page and adapt for your own use. It has established itself as the most effective guide you will ever need – truly the last word on modern business writing.

This is a comprehensive textbook and reference guide on the essentials of good communication skills. It explains the principles of effective communication, both oral and written, and provides solid advice and practical guidelines on how to strengthen communication skills and produce better business communication. Perfect for use as a self-study guide, with answers in the back. (Teacher's resource pack available)

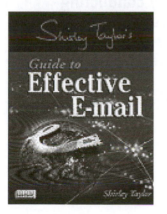

This book contains practical advice on all the essential aspects of e-mail. It aims to establish some 'rules of the road' for e-mail by providing guidelines on common courtesy online, basic rules of netiquette, composing effective messages, using appropriate language, style and structure, the problems and potential of e-mail, managing your e-mail, and much more.

Success Skills for Secretaries and Other Support Staff (one day)

It takes years of experience to achieve respect as an indispensable secretary, administrative assistant or support staff member. There are many essential skills that you need if you are to achieve success in business today. In this practical workshop you will learn how to handle the demands of your job with assertiveness, confidence and professionalism. You will learn how to communicate well, how to handle difficult people, how to priortise, how to manage time and resources, how to handle crises, how to beat stress and much more. **This comprehensive one-day workshop shows you how to make your working life more productive, more rewarding, more successful and much more enjoyable.**

"It's the most fantastic seminar I've attended. Shirley's course awakened my inner potentials and encouraged me to do my job better."

"Shirley, I enjoy your speeches and presentations. They are simply lively and certainly enriching. I am always amazed by the way you capture the attention of the audience."

SHIRLEY TAYLOR
Training and Consultancy

Shirley lives in Singapore and travels extensively conducting her popular workshops and seminars.
Contact Shirley to discuss in-house workshops for your company or to discuss speaking at international conferences.

Telephone: (+65) 6472 6076   Fax: (+65) 6399 2710
E-mail: shirley@shirleytaylor.com
Website: www.shirleytaylor.com